D1486136

BRITISH COOKING

BRITISH COOKING

Caroline Conran

PARK LANE PRESS

First published in 1978 by Park Lane Press,
36 Park Street, London WIY 4DE

Text: © Caroline Conran Ink Ltd. 1978

Editors: Mary Anne Sanders and Fiona Roxburgh
Designers: Yvonne Dedman and Gail Engert
Series designer: Rod Springett Associates
Photographer: David Levin
Props research: Fran Fisher
Diagrams: Marion Appleton
Picture research: Anne-Marie Ehrlich
Production: Georgina Ewer

Text set by SX Composing Ltd., Rayleigh, England
Printed by Chromoworks Ltd., Nottingham, England
Bound by Dorstal Press Ltd., Harlow, England

Contents

Notes

The symbol  denotes that the recipe is a more glamorous and ambitious dish and suitable for special occasions; it may therefore require more preparation as well as possible extra expense.

All spoon measures are level unless otherwise stated.

Plain flour should be used unless otherwise stated in the ingredients.

Egg sizes are specified only where exact quantities are vital to the recipe.

Introduction

Standing back and looking at British cookery now, at a time when outside influences often become muddled up with our own honest and sensible instincts, it is interesting to see how few attempts have been made to adapt real traditional British cooking to modern life.

We have all embraced the pizza, the curry and the chop suey and our own great cookery writers have put us in touch with cooking from the Mediterranean, from the Middle East, and from France; but who has done the same for British cooking?

If you look up Mrs Beeton, scan the pages and savour the flavour of the recipes, and then do the same with a French cookery book of the same period (there is for example a nice one called the *Town and Country Cook* published in Paris in 1881 by a Monsieur Audot), you will find the same old brown recipes, the sago soups, the baked river fish with bready stuffings, the elaborate boring marzipanned puddings, coming through equally strongly in both French and English books. But since then French cookery has been brought to life for us, and its recipes adapted to our modern tastes and standards – it has allure, it has romance and appeal, while poor old British cooking is still cloaked in the thin brown mantle given to it by Mrs Beeton, and her good plain recipes.

The overall tone may seem brown and boring, but a close look is what is needed. We need to illuminate that which is good and colourful and appealing in British cooking, and consign all the dull recipes to the past. For example British soups can be the most savoury, the most appetizing, the most rich of all soups. The pies we make are equal to any. All that is needed is a new approach. We want our recipes, our own good simple recipes, made easy to use in a modern kitchen, by modern women who are busy, but who at the same time regard cooking and food as a very important part of their daily lives. Let us not introduce green peppers into our beef stews – they are lovely when we are making Italian dishes but not to be thrown willy-nilly into British food. And when we are serving steak and kidney pie, let us not go offering ratatouille – a stew of Mediterranean vegetables in olive oil – along with it, but beautifully cooked, wonderfully tender, bright green cabbage, soft and melting in its light coating of butter. In other words, let's try not to talk in more than one language at once. It is bound to end up as nonsense.

There is a myth that traditional British cooking is stodgy, and that it tends to be fattening; but by planning the meal properly you can easily avoid having more than one fattening thing: of course steak and kidney pudding followed by apple pie with cream is fattening. But replace the apple pie with baked apples and all is well.

Finally, British food often relies on lengthy cooking. If you are pressed for time and see that some recipe takes hours to cook, do not be put off. It will probably take the same time actually to prepare as a seemingly quick dish, the difference is that you can go away and do something else whilst the slow dish simmers away, and all the while you will have a nice comfortable feeling that your dish will be ready without much fuss when you want it.

So the intention of this book is to put British cooking into line with French and Italian cooking as a splendid, unassailable institution (which other countries are beginning to recognize as something good and special in its own right).

Caroline Conran

Kitchen equipment

Knowing what equipment to buy so that life in the kitchen runs smoothly is almost as important as knowing how to cook, so here are some suggestions to help you make the right choice.

When spending money on expensive items like knives and saucepans it is essential to buy things of good design and good quality that will last well and feel right and comfortable in the hands, and to use these things in the right way and for the right purpose.

Such pleasure can be had from using properly balanced knives and solid saucepans – and such misery of cut fingers and burned food with badly made or wrongly used equipment.

Knives

The cook's best ally is a set of good knives. She will need to keep them sharp, so a very good-quality steel is important. If you can find a local ironmonger who grinds knives, have them reground every six months or year. (Your butcher may be able to recommend someone – he has *his* reground every week.)

Look for knives with blades that are thin along the cutting edge. Balanced on a finger, handle and blade should weigh about the same. The blade should run down the length of the handle and be riveted in place.

If buying stainless steel, take care to buy good quality Sheffield stainless steel which can be sharpened. Cheap stainless steel, often imported from the Far East, is poor quality and impervious to sharpening by steel or stone or anything else.

Look after your knives. Don't leave them soaking in water, and don't put them in the dishwasher – both will loosen or split the handles.

Don't use them for anything but the preparation of food – don't, most of all, don't let your nearest and dearest use them for their engineering pursuits.

Saucepans

Whether you decide on aluminium, enamelled iron, copper or stainless steel, you will be doing yourself a good turn if you choose thick pans; they do cook best, whether you use electricity, an Aga or solid fuel and need ground-based pans, or whether you use gas and can use any type of pan.

Since your pans will be used every day and for such a variety of purposes, it seems

(*continued on page* 10)

Equipment for a good home-cook
Here and overleaf, you see the traditional equipment which will enable you to go ahead with the great British specialities, plate pies, treacle puddings, jam tarts, steak and kidney and apple pies, and Yorkshire puddings that make British cooking such a different and distinctive thing.

But to see that you have indeed got everything you think you need in your kitchen, use this checklist as a guide – bearing in mind that every piece you own must earn its space by its usefulness to you.

Cutters

A breadknife with a wooden handle and a serrated blade. Two large cooks' knives with wooden handles and tapering blades for chopping, slicing and trimming, two smaller ones for preparing vegetables and fruit. A small serrated knife for slicing tomatoes. A butcher's knife with a curved blade for all heavy meat chopping and slicing. A long carving knife and fork with a guard for carving at table. A hard steel or stone for sharpening. A grater with the greatest possible assortment of rasps. Choose one with a straight blade for slicing cucumbers for sandwiches and a corrugated blade for making game chips, otherwise you will also need a mandoline (*see page* 136). A pair of poultry scissors and a pair of ordinary scissors – useful for quickly dividing strings of sausages and for chopping small quantities of herbs directly on to dishes. An egg slicer.

Boards

Chopping on worktops ruins knives and surfaces – unless these are oak or teak. So, you need a breadboard, and two large wooden chopping boards; reserve one for chopping onions and garlic as their smell remains and can transfer itself to whatever you want to chop next.

Larger utensils

At least three solid thick sauce-pans with well-fitting lids, a non-stick pan for milk and sauces, a round-bottomed pan for things like Hollandaise sauce. Two frying pans, one large, one small, and an omelet pan. A deep pan with a basket for chips. A fish kettle – not essential but nice to have, so is a preserving pan (1) for jams and marmalade: your largest saucepan might serve at a pinch, but if you make your own redcurrant jelly, you need a jelly bag (2). A steamer to fit on top of saucepans is necessary for steaming puddings, so is a double saucepan – for non-curdled custards. For oven-cookery, you need two casseroles with lids: (3) is cast iron, (4) is straight-sided earthenware; a Dutch pot (5), two shallow oval dishes in fireproof porcelain, copper or enamelled iron; a terrine; a roasting tin and grid; two pie dishes (6) with bird or funnel (7); two pie plates, a cake tin, jam tart tins (8), two sandwich tins (9), pastry cutters (10), two baking sheets, or more to make the most of a hot oven, Yorkshire pudding tins, one large, several small; soufflé dishes of various sizes. Two loaf tins (11), and a terracotta 'flowerpot' for bread-making (12), a cake rack where bread and cakes can cool while their moisture evaporates (13); a griddle for oatcakes and Scotch pancakes (14); a large mixing bowl (15) and an assortment of three or four pudding basins (16).

only logical to buy something that is as good as you can afford to let it be. Keep your non-stick pans for making sauces or porridge and for heating milk: they will be most useful for these purposes, but cannot long stand up to heavy everyday use for everything under the sun.

Aluminium is a very suitable metal for pans – it conducts heat well and doesn't weigh too much. Unfortunately it can be affected by acid – and cleaned by it; if you boil rhubarb or sharp apples, your blackish pan will be silver again, but if you leave your rhubarb in the pan for too long you will slightly pit the surface. Aluminium is probably the best buy today, but it takes a bit of cleaning to keep it really shining.

Stainless steel is not an easy metal to use for cooking – it conducts heat badly, scorching food and browning or burning itself. However, it is wonderfully shiny and easy to clean and will never impart a flavour to food or react to it. Some stainless steel pans now have a layer of aluminium sandwiched inside the base and these are the ones to look for since it improves their performance.

Enamelled iron pans are extremely heavy – they are made of iron with a thin layer of enamel over the surface. The smoothness of the enamel makes an ideal surface for the making of sauces, but rather like the non-stick coating, it is not much good for frying foods. This sort of pan will chip or even break if dropped, and the bottom will chip if the pan is left long on the heat with nothing in it, but otherwise enamelled iron is tough and long-lasting and a pleasure to use.

Copper is a precious and pretty metal and a very good conductor of heat, but it reacts very quickly to acids in food, so copper pans must be coated inside, either with silver, stainless steel or tin.

Unfortunately copper is prohibitively expensive and thin copper is not good. Copper pans, to give you the wonderful solid feeling that your food will be cooked evenly and perfectly, must be thick. If tinned, they will need regular retinning as the surface wears out.

Heat-resistant ceramic and glass pans are for people who really take great care of their possessions and are lovely for making sauces, but sadly fragile.

Frying pans

Heavy frying pans in enamelled cast iron with black interiors or in thick steel, are the best to work with. They won't readily burn or tip over, will fry evenly and can be kept spotless without the use of soap-filled wire wool pads which would destroy their inside cooking surface and cause food to stick. Season new steel frying pans by heating a tablespoon of oil in them and then sprinkling in about 2 tablespoons of salt. This must be rubbed round and round patiently with a wodge of kitchen paper, smoothing the surface and helping the oil to sink into the pores of the metal. Now wash well with soap and hot water, oil the inside lightly and your pan is ready. Whenever you put a steel pan away give it a light but thorough rub with a piece of kitchen paper saturated in oil.

Oven dishes

Apart from that plain but familiar and friendly object the roasting tin, there are several oven dishes needed in every kitchen.

First, casseroles or stew-pots, either traditional British brown glazed stoneware specially toughened for the oven, or enamelled iron, the most popular material at the moment because it is tough, distributes the heat as well as stoneware, is less porous, therefore unaffected by food, and can be used on the top of the cooker as well as in the oven.

But for cooking baked beans, hot pot and good old British stews there is nothing to beat the stoneware casserole that our grandmothers used.

Open oven dishes

These include deep pie dishes, wide flat baking dishes, either rectangular, round or oval and made in oven-glass, copper, earthenware or enamelled iron (for cooking such things as macaroni cheese or plaice in cheese sauce that need to be cooked in the oven and then lightly browned under the grill), and oval stoneware pots with lids (useful for the making of soused mackerel and potted shrimps as well as brawns and such like). There are also available little individual pots or ramekins in which eggs can be baked or potted shrimps served.

Lastly, apart from plain roasting tins, there are soufflé dishes, internationally used and nationally useful for all sorts of puddings as well as for their obvious purpose.

Most people who cook will have their own ideas about what they need to make their life pleasant. Some people go out to work and don't feel like doing much when they get home, so a small collection of things will get them by. Others love cooking for their families and like to spend time over it, and for them the basic collection will be quite large.

A measuring jug (17) and two large jugs for decanting liquids into, and a pestle and mortar (18). Ramekin dishes for egg and fish dishes (19), dariole moulds for castle puddings (20); a china mould for jellies and flummeries (21) – the more elaborate, the prettier – will enable you to serve up your puddings in the traditional manner.

Smaller utensils
At least three wooden spoons in different sizes and a wooden fork; keep these in a jug or jar near the cooker, and you will save fumbling for them in the drawer. Depending on the size of this container, it might also hold a spatula, a perforated spoon, and

a fishslice (22) (useful for turning other things besides fish). You also need a large ladle (23), slotted spoon (24), a steak basher, a vegetable brush, a funnel, a lemon squeezer (25), skewers (26), a corkscrew, a tin opener and a bottle opener. A kettle (27), of course, goes without saying, but you also need an enamelled or earthenware breadbin, a salt box to keep by the cooker (28), a pepper mill, a spice box, and a range of storage jars, large and small, for dry goods and herbs (29); if these are made of glass, you will be able to see the stock position at a glance. For baking, you will need a small wire whisk (30), a rubber or plastic scraper for getting all

your sticky mixtures off bowls, a pastry brush (31), a fluted cutting wheel (32) and a rolling pin (33). For toasting muffins by the fire, an adjustable toasting fork (34).

Kitchen machines
A food processor or electric mixer-liquidizer is a good friend to the cook, doing the work of an entire *brigade de cuisine*. If you own one, keep it well in view and in easy reach, or you will not make the best use of it; depending on the services it performs, you may also need a mincer that clamps on to the tabletop; a mouli-légumes, which is an inexpensive hand-operated food mill for puréeing; a rotary egg whisk; a coffee grinder.

Strainers
A colander (35); two wire sieves, one large, one small; a hairsieve, a conical strainer, useful for straining gravy or sauce into a jug or sauceboat. A salad shaker, though you could dry your washed lettuce by swinging it round in a clean tea towel.

Breakfasts

Magnificent British breakfasts – hot cutlets, pink hams, fried soles, devilled kidneys, little crisp rolls of bacon, dishes of scrambled eggs and sausages, a cold grouse or pheasant, a piece of pie and then hot toast in white napkins, fresh rolls, sweet butter, marmalades of all cuts and colours, jams, jellies and pyramids of fruit – 'ah the breakfast', wrote an early nineteenth-century visitor to Scotland, 'that is what redeems the land'.

At the turn of the century the grand English breakfast – designed to boost the inner man for a morning's sport out of doors, was still going strong, but when the First World War arrived with attendant shortages and a new horror of waste, things were modified to what we would now regard as a more seemly level. In 1933 a bachelor cook, discreetly naming himself 'Gourmet', wrote a little book giving up two whole chapters to the British breakfast, which he regarded as a meal to be eaten only after an hour's pottering about – presumably to get up an appetite. His favourite breakfast, eaten in a Lakeland fishing inn, consisted of a modest five courses: Manx kippers, brown trout, Cumberland ham and eggs with fried bannocks, cold boiled bacon, four kinds of scones, three kinds of home-made jam, pukka coffee (by which he presumably means good, strong, hot, fresh coffee).

The magnificent breakfast was on the way out, and by the Second World War parlourmaids and cooks had disappeared along with butter, sugar, and coffee, and the whole thing had condensed to its present-day level – cereal, egg and bacon, toast and marmalade and cups of tea.

But it is an institution worth reviving, even if only at weekends, when there is time to make little special breakfast dishes, and to ponder long over the paper with a hot pot of coffee on the table. So this chapter includes a few of the old breakfast recipes that could make breakfast once more into a most enjoyable meal – and could even turn it into a brunch which would allow more time for pottering, another British institution worth reviving.

A hunting breakfast at the turn of the century

Tea

It would be sheer presumption to offer advice on the making of tea to a nation whose national drink it has been for about two centuries.

The only thing to be repeated about the making of tea, which is second nature to us all, is the adage from the side of the Victorian teapot.

> 'Those who love good tea
> Must please remember me
> Be sure allow the water to boil
> Then the tea you will not spoil'

To which I add – use freshly run water. Water re-boiled is only fit for washing-up.

About keeping a pot of tea going and producing more cups the following advice is worth remembering: 'do not drain the pot dry and then fill it up again; fill half the cups at a time and replace in the teapot the water you have taken from it; always with boiling water.'

Coffee

The delicious fugitive aroma and flavour diminish with every moment that passes between roasting and drinking. It was true in the nineteenth century, when writers of household hints strongly recommended the home-roasting of green coffee beans, and it is true today, although with quicker transport and vacuum-packing we don't have to go quite so far.

The insurance for good cups of coffee is to buy freshly roasted beans, keep them in airtight jars or tins for a maximum of three weeks, and grind them freshly for each pot, not forgetting to drink the coffee as soon as it is made.

Another essential for excellent coffee is to make it strong: a continental connoisseur said of eighteenth-century coffee houses, 'I would advise those who wish to drink coffee in England to tell the waiters how many cups are to be made with $\frac{1}{2}$ ounce, or else people will probably bring them a prodigious quantity of brown fluid'.

For decent coffee use 25 g (1 oz) of beans and about 700 ml (1–1¼ pints) water to make four cups of coffee.

A third vital point concerns the boiling of coffee – 'boil for six minutes then add a chip or two of gelatine and boil for five minutes more' says Warner's *Model Cookery* published in the mid-nineteenth century – a sure recipe for disaster. Coffee must never be boiled, it destroys the flavour and turns it grey and bitter. Make coffee in a percolator, or use the filter method or even infuse it like tea, but on no account let it boil.

For those who like hot milk with their coffee 'without the thick yellow blanket of

Usually, the silver was the butler's province, but in middle-class households, the maid's duties included polishing the breakfast things.

skin which embarrasses all and disgusts many', Lady Jekyll DBE, previous cookery contributor to *The Times*, provides the answer.

Lady Jekyll's frothed coffee

Take 2 teaspoons of cream and froth it well with a rotary beater or blender and pour it immediately over already served coffee. Each cup will then look better and the coffee taste better too.

Chocolate

'Say what you will it is pleasant to awake every morning, to take early breakfast in the balcony room with the sweet fresh air coming up from the garden through the open glass door; to drink, instead of coffee, a cup of chocolate handed one on a tray.'

So thought Tony in Thomas Mann's *Buddenbrooks* and so thought the British in the eighteenth century, devoting many pages in early cookbooks to describing how to make it to perfection, running the gamut from chocolate with a little grated lemon or orange rind, or chocolate with a little pinch of cinnamon, to Dr Todd's Cocoa Nibs which took five hours to prepare. Although nowadays we have cocoa to speed up the process, it is nice to know that the following makes a delicious breakfast drink.

Use 275 ml (½ pint) of milk to every 25 g (1 oz) chocolate.

Heat the milk in a saucepan. When it is very hot gradually add the grated chocolate. Stir all the time until boiling point is reached, draw the pan off the heat and stir vigorously for a little longer. Serve at once or if it is not wanted immediately reheat to boiling point again just before serving. Like tea or coffee it must never boil.

Traditional porridge

TO SERVE SIX

INGREDIENTS
150 g (5 oz) porridge oats, or better still, medium oatmeal
1.2 litres (2 pints) of water
1–2 teaspoons salt

The classic way of starting a British breakfast is with porridge. The subject of much mystery and ritual, porridge was considered best when made with spring water, stirred with a wooden stick and eaten with a horn spoon. Scots always referred to it as *them* – 'aren't they ready yet?' being the constant question, since in the past 'they' took almost an hour to make.

In the Highlands it was customary to eat your porridge walking about, and to dip each spoonful into a separate bowl of cold

milk – a most awkward performance designed to avoid being stabbed in the back while still slightly dulled by the night's sleep. Sugar on porridge was sacrilege although an exceptionally good child might be allowed to trace its initials in treacle on its porridge.

Although cooking methods differed widely, the originator of this recipe was so confident in his version that he called it 'The one and only method'.

Put the cold water into a heavy (and easily soaked and cleaned) saucepan and bring it to the boil. As it reaches boiling point, sprinkle in the porridge oats in a steady rain, stirring all the time with a wooden fork to keep them evenly distributed. When the porridge thickens stir in the salt, cover the pan and simmer very, very slowly for 20 minutes stirring from time to time as you go by, and adding a little water if it becomes too stiff. Pour into hot bowls and serve with *cold* top of the milk.

Scrambled eggs

TO SERVE FOUR

INGREDIENTS
4 pieces of buttered toast
50 g (2 oz) butter
8 eggs
salt and pepper

Scrambled eggs, one of the most comforting and delicious of dishes, is a very old favourite in Britain. Even seventeenth-century doctors, who disapproved of eggs in almost every form, thought scrambled eggs were extremely wholesome.

However, as the old cookery books stress, the quality of the ingredients are of ultimate importance. The butter must be tasted in the shop 'but do not be deceived by a well-scented piece artfully placed in the lump – dig well down with a knife and hold that at once to your nose'. As for buying eggs 'put the great end to your

tongue. If it be warm, it is new; if cold, stale'.

Prepare the toast and keep it hot. Heat the butter just enough to melt it in a non-stick pan. Break in the eggs and season with salt and pepper before beating them lightly, just enough to break them up.

Now over a gentle heat stir and scrape the pan mixing the eggs as they start to set. When the mixture is thick, creamy, and lumpy, remove the pan from the heat, pile it up on the toast, dust with a little freshly ground pepper and serve at once.

Top to bottom: Rumbled eggs, scrambled eggs

Rumbled eggs

TO SERVE FOUR

INGREDIENTS
1 tablespoon butter
6 eggs
1 dessertspoon water
salt and pepper

The beauty of rumbled eggs is that they cook practically on their own, whereas scrambled eggs almost always overcook while you hastily make the toast.

Put a saucepan of boiling water over a low heat. Put the butter in a bowl and stand it in the saucepan to melt, while you beat the eggs, salt, pepper and water. When the butter is hot and clear, pour in the egg mixture and stir twice. They can then be left over the gently simmering water while you lay the table. Give them an occasional stir as you pass by to prevent the eggs at the bottom from sticking.

As soon as the eggs are the consistency of clotted cream remove the saucepan from the heat, and the eggs will keep hot over the hot water until they are needed. Serve on buttered toast.

Eggs and bacon

TO SERVE FOUR

INGREDIENTS
4 rashers preferably
  smoked back bacon (or 8
  thin rashers or 4 back,
  4 streaky)
1 teaspoon butter or lard
4 eggs

One of the most reliably delicious dishes throughout the length and breadth of Britain, breakfast eggs and bacon can be eaten with pleasure and relish at any time of day or night.

Although *'oeufs sur le plat à l'anglaise'*, when served in France, are fried in the sizzling fat of the bacon, British traditionalists insist that bacon grilled or crisped in the oven or toasted on a toasting fork in front of a clear fire is infinitely superior. The object is to get the bacon crisp and this is in fact quite easy to do in a frying pan.

Cut the rinds off the bacon with kitchen scissors and put them in the frying pan with the teaspoon of butter or lard. Let them give up their fat over a low heat for a few minutes, then put in the bacon rashers and fry to a medium brown on each side, turning them only once.

Push them to the side of the pan, break the eggs into the bacon fat and let them fry fairly gently. When they are firm, tip the pan and spoon the bacon fat, sizzling hot, over the yolks to cloud them. Serve straight away or they will go rubbery.

Ham and eggs

TO SERVE FOUR

INGREDIENTS
4 thin slices cooked
  gammon or ham
15 g ($\frac{1}{2}$ oz) butter
4 eggs

Making fried ham and eggs is an extremely good and welcome way of using up a piece of cooked gammon or ham.

Slice the gammon or ham rather thinly. Melt the butter in a large frying pan, put in the ham and break in the eggs. Cover the pan with a lid and let it cook over a medium heat until the eggs are just set.

If you want the ham crisp round the edges, cook it in the butter first before breaking in the eggs and putting on the lid.

For tender ham and eggs, add a teaspoon of water to the butter, and cook gently over a fairly low heat until the whites of the eggs are just cooked.

Bacon and eggs, ham and eggs

17

Devilled kidneys

TO SERVE FOUR

INGREDIENTS
8 lamb's kidneys, skinned,
    cored and diced
1 tablespoon flour
salt and cayenne pepper
2 tablespoons dry mustard
50 g (2 oz) butter
1 dessertspoon Worcester
    sauce
150 ml (¼ pint) chicken
    stock
4 pieces of hot buttered
    toast

This was the most traditional and delicious of breakfast dishes, without which no grand Edwardian breakfast table, with its rows of sizzling silver dishes, would be complete. If you dice the kidneys the night before there will be no problems of early morning preparations, and your family will have reason to be grateful.

Dust the kidneys with flour, salt and plenty of cayenne pepper. Roll them in dry mustard. Melt the butter in a small frying pan and cook the kidneys over a gentle heat for 5 minutes, turning them over now and again. They should be just pink inside. When they are almost done to your liking, pour the Worcester sauce and the stock around them; simmer until the gravy is thick and serve them on hot buttered toast.

Countess Morphy's croquettes

TO SERVE FOUR

INGREDIENTS
25 g (1 oz) butter or 1
    tablespoon bacon fat
3 tablespoons milk
225 g (½ lb) plain mashed
    potato
50 g (2 oz) self-raising flour
salt

These are usefully made from leftover mashed potato and should be very light. Serve with bacon or with fried eggs.

Beat the butter or bacon fat and milk into the mashed potato, then mix in the flour. Season with a little salt, form into little rolls the size and shape of corks, and fry.

Lady Sarah's potato cakes

TO SERVE FOUR

INGREDIENTS
225 g (½ lb) floury potatoes
    boiled and mashed
15–25 g (½–1 oz) butter
salt
1 egg
50 g (2 oz) ham
butter for frying

Mash the potatoes with the butter and salt; they should be rather dry. Add the egg and the ham, finely chopped. Form into little flat cakes and fry in butter until golden.

Lady Sarah's potato cakes, Countess Morphy's croquettes (top left pan); bacon fraize; jolly boys

Oxford sausages

TO SERVE FOUR

INGREDIENTS
225 g (8 oz) lean veal and
    225 g (8 oz) lean pork,
    minced or finely chopped,
    preferably by the butcher
100 g (4 oz) prepared suet
100 g (4 oz) fresh
    breadcrumbs, moistened
    with water
grated rind of a $\frac{1}{4}$ lemon
$\frac{1}{2}$ teaspoon freshly
    ground pepper
1 teaspoon salt
2 chopped sage leaves
grating of nutmeg
pinch dried thyme,
    marjoram or basil

Oxford sausages, still sold today in the excellent Oxford covered market, are no problem to make as they are skinless. Make up the mixture the day before and keep it chilled until it is needed. There is something particularly luxurious about home-made sausages.

Mix everything together thoroughly in a bowl. Form into sausage shapes or little flat cakes and fry in a little oil and butter or lard.

Bacon fraize

TO SERVE FOUR

INGREDIENTS
4 rashers streaky bacon
50 g (2 oz) flour
1 egg
150 ml ($\frac{1}{4}$ pint) milk
pinch salt

This is a very old English dish and a very good way of stretching a single egg round the whole breakfast table.

Cut the bacon into little strips or squares. Make a pancake batter in the normal way, start with the flour in a bowl, then stir in the egg and lastly add the milk gradually stirring and beating as you do so, until you have a smooth lump-free batter. Season it very lightly as the bacon is salty.
    Fry a quarter of the strips of bacon gently, until they are crisp, in a small frying pan. Pour a ladleful of the pancake batter over the hot bacon and when cooked on one side, turn it over and cook the other side. Each person's pancake is made in the same way, and is served folded in half or rolled according to thickness.
    Sausagemeat can be done in the same way.

Jolly boys

TO SERVE FOUR

INGREDIENTS
2 tablespoons flour
1 egg
pinch salt
150 ml ($\frac{1}{4}$ pint) milk
4 rashers of bacon
1 teaspoon butter or lard

When you haven't enough eggs to go round, you could also make these nice little pancakes called jolly boys, originally invented to fill the breakfast plates of hungry young country families when the backyard hens had stopped laying.

Make a batter with the flour, egg and milk and a pinch of salt. It should be the consistency of double cream, and run quickly from the spoon.
    After frying the bacon in butter or lard, remove it to a plate to keep hot. Increase the heat under the frying pan and put in a tablespoon of batter. This will run into an oval shape and rise up in the middle. Baste it with hot fat as you would a fried egg and dish up at once.

Creamed smoked haddock

TO SERVE FOUR

INGREDIENTS
350 g (¾ lb) smoked
  haddock
275 ml (½ pint) milk –
  creamy milk is best
25 g (1 oz) butter
20 g (¾ oz) flour
freshly ground pepper
1 hard-boiled egg
4 rounds of freshly made
  buttered toast or 4
  rounds of fried bread
  with crusts removed

This can be made the day before and simply heated through, but make the toast or fried bread at the last minute.

Put the haddock in a roasting tin with the milk and poach it for 15 minutes over a low heat. When it will flake off the bone, remove it and keep the milk on one side. Flake the fish, discarding skin and bones.

Now make a sauce; melt the butter in a thick saucepan, stir in the flour and when it has combined with the butter and has a glossy look, stir in the milk, a little at a time, stirring until the sauce is smooth

between each addition. Stir in the flaked smoked haddock, the chopped hard-boiled egg and the pepper. While the mixture is heating through make the toast or fried bread. Cut each piece across diagonally to make two triangular pieces and to serve, place these on either side of the creamed haddock. They can either be eaten separately, dipped into the creamed haddock or eaten with it.

Creamed smoked haddock, kedgeree

Kedgeree

TO SERVE FOUR

INGREDIENTS
350 g (¾ lb) smoked
  haddock
100 g (4 oz) long grain rice
4 hard-boiled eggs
50 g (2 oz) butter
¼ teaspoon curry powder
  (optional) or large pinch
  cayenne pepper
salt and freshly ground
  pepper
2–3 sprigs parsley

Kedgeree, a dish still eaten in India as kichiree (rather surprisingly without any fish), was one of the recipes most successfully adopted and adapted by the British Raj, who turned it into a most acceptable breakfast, brunch or even lunch dish. Made basically with lightly spiced smoked haddock, rice and hard-boiled eggs, it should be light, fragrant and moist, and is a wonderful restorative after a late night.

Put the haddock in a roasting tin, cover with water and cook for 10–15 minutes in a moderate oven, 180°C, 350°F, Gas Mark 4.

Cook the rice in a large saucepan of boiling, well-salted water. After 12 minutes, when it is just tender between the teeth, pour it into a sieve and run it briefly under the cold tap to prevent any further cooking. Skin, bone and flake the haddock and shell and chop the hard-boiled eggs. In the cleaned saucepan melt the butter and stir in the curry powder if liked. Add the rice, flaked fish, chopped eggs and the seasoning. Stir in the chopped parsley, heat through gently and serve piping hot.

A few cooked fresh peas are a good addition to kedgeree.

Fishcakes

TO SERVE FOUR

INGREDIENTS
225 g ($\frac{1}{2}$ lb) cooked
    haddock, coley, hake,
    cod, etc.
225 g ($\frac{1}{2}$ lb) potatoes boiled
    and mashed
1 small egg
1 hard-boiled egg
salt, pepper, a few drops of
    lemon juice or vinegar
1 tablespoon finely
    chopped parsley
flour
4 tablespoons dry
    breadcrumbs

Fishcakes can be such dry disappointing objects that they have rather fallen out of favour. However, home-made fishcakes crisp and golden on the outside and soft and creamy within are well worth the small amount of trouble they take.

First flake the cooked fish. To obtain the right amount of dryish mashed potato, peel the potatoes before weighing. You will need about two fairly large ones. Boil them in salted water and mash as dry as possible.

Combine raw egg, mashed potato and flaked fish, and stir in the chopped hard-boiled egg, salt, pepper, lemon juice or vinegar and parsley.

The mixture will be fairly sticky, so work with well-floured hands, forming small fishcakes and turning them over in the crumbs with a fish-slice. Fry on each side in oil or butter until an attractive golden colour. Serve very hot.

Although the recipe is complicated to describe, it is simplicity itself to make and can be prepared the day before, only the frying to be left until breakfast time. (This amount is enough to make eight small fishcakes.)

Fishcakes, fish croquettes

Fish croquettes

TO SERVE FOUR

INGREDIENTS
225 g ($\frac{1}{2}$ lb) cooked fish,
    haddock, coley, hake,
    cod, etc (particularly
    delicious made with
    conger eel)
200 ml ($\frac{1}{3}$ pint) stiff white
    sauce made from 25 g
    (1 oz) of flour, 25 g (1 oz)
    butter, 150 ml ($\frac{1}{4}$ pint)
    creamy milk
1 hard-boiled egg
1 tablespoon chopped
    parsley
salt and pepper
flour, beaten egg and fresh
    breadcrumbs
butter and oil for frying

Flake the fish. Make the white sauce by melting the butter in a small pan, stirring in the flour over a low heat and when it has become glossy, add the cold milk (or fish cooking-liquid and milk, half and half) a little at a time, stirring until smooth after each addition. Mix sauce, with flaked fish, chopped hard-boiled egg and parsley, add salt and pepper to taste and leave the mixture to cool and stiffen.

When it is cold, form quickly into the shape of wine corks, and dip first in flour, then the beaten egg and finally in fresh breadcrumbs. Fry to a golden brown.

Cooking kippers

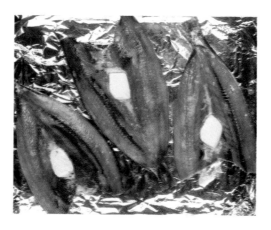

Choose for preference undyed kippers which are a pale golden colour, and have been smoked over oak chips, but this method works equally well for kipper fillets.

Trim heads and tails of kippers with scissors and put them skin side down in a roasting tin lined with foil. Pour boiling water over them and they will plump up and swell Pour it off again straight away, dot kippers with butter and put them under a moderate grill until they are crisp and sizzling.

21

Soup

Soup is not only one of the most enjoyable and reviving foods that can be made; it is also, now with timesavers and up-to-date kitchens, one of the easiest. It serves, too, for absolutely any and every occasion – a bowl of thick pea soup is a great comfort for a cold child coming in from outside, and clear broth, such as the one eaten at Court in Queen Anne's day, a perfect reviver and restorer for people who have stayed up too late. On a hot and heavy summer's day iced tomato soup, or 'tomata' as it used to be called, a clear red, is deliciously refreshing.

Of course British soups have not always had a particularly good reputation and there have been hard times, when 'kidley brose' or 'kettle broth' was all the villagers could afford to eat – a piece of toast in a bowl with boiling water poured over, seasoned with a pinch of salt. By the end of the nineteenth century it was very much the done thing for the ladies of the big house to hand out soup, brewed weekly, to the poor – one manuscript book of that time suggests boiling up kitchen scraps, plate-scrapings, even fishbones, and lumps of broken bread. Poor poor. However, at Court and at the tables of the grand houses, soup had long ago left the area of large pieces of this and that, boiled up in a pot, and had reached a high level of refinement. Turtle soup, or mock turtle or even imitation mock turtle soup (if you were really trying to keep up appearances) were a regular feature, and there are many old engravings showing turtles – some are actually hanging in rows from the kitchen beams alongside deer and pheasants.

The game larder at Windsor Castle in Queen Victoria's day

The well-known early nineteenth-century cookery-book writer Eliza Acton, predecessor of Mrs Beeton, was an avid supporter of soups, and her recipes are almost the first that we could still enjoy today; they were delicate vegetable soups, pearly white soups thickened with almonds and she was also fond of fish soups, which have now almost vanished from our tables, with the one exception of Cornish crab. It was about this time that the first short cuts in soup making start to appear – for example, there were recipes published for an early form of stock cube called 'portable soup' which was stock highly concentrated by boiling until it became a stiff glue. It was then cut into squares and could be kept for years. Captain Cook, in fact, took something similar on his voyage to Australia and a lump of it still sits in Greenwich, proof of its wonderful keeping qualities – a shaving was recently scraped off and diluted and was evidently as good (or just as bearable) as ever.

Nowadays stock cubes sit on the shelf of every kitchen cupboard and save many a cook's skin, although of course for more interesting flavours it is best of all to make fresh stock at home.

However, time is not always on the side of the cook, and thank goodness there are a few decent tinned soups – oxtail, tomato, and thick pea – as well as stock cubes, refrigerators and liquidizers to take the hours out of soup making.

We are so lucky to have all these aids that it seems all wrong not to take advantage of them and eat better soups than ever before.

A word about the stockpot

The old Victorian stockpot has gone by the board. If you want freshness of flavour, it is no longer a good idea to keep popping new bits and pieces into the same pot, which even in its heyday used to be a repository for every leftover as it came along: beef, lamb, vegetables, even fish were kept bubbling away perpetually on the side of the stove, and the resulting brew, strained and boiled, went into the dull brown soups and sauces of the era, Brown Windsor and Espagnole, tasting of mutton fat and flour.

Today we prefer to make a fresh-tasting stock with fresh ingredients and use it within a day or two, or freeze it to use later. The reasons for bothering to do such a thing at all, when useful stock cubes are sitting in the cupboard ready to add any extra flavour that a soup may require, are not immediately clear. But by making stock with fresh vegetables, a new fresh flavour is created, so that each soup made at home has a subtly different taste – much more interesting than tasting the same concentrated stock cube flavour every time, useful though they may be.

Chicken stock

INGREDIENTS
1 chicken carcass from a roast chicken or 900 g (2 lb) veal knuckle bones
2 onions
2 sticks celery
3–4 sprigs parsley
6 peppercorns, salt

The simplest way to make this most useful of all stocks is to take the giblets, carcass and leftovers from a roast chicken as soon as you have eaten it, and put them into a saucepan of water with vegetables and herbs for flavour. Let it simmer very slowly for 2 hours then strain and cook quickly: the resulting delicate jellied stock will be useful for improving the flavour of all your sauces, soups and gravies.

A more classic recipe for white stock which has less flavour and sets to a firm jelly is made with veal bones. Place meat and bones in a large saucepan, cover with water, bring slowly to the boil and skim well. Turn down the heat to a slow simmer, add the chopped vegetables, parsley and peppercorns and simmer slowly for 2 hours for chicken stock, 5 hours for veal stock. Season at the end, because the volume reduces considerably during the cooking. Strain through a fine sieve, allow to cool rapidly and place, covered, in the refrigerator where it will keep for 3 days. It is a good plan to boil some until it is very reduced and then freeze it in an ice-cube tray – making a home version of a stock cube. These last about 2 months in the freezer. This is applicable to all sorts of stock including the beef stock that follows.

Beef stock

INGREDIENTS
225 g ($\frac{1}{2}$ lb) shin of beef
900 g (2 lb) cracked beef bones manageably chopped by the butcher
3 carrots
2 onions in their skins
2 sticks celery
2 or 3 mushrooms, or a handful of mushroom stalks and peelings
1 tomato
1 leek
1 tablespoon either butter or good beef dripping
$\frac{1}{2}$ teaspoon salt
12 peppercorns
bunch of herbs – thyme, parsley, bayleaf

Chop the meat and vegetables except the onions into coarse chunks. Melt the butter in a large heavy pan and fry everything over a low heat, stirring from time to time, until they have absorbed the fat and become dark brown. The onions are fried whole in their skins to give the stock a beautiful golden colour. (You can add extra skins for a deeper browny-gold without spoiling the flavour – put them into the pot after the water has been added.)

Add the cold water, bring slowly to the boil, skim well, add salt, peppercorns and herbs and simmer, covered with a tilted lid, for 3 hours. Sieve into a basin; when cold remove fat. You should have 1.2 litres (2 pints) of excellent stock; it can be further reduced by gentle simmering to obtain a more concentrated, fuller flavoured stock. Rapid boiling will turn it cloudy.

Royal velvet chicken soup

TO SERVE SIX

INGREDIENTS
1 boiling fowl or roasting
   bird 1.4–1.8 kg (3–4 lb)
1 large onion
2 sticks celery
2 fat leeks – white part only
large pinch of salt
small bunch of herbs –
   parsley, bayleaf, thyme
25 g (1 oz) butter
25 g (1 oz) flour
3 egg yolks
100–150 g (4–5 oz) carton
   double cream (optional)

This rich creamy soup is less of an extravagance than it appears since a single chicken will make both the soup and a chicken salad or some other chicken dish. In the past, all laying hens were allowed to reach quite an age, and were then destined to end their days in the pot. Nowadays a boiling fowl is not so easy to find, but this classic soup can also be made with a roasting chicken.

Put the cleaned whole chicken and its giblets, apart from the liver, into a large deep pan. Add the vegetables cleaned and coarsely chopped, the salt and herbs. Cover with about 2.5 litres (4–5 pints) of cold water, bring slowly to the boil and skim off the scum as it rises.

When the soup is free of scum turn the heat right down, put the lid on the pan and allow to simmer for 20 minutes per 450 g (1 lb) and 20 minutes over.

As the level of the broth sinks, remove the tideline from around the sides of the pan with a spatula.

When the chicken is tender remove it from the pan. Taste the broth at this point and boil it further if necessary to end up with about 1.2 litres (2 pints) of liquid.

Now in a separate pan, large enough to hold the soup, melt the butter and stir in the flour. Let it simmer, stirring it, for a minute or two, until it is glistening, then gradually add 850 ml (1½ pints) of your strained chicken broth, stirring to obtain a smooth liquid. Simmer for 15 minutes. Beat the egg yolks in a basin with the remaining hot (not boiling) soup, and the cream, then add it, away from the heat, to the soup, which must on no account be allowed to boil or the eggs will curdle.

Stir, or whisk, over the lowest possible heat until the soup thickens to a velvety cream and then, if you like, add the breasts of the chicken, cut into tiny dice. Heat a moment longer, stirring, then serve at once.

Queen Anne's broth

TO SERVE SIX

INGREDIENTS
1.2 litres (2 pints) of your
   best chicken stock
1 onion, chopped
1 clove garlic
2 sprigs parsley
2 sprigs thyme
2 sprigs mint
2 sprigs lemon balm
12 coriander seeds
large pinch saffron
4 cloves
a little salt and freshly
   ground pepper

Queen Anne's broth, a deep golden chicken broth flavoured with herbs and spices, was taken every morning for breakfast by that large ailing lady. She believed, and it was thought to be true, that the broth was particularly wholesome and nourishing.

Place all the ingredients in a saucepan and simmer for 30 minutes, covered, to infuse the broth with all the delicate herbal and spicy savours. Strain and serve hot, with freshly-made fingers of toast to dip into the soup.

In the summer you can add sorrel and shredded lettuce, as well as some of the more unusual herbs – purslane and borage, 'but green herbs do rob the strength and vigour of the potage'.

English potage

This sparkling elegant first course served like consommé, in cups, is designed to get the gastric juices flowing.

TO SERVE FOUR

INGREDIENTS
225 g (½ lb) shin of beef
900 g (2 lb) beef bones,
   marrow bones if possible
1 or 2 sets of chicken
   giblets (optional but a
   useful addition)
2 carrots
2 onions
2 leeks
2 sticks celery
1 egg white (beaten to a
   soft snow)
salt, freshly ground pepper
   or cayenne
1 glass sherry

The clear broth is also very restoring to a tired or convalescent person, and a great traditional reviver for hangovers. It needs a long cooking time, but not a great deal of preparation, and can, of course, be prepared the day before.

Put the meat, bones, giblets (if you are using them), the vegetables, peeled and cut up coarsely, and a good pinch of salt into a large pan and cover with nearly 3 litres (5 pints) of cold water. Add the beaten egg white last of all. Bring slowly to the boil, whisking energetically from time to time, until the white of egg and impurities form a frothy lid on top. Allow to simmer, almost imperceptibly, for 2½ hours, or even longer, although more than 5 hours will exhaust all the flavours and nutrients.

Now strain the broth into a bowl through a clean tea-towel, rinsed out in cold water and placed over a colander. Rinse the cloth and repeat the performance, to remove the last traces of the egg-white filter. Taste for seasoning.

At this stage, if the potage is to be served hot, return it to the carefully rinsed pan; if cold, put it, cooled, into the 'fridge; it must be either piping hot or properly chilled.

The sherry, like all fortified wines – others include port, Madeira, Marsala – has a short-lived flavour and should be added almost at the last moment.

English potage, Scotch broth

Scotch broth

TO SERVE SIX

INGREDIENTS
900 g (2 lb) lean stewing
   cuts of beef or lamb
2.3 litres (4 pints) water or
   beef stock cube
50 g (2 oz) pearl barley
   soaked for 1–2 hours
50 g (2 oz) dried peas,
   soaked overnight
2 large leeks
2 large carrots
1 small turnip
½ green cabbage
salt and freshly ground
   pepper
grating of nutmeg
1 tablespoon chopped
   parsley

The traditional way to serve Scotch broth was to offer a bowl of broth, clear and plain, as the first course, and follow it with a dish of meat and vegetables. If you follow this tradition use a better piece of meat such as topside or brisket if using beef – shoulder or best end of neck if using lamb.

Trim the meat, put it into a large saucepan with the soaked peas and pearl barley and cover with 2.3 litres (4 pints) of cold water. Bring it slowly to the boil and skim carefully as the scum rises.

Let it simmer while you pare and slice the vegetables, then throw them all except the cabbage into the broth. Cover the pan and allow to simmer very slowly for 2½ hours. Add the shredded cabbage and seasoning of salt, pepper, and nutmeg and simmer on, uncovered, for 20 minutes more.

To serve broth and meat separately, strain the broth and then add a handful of chopped parsley before ladling it out into bowls. Keep a little liquid back to moisten the meat and vegetables which are shared out between the bowls. Pile some of the green cabbage on to the top of each plateful.

To serve all together, sprinkle the parsley into the pan, then fill the bowls with meat, vegetables and broth.

Poacher's soup

TO SERVE FOUR

INGREDIENTS
1 roast pheasant and
   trimmings and any
   leftover gravy
25 g (1 oz) butter
2 rashers lean bacon
1 onion
2 carrots
1 small parsnip
   (or ½ large one)
1 stick celery
25 g (1 oz) flour
1.2 litres (2 pints) beef or
   chicken stock (home-
   made or stock cube)
parsley, bayleaf, thyme
   tied in a bunch
salt, cayenne pepper,
   peppercorns
1 clove
optional: a dash of dry
   sherry

A very good game soup can be made from the bits and pieces left over from a roast pheasant, partridge or pigeon.

Remove any good bits of flesh left on the birds and keep them on one side. Melt the butter in a large heavy pan and fry the chopped bacon and broken up carcass fairly slowly until they are golden brown and glistening, turning them over from time to time.

Meanwhile peel and chop the vegetables, and then add them to the pan, stirring everything around until nicely browned. Finally stir in the flour, and let it sizzle a minute, then remove the pan from the heat.

Heat the stock and when it comes to the boil pour it over the bones and vegetables in their pan. Add the bouquet of herbs, the salt, cayenne pepper and peppercorns and the clove, and simmer everything for 2 hours, skimming away any impurities that rise to the surface.

Strain the soup, add the pieces of reserved meat, cut into dice, and add the sherry. Heat through, season carefully and serve.

29

Light carrot soup with cream

TO SERVE FOUR

INGREDIENTS
450 g (1 lb) new carrots
225 g (½ lb) parsnips
1 dozen silver baby onions
  or 100 g (¼ lb) shallots
275 ml (½ pint) water
4 sprigs parsley
salt and freshly ground
  pepper
850 ml (1½ pints) creamy
  milk
2 egg yolks
150 ml (¼ pint) single
  cream
parsley for garnishing

This soup, made with tender new spring carrots and flavoured lightly with parsnips which have been seasoned by a touch of winter frost, is fresh and delicate – quite unlike the hefty winter version of carrot soup.

Trim and scrape the vegetables and cut them into manageable pieces – if the cores of the parsnips seem woody, discard them as they will be tasteless.

Put all the vegetables into a large saucepan, cover them with cold water and add a pinch of salt. Cook for 15 minutes if you are going to use a liquidizer – up to 25, until everything is very tender, if you are going to use a mouli-légumes.

Now purée the vegetables, add the chopped parsley, seasoning and the milk and heat through to simmering point. Beat together the egg yolks and cream and put them in the bottom of the bowl in which you will serve the soup. Add a ladleful of the hot, but not boiling soup, stir it in, then pour in the rest of the soup, very hot but not boiling or the egg yolk will curdle. Stir well and serve garnished with parsley.

Light carrot soup with cream, English onion soup

English onion soup

TO SERVE FOUR

INGREDIENTS
4 large onions or 6 small
  ones
2 stalks celery
50 g (2 oz) butter
50 g (2 oz) flour
275 ml (½ pint) milk
850 ml (1½ pints) best
  chicken stock
salt, plenty of freshly
  ground pepper, nutmeg
2 tablespoons chopped
  parsley
4 tablespoons single cream

The onion, whose flavour is such an essential part of practically every soup, has been used for more than just flavouring in the past – the juice was rubbed on wasp stings as a pain-killer, and, if you could bear the smell it made an excellent hair restorer – it also helped to cure chilblains, catarrh and hangovers. The famous French onion soup, eaten by market porters for breakfast was therefore part food, part cure, but this English version, creamier and milder, is food pure and simple.

Peel and chop the onions and celery and cook them in a covered pan in a little butter, with a tablespoon of water until they are very soft, about 10 minutes. Then purée them in the liquidizer or sieve through the fine blade of a mouli-légumes. Keep the purée on one side while you melt the butter in the cleaned saucepan and stir in the flour to make a *roux*. When the flour and butter have combined and become smooth and glossy, add the milk a little at a time, stirring all the time until you have a smooth mixture. Add the onion and celery purée and enough stock to make a smooth creamy soup. Simmer for 10 minutes, taste for seasoning, add a little nutmeg, stir in the parsley and lastly enrich the soup by pouring the cream into the middle and letting it swirl up to the top.

Almond soup

TO SERVE SIX

INGREDIENTS
100 g (4 oz) ground
  almonds
275 ml (½ pint) milk
2 tablespoons fresh white
  breadcrumbs
25 g (1 oz) butter
25 g (1 oz) flour
1.2 litres (2 pints) best
  chicken stock
salt, cayenne pepper, mace
275 ml (½ pint) single
  cream
a few whole almonds,
  slivered
1 tablespoon butter

Almonds used to be a great feature of British cookery, when they were used, toasted, as a garnish and flavouring for green beans, or, pounded, as a thickening for sauces or to lighten cakes and puddings. In this recipe they make a pearly and delicate soup.

Put the ground almonds with the milk in a small saucepan and simmer gently for 10 minutes. Add the crumbs and simmer for 3 minutes more, then liquidize or rub to a purée with a spoon. In a large pan, melt the butter, add the flour and stir it in, then stir in the almond purée. Gradually add the stock and when you have a smooth soup, season with salt, cayenne pepper and mace.

Simmer slowly for 10 minutes and then remove from heat and stir in the cream. Heat through gently. Meanwhile fry the slivered almonds to a golden brown and scatter them over the soup just before serving.

Mushroom soup, almond soup

Mushroom soup with cream

TO SERVE SIX

INGREDIENTS
225 g (8 oz) white button
  mushrooms
1 small onion
50 g (2 oz) butter
25 g (1 oz) flour
1.2 litres (2 pints) chicken
  stock, home-made or cube
salt, freshly ground pepper,
  grating of nutmeg
½ wineglass Sauterne or
  other white wine
  (optional)
150 ml (¼ pint) milk

The colour of this soup depends very much on the quality of the mushrooms. It should ideally be a velvety pale brown, only possible if the mushrooms are really young and quite closed, but the flavour will still be very good indeed if you use mushrooms past their first youth.

Chop the mushrooms coarsely and either grate or chop the onion finely. Put them into a large saucepan with the butter and simmer in their own juices for 10 minutes. Add the flour, let it bubble for a few minutes, stirring with a wooden spoon, then add the stock little by little until you have a smooth soup. Bring to the boil and simmer for 20 minutes, then blend to a velvety cream in the liquidizer. Return to the pan, bring back to the boil and simmer 10–15 minutes, to reduce the soup a little – it should be thicker than required since you will be adding more liquid.

Season with salt, freshly ground pepper and nutmeg, add the wine and simmer for a further 5 minutes. Stir in the milk and cream, heat through and serve.

Delicate fresh tomato soup

Tomato soup (or 'tomata' as it used to be) is a foreign soup gone native, and is now one of the most loved of English soups. The home-made sort, a shade less pillarbox red than its useful tinned counterpart is the most delicate and fresh-tasting of dishes.

TO SERVE FOUR

INGREDIENTS
675 g (1½ lb) very ripe tomatoes
1 small bunch of spring onions
50 g (2 oz) butter
1 clove garlic
575 ml (1 pint) chicken stock
1 bayleaf
salt and pepper
a pinch of sugar
1 sprig of mint
4 tablespoons of single cream

Pour boiling water over the tomatoes and remove them after 30 seconds when the skins peel off easily. Cut them in half and squeeze out the pips which are discarded – take care not to discard too much of the liquid.

Chop the pipless tomato pulp coarsely, and skin and chop the onions, using the firm white part.

Melt the butter in a heavy saucepan and soften the spring onions with the clove of garlic until they are tender and trans-

parent. Add the tomato pulp and stir. Let it reduce a little and lose some of its moisture, and then add the stock and bay-leaf. Lower the heat and simmer the soup for 15 minutes until the tomatoes have all but dissolved. Take out the bayleaf and blend the soup in the liquidizer for a few seconds, or purée it in a mouli-légumes. Season with salt, pepper, and sugar and add a sprinkling of chopped mint and a swirl of cream which will rise appetisingly to the surface. Serve hot or cold.

Spinach soup

TO SERVE FOUR

INGREDIENTS
450 g (1 lb) spinach
1 onion, 1 stick celery
15 g (½ oz) butter
15 g (½ oz) flour
575 ml (1 pint) chicken stock either home-made or made with stock cubes
grating of nutmeg
salt and pepper
425 ml (¾ pint) single cream or milk
chopped chives (or chopped parsley if chives are not available)

The beauty of this soup lies in its bright emerald colour which is lost if the spinach is cooked for too long. It gives a taste of spring in the winter as it is both fresh and refreshing.

Wash the spinach, removing tough ribs and stalks and drop it into about 575 ml (1 pint) of boiling, lightly salted water. It does not matter if it doesn't all go under, since it will soon wilt down. When the spinach is tender, after about 10 minutes, cool it a little, put it into the liquidizer and whizz to a smooth purée.

Meanwhile chop the onion and celery finely and soften them over a medium heat in the butter, without letting them brown, in a large saucepan. When they are tender stir in the flour, let it cook slowly, without

bubbling for 5 minutes, then add the chicken stock, adding it gradually and stirring after each addition. When you have a velvety smooth sauce season with nutmeg, salt and pepper, turn down the heat a little and allow to bubble gently for 20 minutes.

Now add all the spinach mixture to your creamy white soup, heat through and lastly swirl in the cream or milk and scatter a few chopped chives over the surface.

Opposite : Spinach soup, green spring soup, fresh green pea and cucumber soup

Green spring soup

TO SERVE FOUR

INGREDIENTS
900 g (2 lb) nettle tops, spinach, lettuce leaves and sorrel mixed
25 g (1 oz) butter or bacon fat
1 bunch spring onions, finely chopped
salt and pepper
3 egg yolks
275 ml (½ pint) milk

It is a tradition in the country among locals, weekenders and untidy gardeners to eat nettle soup at least once in the spring, since as well as being good and refreshing it is supposed to cleanse the blood ready for the summer.

Pick very tiny young nettle shoots and wear gloves to do it. As soon as you get them home put them in a pan and pour a kettleful of boiling water over, and they will lose their sting.

Chop the greenery coarsely. Melt the butter or fat in a large saucepan, add the spring onions and all the chopped greenstuff and let it wilt down, turning it until it glistens. Now pour on 850 ml (1½ pints) of boiling water, season with salt and freshly ground pepper, and simmer, uncovered (covering will spoil the colour of the herbs), for 10 minutes until tender. Allow to cool a little. Beat the egg yolks, and mix with three tablespoons of the hot but not boiling liquid.

Purée the cooked greenery in the liquidizer and pour the resulting thin mossy green soup back into the pan together with the milk.

Heat through but do not boil. Away from the heat stir in the egg-yolk mixture, and serve.

Fresh green pea and cucumber soup

TO SERVE SIX

INGREDIENTS
900 g (2 lb) peas in their pods
a cucumber
1 lettuce (cos if possible)
2 onions
50 g (2 oz) butter
2 sprigs mint
1.2 litres (2 pints) chicken stock, home-made or made with a stock cube
salt and pepper
25 g (1 oz) flour
25 g (1 oz) butter
150 ml (¼ pint) creamy milk
3 tablespoons cream
parsley

This is one of the very best traditional summer soups and perfect for peas that have got a bit too old and starchy to eat on their own. If fresh peas are hard to come by, frozen peas make a reasonable substitute.

Shell the peas. Peel and slice the cucumber. Shred the lettuce – you can keep the inner heart for later sandwiches or salad. Chop the onions fairly finely.

Melt the butter in a large pan and soften the chopped onions for 5 minutes. Add the remaining vegetables and the mint and allow to wilt in the butter for about 5 minutes more before adding the chicken stock. Season as necessary with salt and freshy ground pepper and simmer for 30 minutes.

Remove from the heat and sieve or liquidize when cool enough to do so and put aside in a bowl. You should now have a thinnish soup of a beautiful green. This can now wait while you cook the rest of the meal.

All that remains to be done is to melt the butter, stir in the flour, then add the milk a little at a time to make a smooth sauce. Add all the soup, stir and heat through until it thickens very slightly.

Serve hot (or chilled) with cream and chopped parsley floating on top.

For a slightly grander soup, keep a few cooked peas and some thin slices of cucumber aside. Throw the peas into the soup at the end and fry the slices of cucumber, first dipped in flour, in a little butter, floating them on the soup like waterlily leaves at the last moment.

Golden pea soup

TO SERVE FOUR

INGREDIENTS
350 g (¾ lb) yellow split
    peas
225 g (½ lb) lean streaky
    bacon in a piece or a
    small hock preferably
    smoked
2 onions
1 clove garlic
1 stalk celery
1 leek
1 teaspoon dried marjoram
salt and freshly ground
    pepper

This soup, so thick that a spoon will almost stand up in it, is a great winter standby. Allow to cook for at least 2½–3 hours, and serve as a delicious meal by itself the first time round. Any leftovers can be extended with stock and served at another meal as a first course.

Soak the peas for 2 hours in a large pan of cold water. Put peas and bacon in a large pan, cover with 2.3 litres (4 pints) of cold water and bring slowly to the boil, stirring once or twice to prevent the peas from sticking, and let it simmer. Meanwhile clean and chop the vegetables including the garlic and scoop off any scum on the surface of the soup. Add the vegetables and marjoram and simmer, covered for 2½ hours, until the bacon is tender. If the soup becomes too thick, add more water, 275 ml (½ pint), at a time.

When the bacon is tender lift it out, remove the rind, cut the meat into small cubes and keep them hot. Taste the soup and add salt and pepper if necessary. Share out the bacon pieces between four bowls and ladle the yellow-gold soup over the top. Serve straight away. This soup must be eaten piping hot as it gets even thicker as it cools.

Crisp croûtons of fried bread are delicious thrown into the bowls, hot and sizzling, at the last moment.

Tattie soup

Traditional Scottish peasant soup, easy to make, and made with the most humble and easily obtained ingredients.

TO SERVE FOUR

INGREDIENTS
450 g (1 lb) old potatoes
2 onions
2 old carrots
4 rashers streaky bacon
    (optional)
1.7 litres (3 pints) water or
    stock – made either from
    leftover roast lamb bones
    or beef bones
salt, freshly ground pepper

Peel and slice the potatoes, coarsely grate the skinned onions and carrots, and cut the bacon into squares.

Bring the stock to the boil in a large pan, add the vegetables and bacon. Cover and simmer gently for 1½ hours, until the soup is thick and creamy; season. Traditionally a handful of finely chopped nettle tops is thrown in 10 minutes before serving, but parsley would be a reasonable alternative, just to freshen up the soup.

From top to bottom: Golden pea soup, tattie soup

Country soup of winter vegetables

TO SERVE FOUR

INGREDIENTS
1 large onion
4 carrots
2 small turnips
2 potatoes
1 small swede (the size of a
  tennis ball)
50 g (2 oz) butter or
  margarine
1.2 litres (2 pints) stock –
  chicken or turkey or
  made with stock cube
grating of nutmeg
salt
plenty of freshly ground
  pepper
150 ml ($\frac{1}{4}$ pint) single cream
  (not expensive when the
  cost of the other
  ingredients is added up)

It would be a sad day if cooks lost all sense of the seasons. Even though we can obtain spring and summer produce all the year round there is real pleasure, when the cold intensifies outside, in serving a hefty soup of winter vegetables to warm the insides.

Grate all the vegetables on the coarse side of the grater. Melt the butter in a large heavy saucepan and turn the grated vegetables in this over a gentle heat, until they are softened and glistening. Pour on the stock and bring to the boil. Simmer, covered, for one hour until the vegetables are tender and the soup is lightly thickened. Taste for seasoning, adding nutmeg, salt and plenty of pepper. Stir in the cream, heat through and serve with freshly cut wholemeal bread and unsalted butter.

White fish soup with green fishballs

INGREDIENTS
575 g (1¼ lb) firm white
  fish, fresh or frozen, for
  instance haddock, coley,
  angler, hake – 450 g
  (1 lb) for the soup and
  100 g (¼ lb) for the
  fishballs
3 or 4 stalks of parsley (the
  green is used for the
  fishballs)
1 small glass white wine
50 g (2 oz) butter
50 g (2 oz) flour
salt and freshly ground
  pepper
150 ml (¼ pint) single
  cream
For the green fishballs
100 g (¼ lb) raw fish (see
  soup ingredients)
1 anchovy
2 heaped tablespoons fresh
  white breadcrumbs
cayenne pepper
1 small egg
2 tablespoons chopped
  parsley

Lady Sarah Lindsay was evidently an exceedingly popular country house guest in the early nineteenth century, and was welcome at many of the great English houses. Luckily for us, her round of visits bore fruit in the form of a little cookery book of the most exquisite recipes given by her hosts and hostesses, including this very delicate creamy-white soup on which bobbed green-speckled fishballs the size of marbles.

You can choose any white fish that is fresh and firm – on the bone will give the best flavour, but fillets will do if that is what is easily available.

Skin the fish and cut it into convenient pieces. Place 450 g (1 lb) in a largish saucepan. Pour 1.4 litres (2½ pints) of cold water over the fish and add the parsley stalk, finely sliced onions, glass of white wine and some salt.

Bring gently to the boil and simmer very slowly for half an hour. Strain the soup into a bowl, retrieve all the flesh from the fish and put on one side. Discard the gubbins.

In a separate pan melt the butter, stir in the flour and let it cook gently for 2 minutes without browning. To this *roux* add the strained fish stock little by little. Let it simmer for 10 minutes, then add the best pieces of the fish. Adjust the seasoning and put the soup aside whilst you make the fishballs.

Purée the raw fish, together with all the other fishball ingredients in the liquidizer until you have a fine paste. Form into little balls the size of marbles with lightly floured hands. All this can be done well in advance.

When the time comes all that remains to be done is to bring the soup to the boil, drop in the fishballs and let them poach for

6 minutes in the simmering soup. If they do not rise after a minute or two, free them gently from the bottom of the pan with a wooden spoon.

Just before serving stir in the cream and heat through.

Cullen skink

INGREDIENTS
1 smoked haddock,
  undyed, weighing 675 g
  (1½ lb)
575 ml (1 pint) milk
1 onion
225 g (½ lb) potatoes,
  peeled, boiled and
  mashed, or leftover mash
25 g (1 oz) butter
salt and freshly ground
  pepper

This is a rich and very subtly flavoured Scottish smoked haddock soup with simple ingredients. Try to make it with undyed smoked haddock which should be a pale straw colour.

Place the smoked haddock in a roasting tin with 575 ml (1 pint) of water and the milk. Chop the onion and scatter it round the fish. Bring slowly to the boil and simmer gently for 15 minutes or until the haddock is just tender, and a light cream appears on its surface, between the flakes. Remove the fish from the pan, and flake the flesh from the skin and bones.

Put the haddock trimmings (bones and skin), into a saucepan together with the cooking liquid and onions and simmer, covered, for 1 hour. Now strain this stock

and return it to the pan. Heat it through, add the mashed potato, stirring well to remove any lumps and then add the flaked fish. Stir in the butter, a little at a time and season with salt and pepper to taste.

If liked, you can stir in 2 tablespoons of cream and sprinkle the soup with chopped parsley.

From left to right : Cullen skink, white fish soup with green fishballs, partan bree

Partan bree

TO SERVE FOUR

INGREDIENTS
1 large or 2 small crabs
  (1 1-kg or 2 ½-kg crabs)
  (1 2-lb or 2 1½-lb crabs)
50 g (2 oz) rice
575 ml (1 pint) milk
575 ml (1 pint) chicken
  stock or water and
  chicken stock cube
salt and pepper
dash of cayenne pepper
150 ml (¼ pint) single
  cream

To pick a crab
Buy a ready boiled crab; it should feel heavy for its size. Ask the fishmonger to open it and remove the inedible gills (deadman's fingers) and intestines.

Twist off legs and claws (1). Crack claws with a hammer to extract claw meat. Crack legs and remove meat with a skewer. Remove bony flap from underside of body. Cut body in three as shown (2). Pick white meat from bony cavities inside body with a skewer (3). Put it with claw meat unless the recipe instructs otherwise. Remove brown meat from inside the shell with skewer (4). Keep it separate from white meat.

Remove all the meat from the boiled crab, putting the claw meat on one side. Rinse the rice and put it in a saucepan with the milk. Season with a small pinch of salt and cook until the rice is soft but not a mush. Liquidize the milk and rice mixture together with the main part of the crab meat to make a fairly coarse or smooth purée according to your preference. Clean out the pan and return the soup. Heat it gradually stirring in enough stock to give it

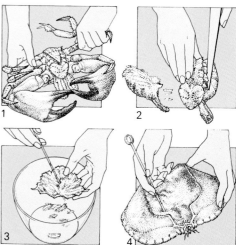

a nice creamy texture. Do not allow to boil. Add the pieces of claw meat, and taste for seasoning, adding salt, pepper and cayenne. At the last moment add the cream and heat through. The result is a pretty pinky soup with a rich and delicious crab flavour.

Fish

The British are an island race and it is not surprising that fish and shellfish from our shores have long been one of our staple foods. But what is surprising is the way that fashions and tastes change. What is scarce is always more desirable than what is plentiful – but how strange nowadays when salmon is so dreadfully expensive to think of the eighteenth-century Irish apprentices who looked on glumly as the great silver salmon leaped up the river Liffey, and insisted on marking in their indenture papers the number of days on which their masters could feed them this cheapest of fish. Oysters too were the food of the poor, they were eaten not by the dozen and half-dozen then, but by the hundreds. (In fact they were so common that they were even made into sausages.)

Nobody in the seventeenth, eighteenth or even nineteenth century thought much of trout; but whale, sturgeon or porpoise were such extra special delicacies that they were saved for the king and were his property alone. In practice though, monarchs often waived their rights and almost inevitably awarded the tongue of the whale, or even the whole head, to the tenant of the stretch of beach where the whale had landed and he would bear it home on a cart and salt it down for the winter.

While whalemeat was a royal perk, kings and subjects alike favoured 'small-fry'. Elvers (tiny transparent baby eels) were a well-loved food together with whitebait, which were caught in the Thames and sold on the quaysides to be cooked on the spot, and eaten by the promenaders, as they strolled about, watching the busy life of the river.

For those who lived inland in earlier times, however, the eating of fish was a far less agreeable business. The people, who at the time, what with the wretched roads

Right : The herring smacks arriving at Lowestoft quay.
Far right : During the winter months these smacks bringing herrings to England's east coast would be met by shoals of migratory Scottish herring-girls waiting to gut and pack the fish on the quayside.
Top : London's famous fish market, Billingsgate, as it looked early in this century. The strange round hats of the porters made good platforms for carrying stacks of baskets filled with fish.

40

and horse transport coupled with no ice, had no possibility of buying sea fish that was anywhere near to being fresh, were obliged by the Church and the State (who were desperately trying to boost an ailing fish industry) to eat fish not only on Fridays and during Lent, but on Wednesdays and Saturdays as well. The result was a heavy diet of salt herrings and dried cod, so hard and salty that it had to be pounded with a stone or hammer for an hour before it was useable. An Elizabethan schoolboy wrote: 'I have ate none other than salt-fish this Lent, and it has engendered so much phlegm within me that it stoppeth my pipes that I can neither speak nor breathe.'

Today we are extremely lucky. Fish, although scarcer than before, is always fresh, and we can buy it with confidence. Whether fish is frozen straight out of the sea on board the deep-sea trawlers, or 'wet' and packed in ice, it has never reached the shops fresher than now.

So freshness is not any longer a problem; our problem, if we have one, is that frozen fish is so easy to buy and to prepare, that we are in danger of forgetting some of the less common varieties of fish available 'wet' at the fishmongers, and as a result the fish-shop may soon disappear. This would indeed be a pity, since many of these fish are so delicious and can bring so much variety to the table.

Do not be put off cooking fresh fish by the idea that the smell will invade the house. Fish baked in the oven covered with kitchen foil makes no smell at all, and if grill pans are covered with foil they will not absorb a fishy smell. Frying fish makes no more smell than frying chips, and if you are worried about cleaning the pan afterwards, rinse it in cold water first before bringing it to the boil with a lump of soda – or use a non-stick pan.

Fried fish in batter

TO SERVE FOUR

INGREDIENTS
175 g (6 oz) flour
1 teaspoon bicarbonate
    of soda
salt
225 ml (8 fl oz) water
4 fillets of fish, cod,
    haddock, hake or plaice
oil or lard for frying

The great British tradition of fish and chips is one which will die hard, even though the batter is not always delicately crisp nor the chips rustling and golden.

The true chip-shop batter is an economical affair made without eggs. Surprisingly enough this frugal mixture of flour and water gives much the lightest and crispest result. Make it thicker or thinner, according to taste.

Put the flour and bicarbonate of soda and a pinch of salt in a bowl, make a well in the centre and add the water gradually, stirring the flour in from round the edges, and incorporating it little by little to make a smooth batter. This can also be done by putting the ingredients in the liquidizer and blending it to a smooth cream. Add more water if the batter is too thick. Let it stand for 1 hour, to develop its texture.

Pat the pieces of fish dry with kitchen paper. Do not skin them as the skin contains much of the flavour. Lay them on a board, dust them lightly with flour and season them with salt.

Heat the oil in a deep wide pan. Try a spoonful of batter. If it rises almost immediately to the surface and sizzles all round its edge, the oil is the right temperature (180°–190°C, 350°–375°F). Dip the fish in the batter, one piece at a time, shake gently to remove extra batter and slide into the hot oil. When it is golden brown all over the fish is done. Transfer to a hot plate and eat as soon as possible with chips and lemon-quarters or vinegar.

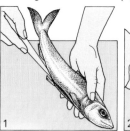

How to clean a round fish: Make a slit along the length of the belly (1). Scrape out the insides. Trim off the gills with scissors (2).

Cod in butter sauce

TO SERVE SIX

INGREDIENTS
½ a medium onion
75 g (3 oz) butter
850 g (1½ lb) small cod
    fillets
salt and pepper
squeeze of fresh lemon
    juice
a little chopped parsley

This excellent and simple recipe can be used with haddock, coley, turbot or brill with equally good results.

Chop the onion finely. Melt 25 g (1 oz) of the butter in a frying pan and soften the onion, without letting it brown, for 5 minutes. Heat the oven to 180°C, 350°F, Gas Mark 4. Put the fish into a buttered, shallow ovenproof dish. Season it with salt and pepper and spoon the onion and butter mixture over the top. Put in the rest of the butter and cover the dish with foil. Bake for 20–25 minutes.

When the fish is just cooked, spoon the butter and cooking juices into a small pan; keep the fish hot. Add a squeeze of lemon juice and a little chopped parsley and whisk it over a very gentle heat with a fork. As you whisk, it will become creamy and opaque. When it is thoroughly whisked pour it over the fish and serve at once.

Plaice with Parmesan cheese

TO SERVE FOUR

INGREDIENTS
4 whole medium-sized
 plaice, lemon sole or
 Dover sole
cayenne pepper
salt and pepper
juice of ½ a lemon
50 g (2 oz) butter
25 g (1 oz) flour
425 ml (¾ pint) milk
50 g (2 oz) finely grated
 Parmesan cheese

In the days of Mrs Beeton, Parmesan cheese was used quite frequently and in large quantities. It is certainly a wonderful cooking cheese, but has now rocketed in price – use Cheddar as a substitute.

Butter a large flat fireproof dish, and put in the whole fish. Season with cayenne pepper, salt, pepper, lemon juice and dot the fish here and there with little lumps of butter, using about 25 g (1 oz). Bake at 180°C, 350°F, Gas Mark 4 for 20 minutes. Meanwhile melt the remaining butter in a

small saucepan, and stir in the flour. When it starts to foam add the milk little by little, stirring until smooth after each addition. Let it simmer for 10 minutes, then stir in the cheese. Taste for seasoning, then, when the fish are ready, pour the sauce over them, and put the dish under a hot grill. Cook until bubbling and browned on top and serve immediately.

Plaice with Parmesan cheese, fried plaice

Fried plaice

TO SERVE FOUR

INGREDIENTS
25 g (1 oz) flour
1 egg (size 2), beaten
75 g (3 oz) fine fresh
 breadcrumbs
450 g (1 lb) plaice fillets or
 4 small whole plaice
salt and white pepper
1 tablespoon oil and 15 g
 (½ oz) butter for frying

This is one of the nicest and simplest of all fish recipes and can equally well be used for soles, flounders, dabs and megrims; Mrs Beeton pronounced it 'excellent'.

The secret of frying fish, or anything else for that matter, in crumbs, is to be well organized. Put the flour, beaten egg and breadcrumbs in three pie dishes and place them side by side on your working top. Put the fillets on a board set down next to the pie dishes, and season with salt and pepper. There is no need to skin the fillets – the skin is very tender, and contains most of the flavour of the fish.

Put a large frying pan ready, with the oil and butter in it, and prepare all the other parts of the dish – the traditional accompaniments of fried plaice fillets are spinach and very buttery creamy mashed potatoes, and lemon wedges, or round pats of parsley butter.

Now take each fillet and dip it first in flour, then egg, then crumbs, patting them in well. Use only the left hand for the flour, only the right for the egg and crumbs, otherwise you will get all stuck up.

Heat the oil and butter and fry the plaice fillets two at a time for 3–4 minutes on each side. Serve very crisp and hot.

How to clean a flat fish: Cut off the head and remove, together with the insides (1). Trim the tail and remove the fins (2).

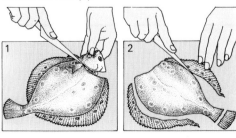

Fried sprats

INGREDIENTS
1 kg (2 lb) sprats
flour
sunflower oil for frying
salt
2 lemons

Many people think the good old sprat is too fiddly to bother with; but fried briefly in oil, a dish of sprats is a tremendously good traditional dish and well worth the trouble it takes.

Cut the heads off the sprats and remove the guts at the same time. This is done by cutting through the top of the body, just behind the head, but not quite cutting through the belly. The knife is then used to pull the head away from the body and the insides will be drawn out at the same time. After a bit of practice it takes literally a few seconds to deal with each fish.

Now pat the fish fairly dry with kitchen paper and dust them with flour.

Heat 2 cm ($\frac{1}{2}$ in) of oil in a large frying pan, add a pinch of salt and drop in one sprat. If it starts to sizzle, immediately drop in several more and fry them on each side until they are brown.

Now take them out with a fish slice and keep them hot in a dish lined with kitchen paper. Sprinkle them with salt to keep them crisp. Fry the rest of the sprats in batches, draining them well on the side of the pan before transferring them to your serving dish to keep hot.

Serve with wedges of lemon and bread and butter. Fried sprats are traditional and quite delicious for tea.

Grilled trout with herb butter

TO SERVE FOUR

INGREDIENTS
2 tablespoons chopped fresh chives, parsley and dill (or dried herbs if fresh are not available)
salt and freshly ground pepper
50 g (2 oz) softened butter
juice of $\frac{1}{2}$ a lemon
4 trout of 175–225 g (6–8 oz) each
a little melted butter

In the past, and until quite recently, trout were seldom bought, but came straight out of the river. Nowadays trout farms abound and 'trout with almonds' has become one of the good old standbys on hotel menus, along with 'smoked trout with horseradish'. A more traditional and equally good dish is a plate of simply fried or grilled trout with herb-flavoured butter.

Put the herbs, seasoning and the butter in a bowl and mash them with a fork until well mixed, then add the lemon juice and work it in. Clean the trout, leaving them whole and pat them dry with kitchen paper. Make three diagonal slashes in each side of the fish, cutting almost through to the bone.

Divide the herb butter into four pieces and put one inside each fish. Brush the fish over with melted butter and grill quickly under a hot grill until nicely browned on each side; it will take about 3 minutes on each side for smaller fish, 5 minutes or so for larger fish.

Mackerel in parcels with watercress sauce

Also suitable for trout

TO SERVE SIX

INGREDIENTS
6 small mackerel
50 g (2 oz) melted butter
salt and pepper
a squeeze of lemon juice
6 squares of kitchen foil
   45 × 23 cm (18 × 9 in)

Watercress sauce
15 g ($\frac{1}{2}$ oz) butter
15 g ($\frac{1}{2}$ oz) flour
425 ml ($\frac{3}{4}$ pint) milk
dash dry cider
salt and pepper to taste
2 bunches of watercress
a hazelnut-sized knob of
   butter

In the old days the parcels or packets in which the fish are cooked would have been made with oiled writing paper, but kitchen foil is easier to handle and gives a very succulent result.

Ask the fishmonger to clean the fish but leave on the heads and tails. Make two incisions across the thickest part of the sides to help them cook quickly.

Brush the squares of foil with melted butter, put a fish on to each square, season with salt and pepper and a squeeze of lemon juice and fold each one into a little parcel, folding the ends so that the juices do not escape.

Place them on a baking tray and put them in a moderate oven, 180°C, 350°F, Gas Mark 4, for 25 minutes – 30 minutes for larger fish.

To serve, put a parcel on each plate, cut open the top with scissors and let each person unwrap their own fish (napkins will be needed). Serve watercress sauce separately.

Watercress sauce
Melt the butter in a saucepan without letting it brown, stir in the flour and when it has foamed up add the milk a little at a time, stirring after each addition, until you have a smooth sauce. Add the cider and a seasoning of salt and pepper and allow to simmer gently, while you prepare the watercress.

Bring a pan of water to the boil, throw in the bunch of watercress, well washed and picked over, and let it boil for 2 minutes. Drain it well in a colander, put it on the chopping board and chop it finely. Stir this chopped cress into the sauce, cover the pan with a tilted lid and let it simmer for a few minutes over a very low heat. Stir in the knob of butter and serve.

Grilled herrings with mustard sauce

TO SERVE FOUR

INGREDIENTS
4 fine fresh herrings
oil
salt

Mustard sauce
1 tablespoon cider vinegar
1 tablespoon softened
   butter
1 teaspon lemon juice
1 teaspoon Dijon mustard
1 teaspoon mustard powder
1 teaspoon brown sugar
1 tablespoon water
1 egg, beaten
salt
cayenne pepper

Scale and clean the herrings and wipe them with kitchen paper. Work all the ingredients for the sauce together into a smooth paste, in the top of a double boiler. Stir gently over hot water until the sauce thickens, but do not allow the water to boil. Keep the sauce warm while you grill the herrings. On each side of the fish make two or three diagonal incisions about 4 cm (1½ in) apart, cutting down to the bone but not through it. Take off the heads and brush the fish with oil. Grill them quickly under a hot grill until brown and crisp on both sides. Serve with the mustard sauce.

It is a good idea to line the grill pan with cooking foil before using it for fish – otherwise rinse it under the tap first with *cold* water and then with gradually hotter water and lastly in a basin with hot water and a lump of soda and the last trace of fish cooking will vanish.

Herrings in oatmeal

TO SERVE FOUR

INGREDIENTS
4 fine fresh herrings
salt
4 heaped tablespoons
   medium or fine oatmeal
   (or porridge oats)
lard for frying

To any Scotsman a meal without oats is a wasted opportunity; this dish of herrings coated with oatmeal has a further claim to fame: it was a great favourite with King Edward VII and enjoyed by him not only in Balmoral but when he was living his grand London life.

The herrings are nicest if you open them out along the back, like kippers, and remove the backbones. To do this, first remove head and guts in one operation (1) without opening the fish. Now scrape off the scales with a blunt knife (2) or a scallop shell – the traditional fish scaler.

Make an incision along the backbone with a sharp knife, open up the fish so that it lies flat like an open book (3), and remove the backbone, easing it out carefully to take out as many large bones as possible (4).

Pat the fish dry with kitchen paper, and then sprinkle them with salt and oatmeal on both sides, patting it in well.

Heat a knob of lard the size of a walnut in a large frying pan, and when it is hot slip in a herring, or two if there is room. Fry them for 8–10 minutes until they are brown and crisp, turning them carefully from time to time.

Serve them with oatcakes and vinegar if you want to be traditional, or with mustard sauce if you want to follow Edward VII's example, but they are very delicious simply served with brown bread and butter.

Top: grilled herrings with mustard sauce, *bottom:* herrings in oatmeal

Soused herrings

Also suitable for mackerel

TO SERVE SIX

INGREDIENTS
6 fine fresh herrings,
    preferably with soft roes
    weighing 175–225 g
    (6–8 oz)
275 ml ($\frac{1}{2}$ pint) vinegar –
    preferably cider vinegar
275 ml ($\frac{1}{2}$ pint) dry cider
salt
4 bayleaves
4 sprigs thyme
12 black peppercorns
4 cloves
2 blades mace

Britain has been a nation of herring eaters, along with Scandinavia and Holland, since earliest times. Yarmouth's herring industry started as early as AD 495 and continued steadily until recently when the catches started to decline. Sad to say, we have fished out many of the old herring waters and it is now becoming a scarce and expensive fish. However, it is still a good buy and still excellent food.

The point of soused herrings is first and foremost that they make a good summer lunch, but also that once soused they can be kept for several days if necessary.

Scrape the scales off the herrings. Cut off their tails and heads, clean them thoroughly reserving the soft roes, then wash them under the tap. Pat them dry, put back the roes and lay them in a large pie dish, heads to tails. Cover with the vinegar and dry cider, half and half. Strew the salt, herbs and spices over the top, cover with a sheet of oiled foil (this will prevent the smell from spreading) and stand the dish in a tin of boiling water.

Bake in a moderate oven 180°C, 350°F, Gas Mark 4, for 30 minutes, then allow to cool.

Serve cold garnished with watercress and with a green salad with hard-boiled eggs chopped into it.

To cook
a whole fish

Salmon trout, sea bass, small cod, mullet, haddock, hake or any large fish

INGREDIENTS
For 4 people buy a 1.3–
   1.4 kg (2½–3 lb) fish
For 6–8 people 1.6–1.8 kg
   (3½–4 lb) fish
salt and pepper
1 shallot
1 tablespoon dry cider or
   white wine
2 sprigs dill
butter

Nothing could be more appetizing than a whole handsome fresh fish splendid on its dish, especially a salmon trout, that prince among fish. The big problem, however, is how to cook a large fish. In the past a fish kettle was the only answer and if your own cupboard did not boast one, then one was borrowed for the occasion. But with the arrival of aluminium foil the process of cooking a whole fish became much more feasible, since a large fish can now be cooked in the oven.

Don't overcook the fish; it should arrive on the table complete, unbroken and in that just-cooked state that gives creamy flakes of fish rather than wet shreds.

Cut off a piece of aluminium foil large enough to enclose the fish. Put it over a baking tin. Spread a very little butter over the inside – usually the non-shiny side.

Season the fish inside and out with salt and pepper and place it on the foil. Slice the shallot finely and scatter it over the fish. Bring the foil up round the fish, pour in the cider to moisten it, put the dill inside it, then loosely wrap.

Bake the fish at 180°C, 350°F, Gas Mark 4. It can be rolled off the foil on to a plate for serving. For a larger fish, too large to fit in the oven, cut it in half and bake the pieces separately. Allow, for a fish weighing 1.3–1.8 kg (2½–4 lb) 40–50

Cooked salmon trout

minutes: for a larger fish, to be cooked whole, 12 minutes per 450 g (1 lb).

To serve the fish hot

Allow to set for 10 minutes, then roll the fish very gently off the foil on to a heated dish. Place some slices of lemon along one side of the dish or on top of the fish if it is large enough, and that is all that is needed, unless the head has become very broken and ugly looking, in which case put a small bunch of watercress just by the gills to cover the worst bits. Serve cod or other white fish with shrimp sauce, parsley sauce, melted butter or Hollandaise sauce, or, in the case of salmon trout (or salmon for that matter) drawn butter sauce, green sauce (*see page* 153) or lots of fresh salted butter.

To serve the fish cold

Allow the fish to cool in the foil, having first opened the top to let the steam escape. When cold lift or roll the fish on to a large plate having first spooned away all the liquid. It can be served with the skin on or carefully skinned. Decorations should again be kept extremely simple; after all the fish is supposed to be eaten, not cast in plaster and stuck on the wall. A row of thin overlapping slices of lemon down the middle of the fish is as fussy as it should be.

Baked grey mullet

INGREDIENTS
4 small (350–500 g/¾–1 lb)
    or 2 large (1 kg/2lb) or
    1 very large mullet
salt, freshly ground pepper
1 tablespoon sunflower oil
4 onions
4 tomatoes
a few sprigs of parsley
1 tablespoon water
squeeze of lemon juice

The grey mullet, which are seen in the muddy tides of Cornish estuaries, are not such delicate fish as the bass, but are still highly thought of by those who know their fish. Since they are now more widely available, here is a very good traditional recipe; if possible choose the smaller fish, and be sure to ask the fishmonger to clean and scale them for you.

Season the fish both inside and out with salt and pepper.

Heat the oil in a frying pan. Slice the onions coarsely and soften them in the oil for about 10–15 minutes, without allowing them to brown.

Put half the onions over the bottom of a fireproof dish and lay the fish on top. Slice the tomatoes and lay them over the fish. Now spread the onions on top and sprinkle their oil over everything. Add the parsley and a tablespoon of water, and a squeeze of lemon juice. Season again lightly and cover the fish with kitchen foil.

Bake at 180°C, 350°F, Gas Mark 4 for 30 minutes for small fish, 35–40 for larger fish. Serve as it is, in the dish. This is also good cold.

Country-house fish pie

TO SERVE FOUR–SIX

INGREDIENTS
450 g (1 lb) white fish:
    halibut, haddock or
    whiting fillets
425 ml (¾ pint) milk
salt and pepper
65 g (2½ oz) butter
25 g (1 oz) flour
100 g (4 oz) white button
    mushrooms
225 g (½ lb) peeled shrimps
    or prawns
3 tablespoons double cream
squeeze of lemon juice
450 g (1 lb) potatoes
    peeled, boiled and
    mashed with milk and
    butter

Put the fish in a baking tin with the milk, season with salt and pepper and bake at 180°C, 350°F, Gas Mark 4 for 15–20 minutes, until it is just cooked through – the time will vary a little according to the thickness of the pieces of fish. Take it out of the oven, flake the fish, removing skin and bones, and strain and reserve the cooking liquid.

Make a sauce by melting 40 g (1½ oz) of butter in a saucepan without allowing it to brown. Stir in the flour and when it foams up, add the cooking liquid from the fish, a little at a time, stirring after each addition until you have a smooth creamy sauce. It will use up almost all the cooking liquid, but there may be a little left over if the pie is not to become too sloppy.

Cut the mushrooms into cubes about 2 cm (½ in) across and soften them in 25 g (1 oz) of butter for a few minutes over a gentle heat. Make the mashed potatoes for the top of the pie.

Now stir the fish, mushrooms and shrimps or prawns lightly into the sauce, add the cream and a squeeze of lemon, taste for seasoning and put the mixture into a 1½-litre (3-pint) pie dish. Cover the top with a layer of mashed potatoes which should be left in rough peaks, not smoothed over. Dot the top with butter and bake at 220°C, 425°F, Gas Mark 7, for 20 minutes until the top is browned and the fish bubbling hot.

Smoked fish pie

TO SERVE FOUR–SIX

INGREDIENTS
225 g (½ lb) smoked golden
    fillet of haddock, cod or
    whiting
350 g (¾ lb) fresh haddock
275 ml (½ pint) milk
2 tablespoons water
1 bayleaf
1 small onion
25 g (1 oz) butter
25 g (1 oz) flour
50 g (2 oz) grated Cheddar
    cheese
2 hard-boiled eggs
3 sprigs parsley
salt and pepper
mashed potato made from
    450 g (1 lb) potatoes
butter

This is a beautiful golden pie with a delicious flavour. Take care when adding salt, as some smoked haddocks are extremely salty.

Put the fish in an ovenproof dish with the milk and 2 tablespoons water. Put in the bayleaf to flavour it and bake uncovered at 180°C, 350°F, Gas Mark 4 for 20 minutes. Take out the fish when it is cool enough to handle and skin and flake it into large flakes. Put these aside, and strain and keep the cooking liquid. Chop the onion.

Melt the butter in a medium-sized saucepan and soften the onion without allowing it to brown. Now stir in the flour and when it begins to foam start adding the milk from the fish. Add enough to make a creamy sauce, pouring it in gradually and stirring until the mixture is smooth after each addition. Add the grated cheese, the flaked fish, the coarsely chopped hard-boiled eggs and the chopped parsley and season

with pepper. Taste the sauce – it may need a little salt but smoked fillet is often very salty, so take care.

Put the mixture into a 1-litre (2-pint) pie dish. Cover with creamy mashed potato, which should be left in rough peaks and not smoothed down. Dot the top with butter and bake at 200°C, 400°F, Gas Mark 6 for 25 minutes until the top is lightly browned and the pie is bubbling round the edges.

Country-house and smoked fish pies

Smoked haddock soufflé

TO SERVE SIX

INGREDIENTS
1 small smoked haddock
  on the bone of 350 g
  (approx $\frac{3}{4}$ lb) or 1 small
  smoked fillet
275 ml ($\frac{1}{2}$ pint) milk
275 ml ($\frac{1}{2}$ pint) water
knob of butter for cooking
  the haddock
25 g (1 oz) flour
50 g (2 oz) butter
50 g (2 oz) grated Cheddar
  cheese
4 eggs plus one egg white

The soufflé, while not being a British invention, has been one of the favourite lunch or supper dishes of the British for well over a century – one of the best and most characteristic being a smoked haddock and cheese soufflé, a flavour combination of which Arnold Bennett was particularly fond (for Arnold Bennett's omelet *see page* 161).

Butter a 1-litre (2-pint) soufflé dish. Preheat the oven to 200°C, 400°F, Gas Mark 6. Put the haddock in a shallow dish with the milk and water, and a knob of butter and poach it in the oven for 15 minutes. When it is cooked strain off the liquid and keep back 275 ml ($\frac{1}{2}$ pint). Flake the haddock, discarding the skin and bones, and chop finely with a knife.

Make a thickish sauce with the flour, butter and 275 ml ($\frac{1}{2}$ pint) of the haddock liquid: melt the butter in a saucepan, stir in the flour and when it foams add the liquid a little at a time, stirring after each addition until the mixture is creamy and smooth. Beat in the grated cheese, add the haddock and remove from the heat.

Beat the egg yolks one at a time into the sauce, and season it with very little salt (the fish is salty) and freshly ground pepper. Beat the egg whites to a firm snow. Stir a quarter into the haddock mixture, fold in the rest with a palette knife, turn it carefully into the soufflé dish, and level out the top. Put it straight into the middle of the oven. Turn down the heat to 190°C, 375°F, Gas Mark 5, and bake for 25 minutes until brown and puffy but still slightly soft and shaky in the middle.

Eat the instant it is out of the oven. The fish makes it a slightly firmer soufflé than usual, but it has a delicious flavour.

Chilled fish mousse

TO SERVE SIX

INGREDIENTS
Fish stock
225 g (½ lb) fish trimmings
  from the fishmonger
bunch of herbs – parsley,
  bayleaf, fennel
1 carrot
1 onion
2 tablespoons dry white
  wine
salt and pepper
425 ml (¾ pint) water
Mousse
350 g (¾ lb) haddock fillet,
  fresh or frozen
15 g (½ oz) gelatine
  (1 packet)
100 g (¼ lb) button
  mushrooms
squeeze of lemon juice
25 g (1 oz) butter
275 ml (½ pint) double or
  whipping cream
1 tablespoon chopped fresh
  tarragon, parsley and
  chives

A creamy fish mousse made a very pretty centrepiece in the summer for a Victorian table. It would probably have been served, then, together with several other dishes such as fried eels and salmon cutlets with horseradish sauce, and would have been called fish cream. However, today it seems quite enough to make the main course with just a nice green salad to keep it company.

Put all the ingredients for the fish stock in a saucepan and simmer them, covered, for three-quarters of an hour. Strain the resulting liquid and boil it fast, uncovered, for 10 minutes to reduce it. Now turn down the heat to keep the stock at a slow simmer. Add the fish and poach it very gently for 10 minutes. Remove the fish and let it cool.

Melt the gelatine completely in a cup with 2 or 3 tablespoons of the hot fish stock, then stir it with the rest of the stock and set it aside to cool. Put it in the refrigerator when it has cooled, until it is just turning 'oily' and starting to set.

Cut the mushrooms into ½-cm (¼-in) dice and toss them with a generous squeeze of lemon to keep them white. Melt the butter in a small pan and sauté the mushrooms in it, without letting them brown, for 5 minutes. Whip the cream to a light snow.

With a fork crush the cooked fish, stir in the mushrooms and their liquid and the chopped herbs. Mix the chilled stock lightly with the fish mixture, and then fold in the whipped cream. Spoon the mixture into a soufflé dish and chill until set. It can be served straight from the dish.

Fish chowder

TO SERVE FOUR

INGREDIENTS
450 g (1 lb) thick haddock
  fillet
1 small onion
850 ml (1½ pints) milk
150 ml (¼ pint) water
3 potatoes
100 g (4 oz) bacon rashers
salt and freshly ground
  pepper
3 tablespoons cream

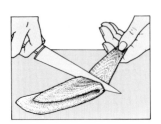

Skin the fillet beginning at the tail end (*see diagram*). Cut into small pieces.

Chop the onion finely and put it in a large saucepan with the milk and water, and bring slowly to the boil. Peel the potatoes and cut them in cubes. Cut the rind off the bacon and cut it into squares.

When the milk and water come to the boil, put in the potatoes and bacon, season with a little salt and pepper and simmer for half an hour. Now add the haddock and cook for a further 10 minutes, taste for seasoning, stir in the cream and serve at once.

Salmon butter

MAKES ABOUT 225 G (½ LB)

INGREDIENTS
175 g (6 oz) cooked salmon
75 g (3 oz) butter
pinch ground mace
sea salt

Remove every scrap of skin and bone and pound the salmon with pestle and mortar, then add the softened butter and pound to a paste. Season with a tiny pinch of mace – it is very strong – and a little sea salt.

Pack the mixture into little pots, chill and spread this delicious soft pink butter lavishly on thin slices of toast for tea or even breakfast.

Salmon hash

Also known as tweed kettle

TO SERVE FOUR–SIX

INGREDIENTS
2–3 potatoes
6 spring onions
40 g (1½ oz) butter
450 g (1 lb) left-over cold,
  cooked salmon
salt and cayenne pepper

Cook the potatoes in their skins. Chop the spring onions and soften them in butter. Cut the salmon into cubes, stir these in with the spring onions, add the potatoes, skinned and cut into cubes, and a little more butter, and fry gently without breaking the fish or potato, until nicely browned.

Top: salmon butter,
bottom: salmon hash

Salmon patties

TO SERVE FOUR

INGREDIENTS
225 g (8 oz) salmon, fresh
  cooked or tinned
100 g ($\frac{1}{4}$ lb) button
  mushrooms
squeeze of lemon juice
25 g (1 oz) butter
15 g ($\frac{1}{2}$ oz) flour
150 ml ($\frac{1}{4}$ pint) milk
1 egg yolk
salt, pepper, and grating of
  nutmeg
1 egg, beaten
50 g (2 oz) freshly toasted
  breadcrumbs
oil for frying

Flake the salmon, remove all bones and set it aside. Cut the mushrooms into little cubes, sprinkle them with lemon juice and stew them very gently in butter in a small frying pan for 5 minutes, tossing them about from time to time.

Melt the butter in a small pan and stir in the flour, then add the milk gradually, stirring after each addition until you have a smooth creamy sauce.

Add the egg yolk and beat thoroughly with a wooden spoon. Add the mushrooms and their juices and stir over a gentle heat until the mixture thickens a little. Season with salt, pepper and nutmeg and stir in the salmon. Put the mixture in a bowl and allow to cool before chilling in the refrigerator. When it is solid enough to handle with floured hands form the mixture into patties about 4 cm ($1\frac{1}{2}$ in) across and dip them first into beaten egg and then breadcrumbs and fry each side to a golden brown in hot oil. Serve very hot with lemon wedges.

Scalloped crab

TO SERVE FOUR

INGREDIENTS
50 g (2 oz) butter
1.4 kg (3 lb) dressed crab
100 g (4 oz) fresh
    breadcrumbs
juice of $\frac{1}{2}$ a lemon
salt, cayenne pepper,
    grating of nutmeg
2 chopped anchovies
150 ml ($\frac{1}{4}$ pint) single
    cream
50 g (2 oz) finely grated
    Cheddar cheese

This is an eighteenth-century recipe and it requires six scallop shells to serve the crab in – you can probably obtain them from the local fishmonger or collect them on the beach; be sure to give them a good scrub before using them for cooking. If you can't find the shells use small ovenproof cocotte dishes.

Melt the butter over a low heat. Stir in the crab meat, both white and brown, and then the breadcrumbs. Add the lemon juice, a tiny pinch of salt, a good sprinkling of cayenne and nutmeg, the anchovies which will add more salt, and cream. Stir till hot and then share the mixture out between the shells. Sprinkle the cheese over the top and brown under a hot grill.

To dress a crab
To pick a crab (*see page* 37). The white meat is served plain, lightly seasoned, in one bowl. The brown meat is mixed with a tablespoon of breadcrumbs, a $\frac{1}{2}$ teaspoon of mustard, salt and cayenne pepper and served in a separate bowl. Serve dressed crab with lemon wedges or home-made mayonnaise, and brown bread and butter.

Grilled lobster with cream and Worcester sauce

From Sir Harry Luke's famous travellers' cookery book 'The Tenth Muse'

TO SERVE FOUR ✿

INGREDIENTS
2 lobsters weighing
    675–900 g (1½–2 lb)
150 ml (¼ pint) double
    cream
50 g (2 oz) butter
1 tablespoon Worcester
    sauce

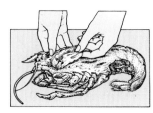

The English way with lobster, which used to be very plentiful, was generally to take it from its shell, mince it up, mix it with cream, breadcrumbs and seasoning and then cook it. But when lobsters are so scarce and also so beautiful, the simplest and plainest ways of serving them are really the best. Try plain boiled lobster served hot with melted butter, a salad of boiled lobster with freshly made mayonnaise, or this grilled lobster recipe, with cream and Worcester sauce.

The secret is never to overcook lobsters, so the counsel of perfection is to buy them live and cook them yourself. The difficulty here lies in despatching the creatures, which have complicated nervous systems. It must either be done by splitting them, still alive, cleanly in half along their backs with a cleaver, or putting them headfirst into a pot of boiling water (when they take a minute to die) and to split them in half afterwards. If you do not like the idea of these procedures, buy cooked lobsters and ask the fishmonger to split them. Take great care to heat them right through and then serve them immediately; any further cooking will toughen the flesh and make it rubbery.

Remove the sandy sac in the head (*see diagram*) but leave the green soft part and the scarlet-orange coral, both of which are edible and delicious. Crack the claws with a hammer. Dot the flesh of the lobsters all over with little pieces of butter, and place under a hot grill in a pan (to catch any juices that escape). A cooked lobster will take 8–10 minutes, a raw one about 25 minutes.

Melt 25 g (1 oz) of butter in a small saucepan, add the cream, season with a hefty dash of Worcester sauce and when the lobsters are hot pour any escaped juices from the grill pan into the sauce. Boil it fast for a minute or two.

Serve bubbling hot with the sauce poured over each grilled lobster half.

Prawn fritters

TO SERVE FOUR

INGREDIENTS
225 ($\frac{1}{2}$ lb) shelled prawns
100 g (4 oz) flour
1 egg
150 ml ($\frac{1}{4}$ pint) water
15 g ($\frac{1}{2}$ oz) melted butter
salt, cayenne pepper
oil for frying

These can be a first course, in which case follow them with a light second course as they are rich.

Chop the prawns very finely until they are almost a paste. Put the flour in a bowl, make a well in the centre and break in the egg, stirring with a wooden spoon to blend in the flour. Gradually add the water until you have a smooth cream. Now add the prawns and the melted butter and beat thoroughly, and season with a little salt and cayenne pepper.

Heat a pan of oil, drop in this delicious mixture in spoonfuls and let them fry to a golden brown. Serve in a crisp mound with lemon wedges.

Morecambe Bay potted shrimps or prawns

TO SERVE FOUR

INGREDIENTS
225 g (8 oz) unsalted butter
1 tablespoon water
1 teaspoon ground mace
2 good pinches cayenne
   pepper
generous grating nutmeg
450 g (1 lb) fresh shrimps
   or 350 g ($\frac{3}{4}$ lb) frozen
   shrimps or prawns,
   defrosted at room
   temperature
salt

Melt the butter gently in a small pan with the water. It must not brown. Pour it into a bowl to cool and then place it in the refrigerator to harden. Remove the solid butter and throw out the liquid which has collected underneath. You now have clarified butter.

Now melt 100 g (4 oz) of the clarified butter together with the spices, put in the shrimps or prawns and let them steep in the hot butter for 10 minutes. They must not cook or they will become tough. Taste for salt at this point. They may be salty enough.

Now pour them, with their butter, into little pots and let them set. Melt the remaining butter and pour enough over the surface of each pot to seal it. Cool and chill. They will keep well for a week or so in the refrigerator.

Before serving allow the chill to go off the potted shrimps or the butter will be hard and tasteless. Serve with hot toast.

Stewed eels

TO SERVE SIX

INGREDIENTS
2 large eels
2–3 onions
25 g (1 oz) butter
25 g (1 oz) flour
275 ml ($\frac{1}{2}$ pint) stock
salt and cayenne pepper
pinch of nutmeg
a few whole allspice
2 bayleaves
150 ml ($\frac{1}{4}$ pint) port
squeeze of lemon
a few sprigs of parsley

Skin the eels and cut them into pieces about 9 cm (3 in) long.

Slice the onions finely and soften them in the butter. Then stir in a little flour, add the stock, a little at a time to begin with, to make a smooth sauce. Add the seasoning, bayleaves, port and pieces of eel. Simmer covered for about 45 minutes. Taste the sauce and add a little squeece of lemon juice if you like.

Serve in a dish with triangular sippets of fried bread round the dish and a sprinkling of chopped parsley on top.

Top : prawn fritters, *centre :* Morecambe Bay
potted shrimps, *bottom :* stewed eels

Smoked eel with creamed eggs

TO SERVE FOUR

INGREDIENTS
225 g (½ lb) smoked eel
  fillets
4 thinly sliced triangular
  pieces of white bread
oil for frying
8 eggs
salt and pepper
50 g (2 oz) butter

Put the eel fillets in a small oval oven-dish, cover it with foil and place the dish in the oven at 190°C, 375°F, Gas Mark 5. Fry the bread sippets (triangular slices of bread) in oil to an even golden brown on each side. Drain them on kitchen paper and keep hot. Break the eggs in a bowl and whisk them lightly with a fork. Season with salt and pepper.

Melt the butter in a thick saucepan, but do not let it get too hot. Pour in the eggs and stir with a wooden spoon. Put the pan over a moderate heat and keep stirring so that the eggs thicken gradually and do not go into lumps. When they are approaching the consistency of soft lightly whipped cream quickly remove the pan from the heat, so that the eggs don't go on cooking. Divide the eggs between four hot plates and place a cross of the hot eel fillets on top of each mound of egg. Serve with the golden sippets of fried bread on the side of each plate.

Poultry and game

Everybody knows the old Christmas song in which the true love gives his lady a partridge in a pear tree, two turtle-doves, three French hens, four calling birds, not to mention swans a-swimming and geese a-laying; what they may not know is that these were traditional Christmas presents – all destined to end up on the table.

The partridge would arrive spiced and garnished with fruit, the doves would be from the domestic dovecote which provided households and farms with pigeons all the year round. The calling birds were song-birds – blackbirds, and thrushes were eaten with relish in pies as were larks and sparrows, threaded on spits like beads on a necklace and roasted in front of the fire. The French hens, previously crammed within an inch of their life, with raisins, breadcrumbs and milk, became so fat that they could barely stand. The swans, swimming on the river Thames in their thousands, were 'eaten by the English, like geese or ducks' to the astonishment of visiting foreigners. And geese were then the most accepted of traditional Christmas fare – (if you couldn't afford a goose you would have an enormous ox-heart and stuff it with sage and onions, calling it 'mock-goose').

In medieval days, when game was a very great part of the winter diet of rich and poor alike, before enclosures made it illegal for the poor to hunt, the stuffings which were designed to flavour, and moisten the birds as well as making them go further, were tremendously rich and spicy – oysters, chestnuts, saffron, prunes, cinnamon, port, oranges and lemons, cloves, and anchovies were all used together with bulky grated bread and a moistening fat such as suet or bacon. Fruit sauces were as popular then as they are today and cranberries, rowanberries, bilberries, redcurrants, and service-berries from the wild whitebeam tree were all liked for their bitter-sweet flavour.

Unfortunately most game has become, if not really scarce, rather costly. Probably the best buys today are hares, which although somewhat gruesome to handle have a quite surprising amount of very good meat on them. Rabbits are also a good buy and so are pigeons and venison.

Pheasants, grouse and partridges (we no longer seem to enjoy, nor are we likely to find such delicacies as herons, bear, wild boar, cormorants, coots, squirrels or swans) are all delicious, either young for roasting, or older for casseroling or stewing. Venison on the whole is a reasonable buy, but can be a dry and disappointing meat – a good plan is to buy it as part of the contents of a mixed game pie, or else stew it to make sure it is tender and juicy.

Bringing down the stag in Jacobean days

Unpacking Christmas game and poultry in the Leadenhall market of Victorian times

Domestic poultry, on the other hand, has become one of the best meat buys there is today; particularly chicken and turkey. However, unlike their ancestors of the backyard and farmyard who scratched a living in the hedgerows and fields, chickens nowadays do need quite a lot of added flavouring; they are grown so fast they have very little time to develop their flavour. Turkeys, too, need assistance to make them really delicious – a moist stuffing is the perfect answer since it also helps to give the somewhat dry flesh a degree of juiciness, and in Victorian times succulent sausages were an essential with a roast turkey, sometimes cooked in strings and festooned round the bird like an alderman's chains.

Geese and ducks are still luxuries, and quite rightly so since they are both exceedingly rich and delicious, but provide a very small amount of meat for their size. Since they are fatty birds it is a good idea to serve something plain, refreshing or sharp with them – turnips or green peas with duck, apples or onions with goose.

Roast chicken with garlic

TO SERVE FOUR

INGREDIENTS
1 chicken weighing
   1.6–1.8 kg (3½–4 lb)
2 cloves garlic
salt, freshly ground pepper
1 bunch parsley or thyme
50 g (2 oz) butter
1 shallot or onion
1 tablespoon oil
275 ml (½ pint) stock made
   from the giblets
1 level tablespoon flour
4 tablespoons double cream
watercress for garnishing

It is odd to find that the British used to love garlic just as keenly as the French. In the fifteenth century spit-roasted chicken was frequently served with garlic sauce and even geese had garlic in their stuffing. In this recipe the garlic does no more than lightly perfume the flesh of the bird with its warm aromatic flavour.

Peel the cloves of garlic and put them inside the bird together with a seasoning of salt and pepper, a bunch of parsley or thyme and a knob of butter.

Slice the shallot or onion and put it in the roasting tin with a knob of butter. Put the chicken on top and rub it over with the oil. Rub the remaining butter over the

breast and legs of the bird, and put it into a hot oven 220°C, 425°F, Gas Mark 7 for 30 minutes, basting once to twice as the butter melts.

Now turn down the heat to 190°C, 375°F, Gas Mark 5 and continue to cook the chicken, covered with foil, for a further 30 minutes. Test to see if it is done by piercing the thick part of the leg with a skewer. If a clear bead of liquid wells out it is done, if rosy, it needs a little longer.

Now tip the bird to allow the juices inside to run into the roasting tin, and remove it to a hot dish. Let it rest in a warm place for 10–15 minutes; this makes it easier to carve.

Meanwhile spoon some of the excess fat from the roasting tin, stir in the flour and let it cook gently over a medium heat for one minute, then gradually add the strained stock, stirring. When you have a nice smooth gravy stir in the cream, and taste for seasoning.

Strain the gravy to remove the shallot and other bits, pour it into a heated sauceboat, stir in a dessertspoon of very finely chopped parsley and serve with the chicken, garnishing the bird with bunches of watercress.

Grilled chicken legs with Gubbins sauce

TO SERVE FOUR

INGREDIENTS
8 chicken drumsticks
oil
Gubbins sauce
50 g (2 oz) butter
3 tablespoons freshly made
   English mustard
3 dessertspoons tarragon
   vinegar
4 tablespoons double cream
salt and pepper

Nathaniel Gubbins, sporting author and a great gourmet of the turn of the century, invented many spicy dishes, of which this is one of the most delicious.

Make the sauce in the top of a double boiler, over gently simmering water which should be low enough not to touch the base of the top pan. Melt the butter, stir in the mustard, the vinegar and lastly the cream.

Season with salt and pepper, and keep the sauce hot, over simmering water.

Brush the chicken drumsticks with oil, season them with salt and pepper and cover the ends of the leg bones with kitchen foil. Now grill under a hot grill for 20 minutes turning from time to time.

Test by piercing with a skewer at the fattest part of the leg, if a colourless bead of liquid falls it is done, if rose-red it needs a little longer. When the chicken legs are done serve them immediately with the Gubbins sauce poured over.

Chicken pie

A creamy rich pie beneath a short golden crust

TO SERVE SIX

INGREDIENTS
1 small chicken weighing
   1.4 kg (3 lb)
2 sticks of celery
½ teaspoon celery seed
1 onion
bunch of parsley
4 hard-boiled eggs
15 g (½ oz) butter, 15 g
   (½ oz) flour worked
   together
150 ml (¼ pint) double
   cream
250 g (9 oz) shortcrust
   pastry (*page* 212)
salt and pepper
1 egg, beaten with a
   dessertspoon of water,
   for glazing

Put the celery, celery seed, onion, and parsley into 2.3 litres (4 pints) of water. Bring to the boil and simmer for 20 minutes. Put in the untrussed chicken, cover the pan and boil until tender, skimming from time to time. After about 50 minutes, when the meat comes away cleanly from the bones, allow the chicken to cool a little and strip off all the meat.

Fill a pie dish with the chicken pieces, cut into manageable chunks, and the coarsely chopped hard-boiled eggs. Put a pie funnel in the centre. Strain the chicken's cooking liquid, reduce it to about 275 ml (½ pint) by boiling, then drop in the butter and flour in little bits, and whisk it in with the cream. Season, and pour it over the

chicken and allow to get cold. Preheat the oven to 220°C, 425°F, Gas Mark 7.

Cover the pie dish with shortcrust pastry, decorate, glaze with beaten egg and bake in a hot oven for 12 minutes, then turn down the heat to 180°C, 350°F, Gas Mark 4 and cook on for a further 15–20 minutes. Equally good served hot or cold. If serving it hot, accompany it with a bowl of buttered new potatoes or with baked potatoes in winter, and a watercress salad.

If eating the pie, which sets to a light jelly, as a cold dish, serve with home-made brown bread and butter, and a large well-dressed salad of lettuce, watercress, cucumber and thinly sliced radishes.

Chicken pie, Kentish chicken pudding

Kentish chicken pudding

TO SERVE FOUR-SIX

INGREDIENTS
1 chicken weighing
   1.6–8 kg (3½–4 lb)
100 g (¼ lb) button
   mushrooms
2 thick slices cooked ham –
   about 50 g (2 oz)
1 tablespoon chopped
   parsley
25 g (1 oz) flour
salt and pepper
275 ml (½ pint) chicken
   stock (make with the
   giblets or use stock cube
   and water)
Suet crust
225 g (8 oz) self-raising
   flour
100 g (4 oz) prepared suet
salt and pepper
water to mix

This pudding would originally have been boiled in a cloth but is lighter and better made in a pudding basin like a steak and kidney pudding. It can be made with a boiling or a roasting bird.

Have the chicken jointed with a small sharp knife; take the meat off the bone and divide into neat pieces. Clean the mushrooms and chop coarsely, together with the ham and parsley. Roll the pieces of chicken in seasoned flour. Make the suet crust by mixing flour, suet and salt and pepper in a bowl. Add enough water to make a soft but not sticky dough. Take two-thirds of the dough and roll it out on a floured surface. Use it to line a greased 1½-litre (2½-pint) pudding basin. Fill the basin with layers of chicken pieces, seasoned and sprinkled with the chopped mushroom and ham mixture.

Pour in the stock. Brush the top edge of the crust with water, and place the remaining crust, rolled out into a disc, on top. Press the edges together well, trim and

cover the top with a loose lid of foil (to allow for rising) tied on with string. Make a handle of string for lifting the pudding out of the pan.

Place it in a large saucepan of boiling water, cover and boil for 3 hours, topping up the pan with more boiling water if necessary.

When the cooking time is up, lift the pudding out of the pan and remove the foil. Wrap the basin in a white napkin and serve the pudding straight from the bowl.

Colonel Kenney-Herbert's chicken curry

TO SERVE FOUR

INGREDIENTS
1 chicken weighing 1.4 kg
  (3 lb), jointed
a little flour
4 small onions
2 cloves garlic
1 piece green ginger
  3×5 cm ($1 \times 1\frac{1}{2}$ in)
  obtainable at
  greengrocers and Indian
  shops
15 g ($\frac{1}{2}$ oz) butter
100 g (4 oz) dessicated
  coconut
1 tablespoon Madras
  curry powder
275 ml ($\frac{1}{2}$ pint) chicken
  stock made with
  chicken giblets or use
  water and stock cube
salt and pepper
squeeze of fresh lemon
  juice
Chutney
150 g (5 oz) plain
  unsweetened yoghurt
2 teaspoons dried mint
2 small green chillies,
  chopped finely
juice of 1 lemon
pinch of salt

Colonel Kenney-Herbert, ex-Indian Army Officer of the 1900 era, was a great expert on the subject of curry. In his opinion a curry cannot be skimped – the process of preparing one takes time and patience. This is his recipe, but we use curry powder where he would have ground and mixed his own spices.

Joint the chicken and roll the joints in flour. Chop the onions and garlic very finely. Peel the green ginger root and crush and chop to a paste.

Melt the butter and in it fry the chopped onions. While they are softening and frying gently bring 275 ml ($\frac{1}{2}$ pint) of water to the boil and pour it over the coconut in a bowl. Let it stand and brew like tea.

When the onions are nice and brown add the garlic and ginger and curry powder.

Stir over a low heat for 3 minutes, then add the chicken pieces. Stir the mixture for a further 5 minutes. Now add just enough of the chicken stock barely to cover the chicken, season with salt and pepper and simmer, uncovered, for 45 minutes, turning the pieces occasionally.

Strain the coconut milk into the pan, add a few drops of lemon juice and continue to simmer until the chicken is done, approximately 10 minutes. Serve with boiled rice and chutney.

Chutney
This mint and yoghurt chutney is typical of the fresh chutneys that are served with this type of curry.

Mix all the ingredients together in a bowl. It will keep in the refrigerator for 5 days.

Devilled chicken

TO SERVE FOUR

INGREDIENTS
4 tablespoons of the liquid
  part of a jar of mango or
  other chutney
4 teaspoons freshly made
  English mustard
4 teaspoons French mustard
1 tablespoon Worcester
  sauce
1 tablespoon wine vinegar
wings and legs of a cooked
  chicken
50 g (2 oz) dried
  breadcrumbs
50 g (2 oz) butter
4 rashers bacon, rolled and
  stuck with cocktail sticks

A 'devil' is a hot sauce in which cold meat is revived and given a new lease of life. It gives an appetizing piquant flavour. This recipe can be used equally well for turkey or chicken.

Mix together the chutney, mustards, Worcester sauce and wine vinegar. Dip the chicken joints in the mixture and then roll them in breadcrumbs. Preheat the oven to 220°C, 425°F, Gas Mark 7. Heat 25 g (1 oz) of butter in a fireproof dish, put in the chicken pieces and the bacon rolls and dot with the remaining butter. Put them in the hot oven for 15 minutes, turning them once or twice. Serve sizzling hot with mashed potato.

Chicken in a blanket

TO SERVE FOUR

INGREDIENTS
1 chicken weighing 1.6 kg
  (3½ lb)
1.7 litres (3 pints) chicken
  stock or water
1 bunch of herbs – parsley,
  thyme and bayleaf
1 sliced carrot
1 sliced onion
salt, cayenne pepper
1 lemon
65 g (2½ oz) butter
25 g (1 oz) flour
100 g (4 oz) button
  mushrooms, wiped clean
3 tablespoons double
  cream

Florence White, the original author of this recipe, changed its title from 'To stew young chickens' to 'Chicken in a blanket', in deference to the sensibilities of a friend who thought stewed chicken sounded horrid.

In fact the chicken is not stewed but poached and served in a wonderful velvety lemon sauce.

Put the chicken stock in a casserole large enough to hold the chicken, together with the herbs, sliced carrot, onion, salt and cayenne pepper. Bring to the boil and lower the chicken into the stock; allow to poach at a gentle simmer for 20 minutes. Put in the lemon rinds, thinly pared, and the juice, and simmer for a further 20–25 minutes.

Lift out the chicken, tipping it to drain off the liquid inside, and keep it hot. Strain the broth into a measuring jug. In a smaller pan melt 40 g (1½ oz) of the butter, and stir in the flour.

Stir over a gentle heat, until it sizzles. Now add 575 ml (1 pint) of chicken broth, a little at a time, stirring in between each addition. Simmer the resulting sauce for 15 minutes, stirring occasionally, taste for seasoning and add the mushrooms, sliced and sautéed gently in the remaining butter for a few minutes until they are just tender.

Lastly stir in the cream and pour the sauce over the chicken.

Roasted bubbly-jock

INGREDIENTS
1 5–6 kg (12–14 lb) turkey, preferably a hen
225 g (½ lb) sausagemeat
100 g (4 oz) fresh breadcrumbs
12 chestnuts boiled, skinned and cooked in stock until tender.
150 ml (¼ pint) milk
3 inner sticks of celery
1 chopped liver from the turkey
25 g (1 oz) butter
4 sprigs parsley
salt and pepper
100 g (4 oz) dripping or butter and oil for roasting
Gravy
1.7 litres (3 pints) water
1 carrot
1 onion
a few peppercorns
a bunch of herbs
1 small glass Scotch whisky
25 g (1 oz) flour
150 ml (¼ pint) double cream

A bubbly-jock is the very descriptive Highland name for a turkey; in earlier days bubbly-jock was often eaten boiled, and served with oyster sauce or a liver-and-lemon sauce such as Hanover sauce (*see page* 153), but now we prefer them roasted – the whisky gravy is modern but the stuffing is traditional.

Stuff the front end of the turkey with seasoned sausagemeat. Make a second stuffing by mixing the breadcrumbs, the slightly broken chestnuts, the milk, and the chopped celery and turkey liver fried in butter. Stir in the chopped parsley, season with salt and pepper and fill the inside of the turkey with this moist mixture.

Preheat the oven to 160°C, 325°F, Gas Mark 3. Spread dripping or butter and oil over the turkey and place it on one side of its breast in the roasting tin. Roast like this for 30 minutes, then 30 minutes on the other side of the breast – the idea is to let the juices run down into the breast of the bird to keep it moist. Baste occasionally. Now finish cooking the bird breast upwards, basting with a little fresh butter from time to time. Cover loosely with foil if getting too brown.

Allow 20 minutes per 450 g (1 lb) altogether, so that a turkey of 5–6 kg (12–14 lb) will have 4 hours cooking, 30 minutes on each breast and then a further 3 hours breast upwards.

While the turkey is cooking make a very good stock by putting the giblets in a pan with 1.7 litres (3 pints) of water, a carrot, a small onion, a few peppercorns, a bunch of herbs, and simmer for about 1½ hours. Skim once at the start and let it simmer very gently; you should end with between 600–800 ml (1–1½ pints) excellent stock.

To make the gravy put the turkey on to a heated serving dish and let it rest in a warm place. Spoon the fat from the roasting tin and pour in the whisky. Let it boil furiously for 2 minutes. Now stir in 25 g (1 oz) of flour and scrape the tin to release the sediment of the cooking juices. Gradually add the strained stock, stirring after each addition.

Lastly pour in the cream and stir to obtain a smooth gravy. Strain this into a large heated sauceboat.

The turkey, if it is allowed to sit in a warm place for 20 minutes after it is taken from the oven (which will leave time to make the gravy and put the vegetables into their dishes) will be much easier to carve, as the meat settles and becomes firmer.

Serve it with watercress, bacon rolls, small fried chipolata sausages, bread sauce and the delicious whisky gravy.

Turkey patties

INGREDIENTS
50 g (2 oz) butter
50 g (2 oz) flour
150 ml (¼ pint) good concentrated chicken stock
150 ml (¼ pint) milk
100 g (4 oz) cooked turkey, chopped
25 g (1 oz) cooked ham, chopped
3–4 sprigs parsley, chopped
1 hard-boiled egg, chopped
salt, freshly ground pepper
flour
1 egg, beaten
dried breadcrumbs
oil for frying

These delicate patties are made with leftover turkey, or they could equally well be made with chicken. Make them in advance and refrigerate so that the mixture has time to cool and stiffen.

Melt the butter in a good heavy-based saucepan. You are making a very thick white sauce and this is one of the easiest things to burn without even noticing. Stir in the flour and let it bubble for a few moments, then start adding the chicken stock gradually, stirring until smooth between each addition. Now add the milk, just enough to make a sauce that has the consistency of a paste. Stir in the turkey, ham, parsley, hard-boiled egg and seasoning. When these ingredients are thoroughly mixed in, and the sauce seasoned to your liking, spread the mixture just over 2 cm (½ in) thick on an oiled plate and let it get quite cold in the refrigerator.

Now cut into 5 cm (1½ in) squares, dip them first in flour, then egg, then breadcrumbs and fry in plenty of oil – not deep fat but about 1 cm (½ in) in a frying pan –

turning them over once, so that they are golden brown all over. Serve hot, well drained, with a green salad, and, if liked, a fresh tomato sauce (*see page* 154).

Manx salt duck with onion sauce

TO SERVE FOUR

INGREDIENTS

850 ml (1½ pints) stock, made with duck giblets or stock cube and water

1 duck

fine sea salt

¼ teaspoon saltpetre (obtainable from the chemist)

1 sliced onion

1 beer-glass cider

freshly ground pepper (no more salt)

Onion sauce

450 g (1 lb) onions, peeled and chopped

275 ml (½ pint) stock from cooking the duck giblets

25 g (1 oz) butter

25 g (1 oz) flour

salt if needed

freshly ground pepper

pinch grated nutmeg

150 ml (¼ pint) single cream

This must be started a day in advance. The flesh of a salt duck is particularly succulent and well-flavoured.

Remove the duck giblets and use them to make the stock. Sprinkle a deep earthenware dish liberally with salt. Put a small handful of salt inside the duck, place it in the dish and sprinkle with more salt and the saltpetre on top. Leave for 24 hours, turning once or twice. The following day wash the salted duck and pat it dry with kitchen paper.

Lay the onion slices over the bottom of an ovenproof casserole. Put the duck on top and pour in 575 ml (1 pint) of stock and the cider. Bring to the boil on top of the stove, skim and then cover and put into a moderate oven – 180°C, 350°F, Gas Mark 4 for 1¾ hours.

Meanwhile start the onion sauce. Chop the onions very finely, put them in a saucepan with 275 ml (½ pint) stock (use the re-maining duck stock) then simmer for 20 minutes until the onions are tender. Transfer to a bowl. Melt the butter in a saucepan, stir in the flour and gradually incorporate the onion liquid and onions. When you have a smooth sauce, simmer for 15 minutes, taste for seasoning, add the nutmeg and stir in the cream.

Serve the duck with the creamy onion sauce and a lovely green purée made by mashing together potatoes and green cabbage cooked separately until very tender. The liquid in which the duck was cooked can be skimmed of fat and used to make a soup, or you can borrow some of it for the sauce.

Roast duckling with green peas

TO SERVE FOUR

INGREDIENTS
1 duckling or young duck
a little flour
salt, freshly ground pepper
50 g (2 oz) butter
1 tablespoon sunflower or olive oil
2 onions, finely chopped
1 lettuce, shredded
bunch of herbs – parsley, thyme and bayleaf
275 ml ($\frac{1}{2}$ pint) stock made with duck giblets or chicken stock cube and water
pinch of ground nutmeg
350 g ($\frac{3}{4}$ lb) shelled green peas, fresh or frozen
1 level tablespoon flour
3 tablespoons double cream
12 triangular pieces (sippets) of fried bread, about 5 × 5 cm (2 × 2 in)

In the eighteenth-century version of this famous English dish, the duckling and peas were cooked together in the same pot – this no doubt made the peas very tasty but we prefer our peas to be lightly cooked and bright green, so nowadays they are added at the end of the cooking, making it a dish to remember.

Dust the duck lightly with flour and season it inside with salt and pepper. Melt 25 g (1 oz) of butter and 1 tablespoon of oil in a flameproof casserole into which it will just fit, and brown it on all sides. Now remove the duck and put the chopped onion, shredded lettuce and bouquet of herbs into the casserole. Cover the pan and allow them to wilt over gentle heat for 5 minutes. Spoon off any excess fat, place the duck on top of the vegetables and pour in the stock. Cover the pot and stew gently either on top of the stove or in a very moderate oven 160°C, 325°F, Gas Mark 3. After 35 minutes sprinkle in the nutmeg and shake the casserole to make sure the duck is not sticking. It will take about 25 minutes more to cook, making roughly 1 hour in all but it depends on the size of the bird, so test for tenderness with a skewer. Meanwhile cook the peas for 10 minutes in boiling salted water, strain them and keep them on one side. Now remove the duck to a heated dish. Work together 25 g (1 oz) of butter and a level tablespoon of flour to make a paste. Remove the herbs from the casserole, skim off the excess fat and drop in little pieces of the butter and flour paste, stirring the pan over a gentle heat. When you have a velvety mixture stir in the peas and cream; heat through. Lastly pour the peas and sauce over the duck, surround it with the fried bread sippets and serve hot with puréed potatoes.

71

Duck with glazed young turnips

TO SERVE THREE–FOUR

INGREDIENTS
1 duck weighing 2 kg
  (4½ lb)
salt and pepper
1 bunch herbs – parsley,
  thyme and marjoram
1 shallot or small onion
1 large glass dry white
  wine
275 ml (½ pint) stock made
  with duck giblets
12 small young turnips
25 g (1 oz) butter
1 dessertspoon sugar

This is a very ancient combination, the Romans served both duck and crane with turnips and in Elizabethan times older birds were often served boiled with turnips. Now we prefer to eat young crisp-skinned roast duck with young turnips glazed to a beautiful bronze in sugar and butter.

Put the duck, salted inside and out, in the roasting pan. Slip the herbs inside it and place the sliced shallot in the pan with the duck. Pour in the glass of white wine and put the duck in a fairly hot oven 200°C, 400°F, Gas Mark 6 for 1¼–1½ hours. Every now and then baste the duck with the wine and prick its skin here and there with a fork or cocktail stick to allow the fat to escape. It will become deliciously crisp.

In the meantime cook the giblets in 575 ml (1 pint) of water letting it simmer and reduce for an hour, to obtain 275 ml (½ pint) of stock.

While the duck is cooking peel the turnips carefully and put them in a pan of cold salted water. Bring to the boil and simmer for 15–20 minutes until just tender. Drain the turnips and return them to the pan together with the melted butter and the sugar. Cook them in this glaze for 15 minutes until they are nicely bronzed and shiny, give them a shake from time to time, to brown them evenly.

When the duck is cooked, remove it to a hot serving dish, place the turnips round and keep it hot.

Spoon all the fat from the juices in the roasting tin. Bring them to the boil, stir in the strained giblet stock and let it simmer for 5 minutes, scraping up the juices from round the tin with a wooden spoon; taste for seasoning, and add further salt and pepper if necessary. Strain into a sauce-boat and serve separately.

Roast goose with apple sauce

TO SERVE SIX

INGREDIENTS

1 goose weighing 5 kg (12 lb)
1 glass white wine
575 ml (1 pint) stock made
   with goose giblets
1½ tablespoons flour

Sage and onion stuffing

4 large onions
25 g (1 oz) butter
100 g (4 oz) fresh
   breadcrumbs
salt and pepper
10 freshly chopped sage
   leaves or 1 teaspoon
   dried sage
1 egg beaten with
   1 teaspoon milk

Apple sauce

900 g (2 lb) cooking apples
15 g (½ oz) butter
2 teaspoons sugar

Traditionally geese are eaten at Michael-mas on 29 October, having just been fat-tened on the gleanings from the wheat and barley. As goose is served so seldom it would be a pity not to do it properly in the old way and make a home-made sage and onion stuffing.

Bring a pan of salted water to the boil and boil the skinned onions for 30 minutes until they are tender. Strain, cool and chop the onions, then cook them in the butter for 10 minutes. Now allow them to cool and mix them with the remaining stuffing ingredients in a bowl.

Preheat the oven to 220°C, 425°F, Gas Mark 7. Salt the goose inside and out, pick-ing off any stray quills. Fill the cavity with the stuffing and put the goose on a rack in a large roasting tin. Prick the skin here and there with a fork to let out the fat which lies under the skin.

Pour the glass of white wine and 575 ml (1 pint) of water into the roasting tin and roast for 1 hour, basting with the liquid from time to time. Turn down the heat to 190°C, 375°F, Gas Mark 5 and roast for a

further 1½ hours, continuing to baste. Cover with foil for the last hour.

When it is done, remove the goose to a large serving dish and put it back in the oven which can now be turned off. The meat will settle, making it easier to carve.

Meanwhile scoop out most of the fat from the roasting tin. Add 1½ tablespoons of flour to the gravy left in the tin, stirring it round until it has cooked and thickened.

Taste the gravy for seasoning and add the boiling goose giblet stock if it is too concentrated. Strain it into a gravy boat and serve the goose with this sauce and the sage and onion stuffing as well as the following apple sauce.

Apple sauce

Peel and core the apples and put them over a low heat in a covered pan with very little water. When they are soft and fluffy beat them with a fork, adding the butter and sugar to taste (this rather varies according to the tartness of the apples, but do not make the sauce too sweet). Serve apple sauce very hot.

Roast pheasant

TO SERVE FOUR

INGREDIENTS
brace of young pheasants
50 g (2 oz) butter
flour
4 rashers of fat bacon
salt and pepper
1 small glass sherry
150 ml ($\frac{1}{4}$ pint) stock or
  water
pinch sugar
2–3 drops wine vinegar
knob of butter, about
  15 g ($\frac{1}{2}$ oz)

This is one of the great party pieces of an English autumn lunch or dinner. Suspect any pheasants seen in the shops before 4 October; the season starts on 1 October and they need to hang 3 or 4 days before they are ready to eat. It is from about mid-October to the end of December that they are at their best, plump and tender.

Preheat the oven to 200°C, 400°F, Gas Mark 6. Pick any stray quills and feather stubs from the pheasants. Melt the butter in a roasting tin. Dredge the birds lightly with flour and brown them gently, breast downwards, in the butter, turning them this way and that, so that they are evenly coloured.

Now turn them breasts upward and put a cross of bacon rashers on each breast. Roast the pheasants for 35 minutes, basting occasionally. If you like them pink,

take them out of the oven, keep them hot and let them rest for 10 minutes before carving. If you prefer them well done, allow 40–45 minutes cooking and 5 minutes rest. Serve roast pheasants garnished with watercress, and serve with fried bread-crumbs. Make the gravy as follows.

Spoon off most of the fat from the roasting tin. Stir in the sherry and scrape and stir the roasting juices which have cara-melized in the tin over a moderate heat until the sherry has reduced to half. Now add a scant 150 ml ($\frac{1}{4}$ pint) of stock or water and let it boil rapidly for 2–3 minutes. Taste for seasoning, add a pinch of sugar and 2–3 drops of wine vinegar and reduce more if it seems watery, but this is essenti-ally thin gravy. Lastly stir in a knob of butter and swirl it round, let it boil rapidly for a minute longer, then strain into a gravy boat.

74

Pheasant with apples

TO SERVE FOUR–SIX

INGREDIENTS
1 young pheasant
75 g (3 oz) butter or
  3 tablespoons oil and
  25 g (1 oz) butter
6 medium cooking apples
15 g ($\frac{1}{2}$ oz) sugar
1 bayleaf
salt and pepper
4 tablespoons single cream
25 g (1 oz) breadcrumbs
  fried in 25 g (1 oz) butter
1 bunch watercress

This recipe, which is made in the autumn with a young pheasant and windfall apples, can be used equally well for an old pheasant by lengthening the cooking time to $1\frac{1}{2}$ hours.

Heat 75 g (3 oz) of butter or the oil together with 25 g (1 oz) butter in a casserole and brown the pheasant on all sides.

Meanwhile peel and core the apples and cut them into slices. Transfer the pheasant to a dish and put the sliced apples into the casserole, sprinkle them with the sugar and let them cook gently until they start to soften. Place the bird on top and add the bayleaf and seasoning. Cover and cook for $\frac{3}{4}$ hour in a moderate oven, 180°C, 350°F, Gas Mark 4.

Now pour in the cream, mix it into the apples and serve the pheasant resting in its apple-bed, which can be sprinkled with golden fried breadcrumbs, and which serves as sauce and gravy at the same time.

Place a small bunch of watercress on each plate and accompany the dish with a fresh vegetable such as brussels sprouts and perhaps a dish of plain steamed potatoes.

Sir Andrew Barnard's partridge stew

Also excellent with pigeons

TO SERVE FOUR

INGREDIENTS
4 partridges or pigeons
225 g ($\frac{1}{2}$ lb) streaky bacon
1 tablespoon oil
4 small onions
12 peppercorns
3 bayleaves
2 tablespoons wine vinegar
275 ml ($\frac{1}{2}$ pint) chicken
  stock (home-made or
  stock cube)
150 ml ($\frac{1}{4}$ pint) cooking port
salt and pepper
nut of butter
1 dessertspoon flour

Schoolboys, it seems, have always complained about school food – a fifteenth-century schoolboy wrote to his parents 'I have no delight in beef and mutton and such daily meats, I would only have a partridge set before us or some other such, in especial small birds that I love passing well'. He was right, partridges are extremely good, particularly plain roasted. However if you can only obtain older birds – partridge or pigeon, this recipe will make them tender and delicious.

Cut the bacon into 3 cm (1 in) squares. Put the bacon in the bottom of a casserole with the oil and let it render some of its fat over a gentle heat. Brown the partridges all over in this and remove them to a dish. Now add the onions, cut in quarters and let them soften a little in the bacon fat. Add

the pepper, bayleaves, vinegar, stock and port, a very little salt and plenty of freshly ground pepper.

Season the partridges and return them to the casserole, cover with a sheet of kitchen foil and then a well-fitting lid and place in a moderately low oven 160°C, 325°F, Gas Mark 3 for 1$\frac{1}{2}$ hours.

Remove the birds, place the onions round them with a slotted spoon, skim the fat from the liquid, strain it and thicken it with a knob of butter the size of a walnut mashed to a paste with a dessertspoon of flour. Let it boil over a moderate heat while you drop in pieces of the paste. When the sauce has thickened cook it for 2–3 minutes more, taste for seasoning, then pour it over the birds and onions.

Braised pigeons and cabbage

TO SERVE FOUR

INGREDIENTS
4 pigeons
flour
50 g (2 oz) butter
4 rashers streaky bacon
2 onions, chopped
1 stick celery, chopped
1 firm white cabbage
1 glass red wine
thyme, bayleaf
salt and pepper
3 cloves
3 allspice
grating of nutmeg
knob of butter mashed
    with 1 teaspoon of flour

Dust the pigeons with flour. Melt the butter in a heavy ovenproof casserole and fry the bacon rashers, cut in strips, for a few minutes to extract some of their fat. Remove with a slotted spoon and keep on one side. Now fry the pigeons in the same casserole, browning them on all sides. Remove them to a plate and add the chopped onions and celery to the pan. Let them soften for 10 minutes over a low heat, then add the cabbage, cleaned and coarsely chopped. Stir it round, then cover the pan and let the cabbage wilt down for 5 minutes. Stir in the bacon pieces, place the pigeons on top of the cabbage and pour the wine over the top. Let it bubble up, add the herbs and spices and season with salt and pepper. Cover the pan and simmer for $1\frac{1}{2}$ hours, until the pigeons are tender.

With a perforated spoon, pile the cabbage in a deep heated dish with the pigeons on top. Reduce the braising liquid and thicken it a little by dropping in a knob of butter mashed with one teaspoon of flour – (a palette knife or your fingers will do the job). Stir until the sauce thickens, then pour it over the birds and serve piping hot.

Mashed potatoes are a good accompaniment to this dish.

Wild duck with fowler's sauce

TO SERVE FOUR

INGREDIENTS
4 wild duck–mallard or
    teal
50 g (2 oz) butter
1 tablespoon oil
1 bunch watercress
Fowler's sauce
2 tablespoons port or
    red wine
juice of 1 lemon
6 drops tabasco sauce
salt and pepper

Major Hugh Pollard, author of *The Sportsman's Cookery Book*, says of wild duck 'above all things duck should not be overdone, but brought piping hot to the table, not partly cooked, but just on the juicy underdone side . . . Overcooking not only destroys the·virtue of wild duck, but toughens them mightily.'

Preheat the oven to 220°C, 425°F, Gas Mark 7. Put a trickle of oil and a few slips of butter on the breasts of the wild duck and place them in a roasting tin. Put the remaining butter in the tin and roast the ducks for 30 minutes (teal for 25 minutes as they are smaller) basting occasionally.

Remove them to a serving dish. Into the roasting tin, from which you have spooned all the fat, pour the port or red wine, lemon juice, and tabasco. Stir it well and season. Now add any juices from the dish on which you have placed the ducks, and heat it

Rabbit stewed in cider

TO SERVE FOUR

INGREDIENTS
1 young tame rabbit or
   1 small wild rabbit, cut
   into pieces
25 g (1 oz) flour
25 g (1 oz) butter
1 dessertspoon oil
2 onions, peeled and
   chopped
4 carrots, cut into rounds
425 ml ($\frac{3}{4}$ pint) dry cider
salt, freshly ground pepper,
   grated nutmeg
1 bayleaf
225 g ($\frac{1}{2}$ lb) shelled peas
4 tablespoons top of the
   milk or single cream

This dish is a very traditional, meltingly tender stew; when peas are not available it can be made with a large handful of coarsely chopped herbs, parsley, chives and either tarragon or marjoram, thrown in at the end instead of the peas. Originally there would have been a few rashers of bacon, chopped up coarsely, fried with the rabbit pieces; by all means add bacon but I have left it out as it turns the whole stew a rather odd pinkish colour.

Dredge the clean dry pieces of rabbit with some of the flour. Heat the butter and oil in a flameproof casserole and fry the pieces lightly to a pale golden colour. Remove them to a plate and add the carrots and onions to the pan. Stir them round, cover the pan and let them sweat for 5 minutes. Stir in the remaining flour and let it coat the vegetables. Return the rabbit pieces and pour in the cider. Let it bubble up and then turn down the heat very low and add the salt, pepper, nutmeg, and a bayleaf. Cover the pan and let it simmer gently for 1 hour. Now throw in the peas and let them cook in the rabbit gravy for 15 minutes.

Lastly stir in the cream or top of the milk and remove the bayleaf. This stew is served with plainly boiled or steamed potatoes.

through. Make cuts in the breasts of the ducks parallel to the breastbone, pour over the fowler's sauce and serve. (The cuts are made so that the juices of the birds can mingle with the sauce.)

Serve one bird to each person, and let each do his own carving. A watercress, orange and celery salad is ideal with these birds.

Jugged hare

TO SERVE FOUR

INGREDIENTS

1 hare and its blood (ask the butcher to cut up the hare for you and put it into a plastic container for carrying home)
25 g (1 oz) seasoned flour
50 g (2 oz) butter
2 tablespoons oil
100 g (4 oz) streaky bacon
4 carrots
4 medium onions
2 glasses red wine
good pinch of ground cloves, cinnamon, and nutmeg
salt and pepper
15 g ($\frac{1}{2}$ oz) butter and 15 g ($\frac{1}{2}$ oz) flour for finishing the gravy
1 teaspoon redcurrant jelly
250 ml ($\frac{1}{2}$ pint) stock, either home-made chicken stock or stock cube and water

Jugged hare, now cooked slowly in a casserole, used to be made in a jug. The pieces of hare would be placed in the jug with onion, cloves and lemon. The jug was put in a deep pan of water, and the water simmered for about four hours until the hare was done. A little port was poured into the gravy towards the end. The rich taste of port would still be a good addition to the gravy; if you have some, add a dash with the blood of the hare at the end.

Roll the hare joints in plenty of seasoned flour. Heat the butter and oil in a large casserole and fry the joints to a rich mahogany-brown all over. Transfer them to a large plate and then throw in the bacon, cut into pieces about 3 cm (1 in) square, the carrots cut into rounds and the sliced onions. Sauté them in the butter and oil until the onions are browned, then pour off any excess fat and return the pieces of hare. Sprinkle with any remaining seasoned flour, pour in the red wine and let it bubble gently for 10 minutes to reduce a little and drive off some of its alcohol. Add the spices, and a good seasoning of pepper and salt, and pour in enough stock to bring the level two-thirds of the way up the meat. Let it come to the boil, then cover the casserole and transfer it to a low oven (150°C, 300°F, Gas Mark 2 to 160°C, 325°F, Gas Mark 3) for 1$\frac{1}{2}$ hours for a young hare or for 2 hours for a larger, older hare.

Remove the pieces of hare, carrots and onions with a slotted spoon and put them in a heated, deep serving dish. In a small pan melt the last 15 g ($\frac{1}{2}$ oz) of butter and stir in the flour. Gradually add the hare gravy, stirring well between each addition; stir in the redcurrant jelly and when you have a smooth sauce remove the pan from the heat and taste for seasoning. Now stir in the blood of the hare and blend it in thoroughly. (If you find this very distasteful you can leave it out, but it does add to the richness of colour and flavour for which this traditional dish is so well-known.)

Pour this gravy over the pieces of hare in the serving dish and keep hot for 5 minutes before serving to allow the dish to mellow.

Serve accompanied by plain boiled potatoes, watercress, perhaps a vegetable such as brussels sprouts, and redcurrant jelly. This dish reheats well, but do not boil or the sauce may separate.

Roast saddle of hare

TO SERVE TWO

INGREDIENTS

1 saddle of hare (use the rest for jugged hare)
flour for dusting
50 g (2 oz) butter
2 rashers smoked bacon
Marinade
15 ml (1 dessertspoon) wine vinegar
1 glass red wine
25 ml (1 tablespoon) oil
2 carrots, sliced into rounds
2 bayleaves
12 peppercorns
2 sprigs thyme

In season between late August and March, hares are best in December when they still have much of their 'stubble-flesh' and are fit and fat. The saddle is the part of the hare that lies between the ribs and the hind-legs; it is in fact the loin, and is surprisingly meaty. The rest of the animal can be 'jugged' – made into a delicious rich dark stew (see above).

Remove the thick silver skin which covers the saddle with a sharp knife. Put the marinade into a suitable earthenware dish and place the hare in it. Let it steep in the tenderizing marinade for 24 hours if possible but at least 3–4 hours, turning it over occasionally.

Preheat the oven to 200°C, 400°F, Gas Mark 6. Remove the saddle from the marinade, wipe it dry, and dust it with the flour. Heat the butter in a roasting tin, put in the hare and let it brown all over. Then cover with bacon and roast in a fairly hot oven for 30 minutes.

To make the gravy strain the marinade. Spoon some of the fat from the roasting tin, pour in the marinade, let it reduce to half and taste for seasoning.

Serve the roast saddle with home-made redcurrant jelly (see page 222), the gravy, and with roast or puréed potatoes.

Jugged hare, roast saddle of hare

An English game pie

INGREDIENTS

1 small hare
1 roasting chicken
  weighing 1.4 kg (3 lb)
1 thick slice of ham
  weighing 175 g (6 oz)
350 g (¾ lb) sparerib or
  pork belly, coarsely
  minced
1 egg, beaten
1 onion or 2 shallots,
  finely chopped
½ teaspoon ground
  cinnamon
½ teaspoon grated nutmeg
1 teaspoon Worcester
  sauce
grated rind of 1 lemon
15 g (½ oz) salt
½ teaspoon coarsely ground
  black pepper
1 glass red wine

For the hot-water crust
225 g (8 oz) lard
275 ml (½ pint) water
675 g (1½ lb) flour
1 heaped teaspoon salt
1 egg beaten with a pinch
  of salt

For the jelly
all the carcasses and
  trimmings from the meat
2 carrots
1 onion
2 sticks celery
dash red wine
bayleaf
1 clove
15 g (½ oz) or 1 packet
  gelatine
salt and pepper

The English have always been fond of cold game – and poultry – pies; huge great gilded tower-shaped pies were the impressive centrepieces at Elizabethan feasts, in which meat and fruit and little birds were mixed together. (It was not usual then to eat the pastry.) A celebrated pie from Yorkshire contained turkey, goose, chicken, partridge and pigeon, all boned and put one inside the other. This sort of pie was sometimes filled with up to nearly 2 kg (4 lb) of butter and sent across the country as a Christmas present. The game pie given here, a more modest effort, would also make a handsome present.

With a sharp knife remove as much meat as you can from the raw chicken and hare, and remove the skin and sinews. Keep the breast meat of the chicken and the saddle meat from the hare on one side, and cut them into 2-cm (¾-in) cubes. Mince or chop the rest of the meat fairly coarsely and mix it with the minced pork, egg, onion, spices, Worcester sauce, lemon rind and seasoning. Moisten with the red wine and allow to mellow in a cool place while you make the stock.

Put the carcasses and trimmings of the chicken and hare in a large saucepan together with the carrots, onion, celery, wine, bayleaf and clove. Cover with 2.4 litres (5 pints) of water, bring to the boil, skim carefully to remove impurities and simmer very gently for 2½ hours.

Make the hot-water crust as follows: put the lard and water in a saucepan and bring it to the boil. Sieve the flour and salt into a bowl and pour in the hot liquid. Mix with a wooden spoon and when the dough is cool enough to handle, knead it well and let it sit in a warm place, covered with a cloth, for 20–30 minutes until you are ready for it.

Use two-thirds of this crust to line a round 25-cm (10-in) spring-clip cake-tin, which you have greased thoroughly. Roll out the pastry to a thickish disc and then spread it and press into the tin so that it fits snugly without any holes (this is vital) and leave a little hanging over the top edge.

Now fill the pie, first with a layer of half the minced pork, then with the pieces of

breast meat, saddle meat and the ham cut in cubes the same size.

Press them down a little and then finish filling the pie with the remaining minced pork. Press down gently to eliminate air holes. Brush the top edges of the pastry with water. Cover with the rest of the pastry, pinching the edges together firmly.

Decorate with any trimmings (*see diagram*) and leave two nice round holes in the top to allow the steam to escape.

Bake at 200°C, 400°F, Gas Mark 6, for 30 minutes. Brush the top with beaten egg and salt, then bake for 1½ hours at 180°C, 350°F, Gas Mark 4. After 30 minutes cover loosely with kitchen foil to prevent the top getting too brown. When it is cooked let it cool in the tin.

When the stock has simmered for 2

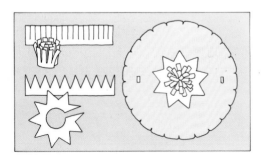

Decorating a game pie

hours strain it, and let it cool so that you can remove the layer of fat from the top. Now measure out 575 ml (1 pint) of the stock, season it and bring it to the boil again. Draw it off the heat, and pour a small quantity into a small saucepan. Keeping this just below boiling point, dissolve the gelatine in it. Stir briskly until all granular or thick jellified bits are completely melted away. Then mix it into the rest of the stock, and allow to cool.

When the pie is cool put a funnel into one of the holes and pour in as much of the cool but melted stock as will come up to the level of the holes in the crust. Allow to set in the refrigerator at least 24 hours before removing the tin and cutting the pie in wedges like a cake.

Ghillies' venison stew

TO SERVE FOUR

INGREDIENTS
900 g (2 lb) venison, from
   leg or haunch
25 g (1 oz) flour
50 g (2 oz) bacon fat or
   2 tablespoons vegetable
   oil
2 onions, coarsely chopped
2 rashers bacon, chopped
squeeze of lemon juice
1 glass port
275 ml ($\frac{1}{2}$ pint) beef stock
   made with stock cube
   and water
4 juniper berries, crushed
salt, freshly ground pepper

Venison is often available in country markets and can be a good, inexpensive buy. The ghillies like to stew their venison to counteract the dryness of the meat.

Cut the trimmed venison into cubes and roll them in seasoned flour.

Melt the bacon fat or oil in a heavy casserole and fry the chopped onions and bacon until the onions are turning colour. Now add the meat and fry, turning the pieces of meat over in the fat as they brown. Add a squeeze of lemon juice, the port, stock, and juniper berries and any remaining flour. Season with salt and pepper, cover and simmer for $1\frac{1}{2}$ hours or until the venison is tender. Serve with baked potatoes and redcurrant or rowan jelly.

English game pie, Ghillies' venison stew

Meat

British meat, and beef in particular, has long been the envy of the world; for flavour and quality there is none so consistently good. An eighteenth-century visitor from the Continent found that our ox, calf, sheep and swine (today's beef, veal, lamb and pork) were of 'unsurpassed fatness and delicious taste, either because of their excellent pasture consisting of nourishing sweet-scented hay, or, owing to some way of fattening . . . known to their butchers alone'.

In fact, until the mid-eighteenth century our cattle were not specially fat, but small and tough. It was largely due to the work of a single man, Robert Bakewell of Loughborough, that our beef became such a splendid example of fine-boned meatiness. Bakewell's breeding experiments were followed by more work, this time on the Aberdeen Angus, by a Victorian farmer-drover, McCombie of Tillyfourie. He was responsible for the fame of this great beef breed, and the result was that Britain became the stock-market of the world.

But long before the days of Queen Victoria and her beef-*breeders*, the British had been renowned as a nation of colossal meat-*eaters*. Although today we eat less than 225 g ($\frac{1}{2}$ lb) of beef per head each week, there was a time when the Englishman was advised, for his health's sake, to consume not less than 3 kg (6 lb) of meat per week, with 2 kg (4 lb) bread, and a daily pint of beer. Dr Kitchiner, author of this hefty diet, which appeared in the *Cooks' Oracle of Health*, was not over-estimating the British appetite of 1817.

In those days meat was cooked in huge pieces, carefully balanced on a revolving spit before a glowing fire. The joints had to be large or they would have dried out long before they were cooked. Besides, houses with large fireplaces were generally inhabited by very large households who could do more than justice to large joints of meat – one of 5 kg (10 lb) was called a Tom Thumb joint in an early cookery book.

Spit-roasting was an ancient art; the joint was treated with great respect, basted and dredged with flour continuously in front of the much-tended fire. It would then go up to the table where the carver would give the choicest cuts to the master and his favoured guests while the less juicy pieces would be sent further down the table to those who sat below the salt. (In Tudor times, this term was literally true, less well-born guests sitting well-down the table beyond the salt cellars.)

In less well-to-do-houses, fireplaces were economically small for, while meat was cheap and plentiful, fuel was expensive and hard to come by. So the poorer families, when they had a piece of meat to be cooked, would stop by at the baker's on their way to church on Sunday morning and put a large joint in his big brick oven, empty and cooling, since bread was not baked on Sundays. The service was often tediously long, but the joint was large enough to hold its succulence, and the family could depend on bearing home a beautifully cooked Sunday lunch.

These Sunday joints, ancestors of our own delicious weekend feasts, were often destined to last all through the following week; hot on Sunday, and then reheated, or cold in endless succession through the next five or six days, in hash, bubble and squeak, rissoles and cottage pie.

Even fifteen or twenty years ago there were still many households whose nightly suppers consisted solely of cold mutton, beetroot in vinegar and the pickle jar, followed by cheese and the biscuit barrel. In middle-class households this meal would be laid out on lace mats, with shining silver, but what an ineffably dreary occasion it was on the whole.

Nowadays, although we still cling to the comfortable notion of a Sunday joint, our ovens are designed to cook small pieces of meat to perfection, so the burden of eating reheated meat has been largely removed, and small joints can appear on the table in top condition and disappear in a single meal. This means that we can have fresh meat, braised, grilled, stewed, fried, or boiled, during the week and enjoy different cuts, differently treated, as often as we like.

There are all sorts of interesting cuts which a good butcher can prepare for you if you give him a day's notice. Ask for a Guard of honour – two best ends of lamb joined back to back – their neatly trimmed bones crossed at the tips, like swords at a military wedding. Or a top-rib of beef for braising – or griskin of pork, the loin of a large bacon pig with the fat and chine-bone removed. I have bought griskins in the West Country so good that the whole family has remembered them ever since. It is true that from Marlborough, westwards through Colne and on to Stroud and the South Midlands, lies good pig country and in this area bacon factories abound, and pork-butchers too. Here, it is possible to find home-made faggots and pork pies, salt-pork, cooked trotters, creamy, freshly made lard, crackling by the quarter, pig's head brawns and excellent fresh pork.

Further west and into the hill-country of Wales, lamb is the thing. In late spring, the legs of lamb, slender and small, are exceptionally sweet and light, and the shoulders have a tender melting quality found in no other country. (Queen Victoria would eat no other.)

But as the poacher's poem says,

> The mountain sheep are sweeter,
> But the valley sheep are fatter;
> We therefore deemed it meeter
> To carry off the latter.

Fatter sheep come from Sussex and Kent and the low-lying salt-marshes. It is said that the salt gives a most particular and fine flavour to the lambs that graze these windy marshes and certainly the local lamb of the area is excellent.

On the other hand, British veal in the recent past has fallen into something like disgrace; ever since the last war, calves have been badly reared and their meat is dry and grey and very expensive. The result is that veal is almost never eaten in this country today, although it was, up to Edwardian days, a great favourite.

It is possible that things may change again. Today's British veal is humanely and properly reared, and if we could only buy it at a reasonable price, roast veal could once again be a British favourite. It is already possible to buy stewing and braising veal without spending a fortune. Your butcher will be pleased to advise you. If he is a man who cares about his customers and the quality of his meat, you can safely ask him which cuts to buy for which purpose. Then with the basic rules of simple British meat cookery, which we have set out over the next few pages, in your head, you will be able to make delicious dishes out of any bit of any animal. (For, once you understand the art of braising, you can braise a pig's ear as easily as a piece of topside. It may not turn out to be a silk purse, but like so many of the lesser known cuts of meat, it will repay the trouble by being delicious and quite different in character from anything else.)

Southdown sheep owe much of their present appearance and succulence to Coke of Holkham, seen here with an early nineteenth-century herd.

This Victorian butcher's shop is a museum piece now, but began life as an educational toy for little girls – the housewives of the future who would need to trust the butcher to advise them. Today, our shopping habits have largely changed. We still have friendly, knowledgeable butchers but self-service has come to stay and however helpfully supermarkets label their meat we still need to remember the different methods of cooking most suited to the different cuts, bearing in mind that a good piece of meat can be used for humbler processes but not the other way about.

Grilling

Grilling means exposing 3–6 cm (1–2½ in) thick pieces of very good quality meat, which have first been rubbed with either oil or butter to prevent them drying out, to the dry heat of a preheated grill. They can be flavoured beforehand by rubbing with pepper, garlic, etc., but salt should not be added until halfway through the cooking as it keeps the surface of the meat moist and prevents it from sealing; this means that juices are lost and the meat will not brown easily. The pieces of meat should first be sealed by searing on each side under a hot grill (or over charcoal, glowing embers, etc.). The heat is then turned down, or the meat put further away from the heat and it finishes cooking more slowly with all its juices sealed inside.

Grilled meat is often served with a sauce or a pat of herbed butter, as there is no natural juice or gravy produced by this method of cooking.

Grilling over a wood fire Meat grilled over a wood fire is really quite different from anything else. The smoke, of which there should be rather little, since an intense bright fire is the best for grilling, gives a very subtle taste.

Oil the well-trimmed meat lightly before grilling. Try not to let too much fat drip into the fire, as this may burst into flame and blacken the meat.

A sandwich-type grill, which encloses the meat, is best for this kind of cooking, since it can be turned without anything dropping into the fire. Clean it immediately after use and keep it well oiled.

Frying

Frying is cooking small pieces of good quality meat in a little fat or oil in a heated shallow pan. Always see that the meat is at room temperature before you start cooking. The pan and fat must be hot when the meat goes in, so that it is sealed immediately on contact with the heat. As in grilling, salting should be done after the meat has been sealed.

The meat can be turned once or twice during cooking, but should not be pierced with a fork, as this will let the juices escape.

Do not use too much fat during frying, as this produces a hard crust. Keep a fairly brisk heat going, but do not overheat the pan or the fat will overheat too and burn any loose particles of meat, giving the food a bitter flavour and beastly appearance.

Roasting

Roasting in the oven is really baking. The meat, which must be top quality, is cooked in a shallow open tin and basted frequently with hot fat to seal the outside, imprisoning most of the meat juices, and to prevent it from drying out. Many people like to put meat on a rack to keep it out of the fat in the roasting tin, and to turn the meat from time to time as it cooks.

Roasting times and temperatures vary according to quality and type of the meat, which should always be at room temperature before going into the oven. Meat should not be seasoned until after roasting, and then again after carving.

Allow all roast meat to rest, covered, in a warm place (either on top of the stove or in the oven, turned off and with the door slightly open) for 20–30 minutes before carving. This settling time makes it firmer and easier to carve. Kitchen foil makes a good cover.

The juices which collect in the tin, when skimmed of fat, form the basis of the most delicious gravy, and the fat (except in the case of lamb fat, which tastes too strong when reheated), can be kept and used for frying potatoes and so forth.

Some people like to add a glass or two of wine or cider to the fat in the roasting tin half an hour before the end of the cooking, to improve the juices for the gravy. This can also be used to baste the joint.

Braising

Braising – used for large pieces of medium quality or dry meats – can be done in the oven, or on top of the cooker. The meat, previously browned and sealed, is placed on a rich bed of chopped vegetables, bacon and herbs, which can also be fried and lightly browned in fat beforehand. It is then moistened by pouring in enough liquid – stock, water, wine, cider or beer – to cover the vegetables. A tight lid is put on the pan and it is cooked at a very moderate temperature, 160°C, 325°F, Gas Mark 3, until tender. This normally takes about 30–35 minutes per 450 g (1 lb) and 30 minutes over.

The meat should be turned and basted once or twice during cooking and seasoned halfway through. Serve with the braising vegetables and the juices skimmed of their fat, and reduced a little by boiling.

Potroasting

Potroasting is cooking a medium-quality or dry joint of meat in a tightly covered pan or casserole with fat to prevent drying, but without liquid. The steam from the cooking meat condenses on the lid and bastes the joint.

Potroasting is done slowly, or moderately slowly and the meat is sealed and browned before seasoning and before you cover the pot. (Veal should remain nearly white.) Turn the joint once or twice. The juices, skimmed of fat, make very good gravy to serve with the meat; this can be stretched by the addition of wine or stock shortly before the end of the cooking time.

Stewing

Stewing consists of cooking the tougher cuts of meat slowly and long in a liquid, either water or stock with wine, beer or cider, or whatever your recipe specifies, to break down the tough fibres and connective tissues. To improve the flavour of the meat, onions, garlic, carrots and other vegetables, herbs, spices and seasonings are added.

The meat to be stewed must be carefully trimmed and cut into smallish pieces – this helps the cooking process. It can then be fried and sealed, or left plain, depending on whether you want to have the juices from the meat completely mingled with the gravy or not.

The cooking liquid can be thickened with flour and in Britain this is normally done by frying the meat with flour before the liquid is added. Some stews are not thickened, in which case some form of starchy vegetable, such as boiled potatoes, is necessary to mop up the gravy. These are very often placed on top of the stew where they absorb any fat that rises. (Hot pot is a good example.)

Stew generally takes from $1\frac{1}{2}$–$3\frac{1}{2}$ hours, according to the quality of the meat and the oven is always kept very low, or the meat will shrink, 140–150°C, 275–290°F, Gas Mark 1–2.

Boiling

Boiling is used for large joints of medium-quality meat, either fresh or salt, but boiling is really a misnomer, since the meat should actually be simmered very lazily and steadily throughout the cooking, and never boiled. The liquid is normally flavoured with vegetables, spices and herbs, but not seasoned with salt until halfway through the cooking, or not at all, in the case of salted meat, which may need soaking before the cooking starts.

There are two schools of thought about boiling: the meat can either be started in cold water and brought to the boil, or plunged straight into boiling water or stock. The first method is the more traditional one, but means that you must skim very carefully for the first half hour as masses of scum will rise. Then cover the pan and keep the heat fairly low so that the water simmers steadily. This method gives you a very good rich broth; by the second method, plunging into already boiling water or stock, most of the flavour remains trapped inside the meat. Either way the meat absorbs some of the flavour from the liquid and gives some of its own flavour in return.

The liquid must only simmer. As a rule allow 20 minutes per 450 g (1 lb) and 20 minutes over for large pieces over 3.6 kg (8 lb), 30 minutes per 450 g (1 lb) and 30 minutes over for smaller joints.

Of the vegetables chosen for flavourings, probably carrots, leeks and onions, with a bit of turnip, swede or celery, are the most usual. Parsley, bayleaves and peppercorns are also good flavourings for boiled beef.

Cuts for frying and grilling:

Rump steak	**Skirt steak**
Sirloin steak	**Flash steak**
Fillet steak	**Minced steak**
T-bone steak	

All this meat is suitable for frying or grilling, except for **minced steak,** which you would use, only fried, for hamburgers, or eat raw as beef tartare. Timing depends on the thickness of your steak, and on how you like it done. Never overcook a steak. Even well-done, it must still be faintly rosy in the middle. As you cook the meat, turning it two or three times during the process, test it by pressing it with your finger. Wobbly and soft inside, it is very rare; pliable, it is medium-rare (and pinky-red inside); firm, it is well-done. Serve steaks with shallot relish, fried onions or parsley butter, and chips or baked potatoes, plus a green salad.

Cuts for roasting:

Sirloin	**Middlerib**
Forerib	**(toprib and**
Fillet	**backrib)**
Aitchbone	**Topside**

The prime cuts – **sirloin, forerib, fillet** – respond best to high temperature roasting which makes them crisp outside and deliciously pink inside. Roast at 220°C, 425°F, Gas Mark 7 for 15 minutes per 450 g (1 lb) and 15 minutes over for rare meat, 20 minutes per 450 g (1 lb) for medium. The coarser cuts – **aitchbone, rib cuts, topside** – should be roasted at a medium temperature: 190°C, 375°F, Gas Mark 5, 25 minutes per 450 g (1 lb) for thin or unboned pieces, but 30 minutes for pieces which are thick or boned and rolled. Before you put your meat in the preheated oven, cover it generously with butter or dripping and oil, and baste frequently. Serve roast beef (*see page* 94) with unthickened gravy, horseradish and Yorkshire pudding plus brown pan-roasted potatoes and a green vegetable or carrots.

Cuts for potroasting*** braising** stewing*:

Top rump★★★	**Oxtail**★★
Brisket★★★	**Leg**★
Top ribs★★★	**Shin**★
Flat ribs★★★	**Skirt**★
Topside★★★	**Clod**★
Flank★★	**Neck or**
Thin flank★★	**sticking**★
Silverside★★	**Chuck and**
Liver★★	**blade**★
Oxcheek★★	**Tripe**★
Oxtongue★★	

For potroasts allow 30–40 minutes per 450 g (1 lb) over medium heat, and 40 minutes per 450 g (1 lb) in the oven at 160°C, 325°F, Gas Mark 3 for thin, or unboned pieces, 45 minutes per 450 g (1 lb) for thick or boned and rolled ones. These cuts can also be braised, allowing the same times and temperatures. The cuts marked ** are good for braising but not potroasting, being too dry in themselves or the wrong shape altogether. To braise allow 30 minutes per 450 g (1 lb) depending on the quality of the meat. The cuts marked * all make lovely stews (as do, of course, those marked ** and ***). Serve potroasts and braises with mustard, boiled potatoes and its own vegetables plus a lettuce salad. Dumplings are the classic accompaniment for beef stew.

Cuts for boiling:

Silverside	**Salt topside**
Topside	**Salt brisket**
Thick flank	**Salt tongue**
Salt silverside	**Cow heel**

Boiled beef, salt or fresh, is one of the great British dishes. Cook it with plenty of vegetables, which will give up their goodness to the broth 20 minutes before serving, ladle some of the liquid into another saucepan, and in it cook a second lot of vegetables to serve with the meat. Do not forget the dumplings. **Salt beef** and **tongue** should be soaked overnight unless the butcher specifically says this is not necessary. Boil all cuts for 1 hour per 450 g (1 lb) up to 1.4 kg (3 lb); 4 hours for a piece of 1.8–2.3 kg (4–5 lb). A hefty **cow heel** must cook for 3–4 hours, until the meat comes cleanly off the bones. Discard the bones before serving.

HOW TO MAKE THE MOST OF VEAL

Cuts for frying and grilling:

Chop	**Fillet**
Cutlet	**Liver**
Escalope or	**Kidney**
scallop	**Minced veal**

All these cuts are more often fried, with the exception of **liver** and **kidneys** which are sometimes grilled – lightly – so that they are still pink inside. Up to one hour before cooking any of the other cuts, sprinkle them with a little lemon juice. Then pat them dry, and fry them over medium heat in a mixture of oil and butter until barely cooked through – just firm but still supple when pressed with the finger. Serve with pan juices and lemon wedges. **Escalopes**, beaten flat, are also good egg-and-bread-crumbed, fried golden and served with a rolled anchovy fillet in a nest of chopped hardboiled egg on top of each.

Cuts for roasting:

Leg (fillet and	**Fillet or**
knuckle end)	**cushion**
Saddle	**(tenderloin)**
Loin	

All veal must be thoroughly cooked, so even the best cuts – **fillet, saddle** or a single **loin** – should be roasted at a medium temperature: 190°C, 375°F, Gas Mark 5. Allow 25 minutes per 450 g (1 lb), 20 minutes over for thin joints or those on the bone, 35 minutes per 450 g (1 lb) for thicker joints or those that are rolled and boned. **Leg of veal** can be a little dry, but makes a succulent dish if you sprinkle the meat with flour and cover it with bacon rashers, and roast it on a bed of sliced onion with plenty of butter and oil in the dish, at 160°C, 325°F, Gas Mark 3, for 30 minutes per 450 g (1 lb) in the case of thin or unboned joints, 35 minutes for thicker or boned and rolled pieces.

Cuts for potroasting*** braising** stewing*

Loin★★★	**Knuckle**★★
Oyster★★★	**Sweetbread**★★
Leg★★★	**Tongue**★★
Breast★★★ **(stuff-**	**Middleneck**★
ed and rolled)	**Neck or scrag**★
Chop★★	**Shin**★

Potroast or casseroled, any of these cuts of veal make a delicious Sunday lunch. Allow 40–50 minutes per 450 g (1 lb) at 160°C, 325°F, Gas Mark 3. (A potroast **breast of veal** with a spinach and egg stuffing, allowed to cool, is a good summer dish.) Braised **chops** – allow 30 minutes – on a bed of savoury vegetables are a great treat. Serve mashed potatoes or buttery noodles with veal plus tiny vegetables: button mushrooms, new silver onions, young carrots, and gravy made from the skimmed pan juices. If you stew veal – allow 2 hours or so – enrich the skimmed cooking liquid with a roux, cream and egg yolk, or flavour it with tomatoes, lemon rind or orange juice after cooking. Stewed veal can lack character, and look rather sad without a velvety sauce. Serve with new potatoes, noodles or rice, and spinach or chicory.

Cuts for boiling:

Feet	**Boned rolled**
Head	**breast**
Bones	

Calves' feet and **heads** are extremely gelatinous and produce wonderful jellied stock for galantines. Cooked **feet** (3 hours) and cooked **heads** (6 hours) are boned, sliced and served with a mustardy French dressing. **Breast of veal,** with a stuffing of sausagemeat, mushrooms, and hazel or pistachio nuts, can be simmered with a split **calves' foot** for about 5 hours, pressed under a board and covered with a coating of deep golden aspic made from the reduced cooking liquid. With a salad, this is perfect for a hot summer's day.

Cuts for frying and grilling:

Chump chop	Fillet
Leg steak	Liver
Loin chop	Kidney
Cutlet	

All these little cuts, nicely trimmed, are equally good fried or grilled. Timing depends on thickness, but do not overcook – they should be pink and succulent inside. Finger-test during cooking: when they are firm but still supple, they are done. **Liver** and **kidneys**, too, should be rosy inside. Serve lamb **chops** and **fillets** with mint sauce or redcurrant jelly, mashed potatoes and fried tomatoes, plus a little bunch of green watercress.

Cuts for roasting:

Leg	Loin
Shoulder	Best end
Saddle (2 loins together)	Breast

Some people like roast lamb rosy pink inside, others well-done. The **leg**, **best end** and **saddle** or **loin** are best rare, the **shoulder** more sweet and succulent if well done, as is **boned, rolled, stuffed breast**. Roast **leg, loin, saddle** or **best end** at 190°C, 375°F, Gas Mark 5, for 25 minutes per 450 g (1 lb), and **shoulder** or **breast** at 160°C, 325°F, Gas Mark 3, allowing 40 minutes per 450 g (1 lb). Served on a preheated dish with redcurrant jelly, mint sauce or onion sauce, and gravy made of the skimmed and strained pan juices. Accompany with potatoes and a green vegetable or butter or haricot beans.

Cuts for potroasting* **braising** ** **stewing***:

Leg***	Heart**
Shoulder***	Sweetbreads**
Chop**	Tongues**
Cutlet**	Scrag*
Middleneck**	Lambs' tails*
Breast**	

Leg and **shoulder** of lamb need $2\frac{1}{2}$ hours at 150–160°C, 300–325°F, Gas Mark 2–3. A lamb hotpot takes about the same time, at the same temperatures. For braised lamb allow $1\frac{1}{2}$ hours, at these oven temperatures, or a little less if you cook it over a low flame. When cooking lamb in the oven, it is traditional to add plenty of potatoes to absorb the fat. If you do without this natural 'sponge', be sure to spoon off the excess fat before serving, or better still, allow it to cool when you can remove it in one solid layer, before reheating the dish. Lamb stew is better if care is taken in trimming the meat beforehand – otherwise the stew can look rather unappetizing, although the taste is quite marvellous. Eat braised or stewed lamb with stout pulse vegetables, or carrots, or cabbage, with which it has a natural affinity.

Cuts for boiling:

Leg	Breast
Middleneck (scrag)	Sheep's head

Boiled **leg of lamb** is a noble English classic, not often seen today but well worth trying (*see page* 109). **Breast**, boiled for 30 minutes per 450 g (1 lb) and relieved of much of its fat, can be cut into squares and fried, egg-and-breadcrumbed: much the best way of dealing with it. **Middleneck**, boiled for 2–3 hours with plenty of vegetables, gives an excellent broth. Boiled **sheep's head** is good: the meat is arranged either side of the skinned tongue, but the business of cleaning, soaking and boiling (4 hours) is rather daunting. It is eaten with onion, caper or tomato sauce.

HOW TO MAKE THE MOST OF PORK

Cuts for frying and grilling:

Loin chop	Tenderloin
Chump chop	Sliced belly
Cutlet	Kidney
Leg fillet	

Never serve fried or grilled pork under-done – all these cuts must be cooked through. A medium **chop**, trimmed of its excess fat, will take about 20 minutes gentle cooking altogether. Turn it from time to time as it fries or grills, test it by piercing with a knife: only when the juices run clear, not rosy, is it ready. Serve these cuts with their pan juices, and apple or tomato sauce and with creamy mashed potatoes. A lettuce salad eaten off the same plate in any juices left over is most delicious.

Cuts for roasting:

Leg (divides into knuckle and fillet)	Belly
	Loin
	Tenderloin
Shoulder (divides into spare rib and blade)	Griskin (boned loin of bacon pig)
Hand and spring	

Roast pork must be very well done, so allow a full 30 minutes per 450 g (1 lb) for smaller, thinner joints, such as **loin** and **belly**, and 20 minutes over at 190°C, 375°F, Gas Mark 5, and 35 minutes per 450 g (1 lb) and 25 over for thick cuts such as **leg**, or **hand** and **spring**. For good crackling, rub the skin, which should be scored by the butcher, with oil and place the joint on a rack in the tin. Baste frequently. Serve with apple sauce, sage and onion stuffing, thick gravy made with skimmed pan juices, and a fresh vegetable such as spinach, bright green or braised red cabbage and mashed or roast potatoes.

Cuts for potroasting*** braising** stewing*:

Chop***	Belly***
Sparerib chop***	Liver**

Pork is a well-lubricated meat so only resort to potroasting, braising, or stewing if you want a change. **Pork chops** or **sparerib chops** can make very good dishes, cooked on a bed of chopped vegetables, but the secret is always to trim away the excess fat before the meat goes into casserole or pot. This applies particularly to **belly of pork,** which makes an excellent main course cooked in a closed casserole with lentils or beans. The remaining fat from the pork – and there will be plenty, even if most of the visible fat has gone – is absorbed by the pulses which become creamy and delicious. **Pig's liver** is good braised, with bacon and vegetables and a glass of red wine or cider. Times vary greatly according to what is being cooked, but the best temperature for oven cookery is 160°C, 325°F, Gas Mark 3.

Cuts for boiling:

Pickled belly	Trotters
Pickled blade	Head

Boiled pickled pork has no equal as a solid winter standby – with pease pudding it is a luxurious dish whatever its reputation. All the pickled cuts need soaking before boiling – ask the butcher for how long: he is the one who will know how long the meat has been salted. Start them off in cold water, bring slowly to the boil, skim and keep simmering slowly allowing 45 minutes per 450 g (1 lb) for a piece up to 900 g (2 lb) and 30 minutes per 450 g (1 lb) for larger pieces. Add vegetables for flavour halfway through, and remove rind before serving with plenty of mustard. **Trotters**, boiled for 2–3 hours, can be eaten hot with vegetables, cold with a plain salad dressing, or be egg-and-bread-crumbed and fried or grilled. **Pig's head** now only makes brawn or galantine, but used to be elaborately dressed in imitation of a boar's head, and served with an apple in its smiling mouth.

Roast forerib

INGREDIENTS
1.8 kg (4 lb) of forerib on
  the bone
50 g (2 oz) butter or beef
  dripping
2 tablespoons oil
salt and pepper
water or stock, either
  home-made or made with
  a stock cube

If possible cook forerib on the bone as this helps to make it really full of flavour and juice. It is delicious for any lunchtime family feast; everybody appreciates a really good piece of roast beef.

Preheat the oven to 220°C, 425°F, Gas Mark 7. Put the beef in a roasting tin, fat-side upwards and coat it all over with butter or dripping. Pour on the oil and put the meat in the oven.

Baste it frequently while it cooks – it will take 1¼ hours for rare beef, 1½ for medium, but must sit in a warm place, covered loosely with a sheet of foil, to settle for 30 minutes or so after cooking and before you start carving.

To make the gravy, skim almost all the fat from the pan juices. Pour in the water or stock and boil it, scraping the tin to lift the brown juices from the bottom and sides to add their flavour to the gravy. This should be all that is needed to make really good gravy. Season it well and serve it very hot. (But if the gravy is not good, for instance should the meat not have produced much in the way of juices, in which case it can be a bit tasteless, then add the corner of a beef stock cube, about the size of a large pea, a tiny pinch of sugar and ½ teaspoon red wine vinegar and boil for a further 3–4 minutes.)

Roast forerib with Yorkshire puddings

Yorkshire pudding

TO SERVE SIX

INGREDIENTS
100 g (4 oz) flour
good pinch of salt
2 eggs (size 2)
150 ml (¼ pint) water
2–3 tablespoons good
    dripping or oil
1 small roasting tin or 6
    individual baking tins

Make in plenty of time as it needs to stand for 1 hour, before cooking. The traditional North Country pudding, eaten before the meat to take the edge off large appetites, was made with water, not milk, and placed beneath the beef turning on its spit in front of the open fire. Here it would cook and at the same time catch the juices and drippings from the meat, which gave it extra flavour. Nowadays, made in the oven, and served with good gravy, Yorkshire pudding is usually served with the meat but tastes as good as ever.

Sieve the flour and salt into a large bowl and make a well in the centre; break in the eggs. With a wooden spoon break up the eggs and start stirring, taking up a little of the flour with each turn of the spoon. Gradually add the water, a couple of teaspoons at a time, so that the mixture can be beaten smooth. Gradually add more and more water until you have a smooth batter. Beat it well for several minutes, then allow to stand for 1 hour, in a cool place. The oven will probably already be hot, roasting a nice piece of beef; but if not, heat it to 200°C, 400°F, Gas Mark 6. Put 1–2 tablespoons of oil or dripping in the tin and place it in the oven to get very hot. Now remove the tin, pour in the batter and put it straight back into the oven. Bake the pudding for 35–40 minutes, moving it to a lower shelf if it starts to become too brown. It should rise and puff but still be slightly juicy in the middle.

Beef Wellington

TO SERVE SIX–EIGHT

INGREDIENTS
900 g (2 lb) fillet of beef
225 g (½ lb) mushrooms
1 small onion
25 g (1 oz) butter
salt, freshly ground pepper
1 teaspoon chopped
    parsley
1 egg (size 4), beaten
450 g (1 lb) home-made
    puff pastry (see page 212)

Have the beef at room temperature. Chop the mushrooms and onions and soften them in the melted butter over a gentle heat. When the onions are tender add the seasoning and chopped parsley and allow to cool in a bowl. Stir in half the beaten egg, and chill the mixture.
Heat the oven to 220°C, 425°F, Gas Mark 7. Coat the beef lightly with oil and place it on a rack in a roasting tin. Sear it for 10 minutes in the oven (15 minutes if your piece of fillet is rather chunky and thick). Allow to cool completely.
Cut the pastry into two pieces – one of three-quarters and one of a quarter of its total weight. Roll out the larger piece on a floured board making an elongated oval shape, large enough almost to enclose the meat. Put it on a roasting tin, place the beef in the centre and spread the mushroom and onion mixture over the top of the meat.
Roll out the remaining piece of pastry into a long strip, large enough to make a cover. Bring the lower piece of pastry up and over the top of the beef. Brush the strip with water and place it over the top. Use any pastry trimmings to make rows of leaves along the top, attaching them with egg. Brush the pastry with egg to glaze it, prick holes in the top, and place the beef in the middle of the oven. Bake for 15 minutes, cover loosely with foil, turn down the heat to 190°C, 375°F, Gas Mark 5, and bake a further 15 minutes. Allow to set for 15 minutes in a warm place before slicing about 3 cm (1 in) thick.
You should have beautiful pink-centred beef with a golden crust. Serve with horseradish sauce (see page 155) to which you have added 4 tablespoons of single cream.

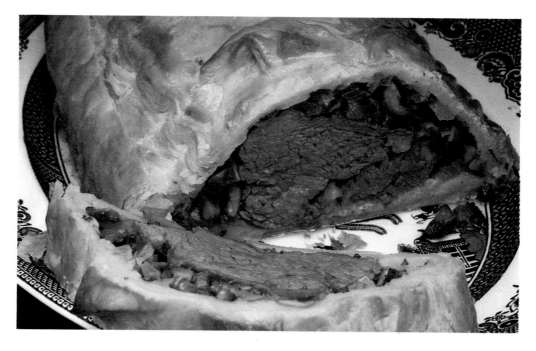

Spiced beef or Christmas beef

TO SERVE SIX

INGREDIENTS

½ teaspoon powdered
  cloves
½ teaspoon powdered mace
½ teaspoon coarsely crushed
  black pepper
½ teaspoon coarsely crushed
  allspice
1 dessertspoon dried thyme
225 g (½ lb) moist dark
  brown sugar
piece of beef (e.g. silverside,
  top rump, thin flank
  or top rib) weighing
  2.5–3 kg (5–6 lb)
225 g (½ lb) sea salt
15 g (½ oz) saltpetre
6 fresh or dried bayleaves
12 juniper berries, crushed
1 bouquet of herbs
2 carrots, chopped
2 sticks celery, chopped
1 onion, chopped
2 wineglasses port
575 ml (1 pint) beef stock
15 g (½ oz) gelatine
1 large bunch parsley,
  finely chopped

The British have always liked their spiced beef, and before Christmas the most enormous pieces of meat, weighing 18 kg (40 lb) or more, would be eaten as part of the 'cold collation' to which guests were treated any time of day or night over the days of celebration.

Although not often seen today, spiced beef is not a complicated dish to make. All that is needed is a week's notice.

Mix the powdered and crushed spices, and the thyme. Mix half the mixture with the sugar. Cover the meat with it in a shallow earthenware dish, and leave to stand for 24 hours. Now add the salt, saltpetre, bayleaves and crushed juniper berries, rubbing them into the meat, and let it steep in the mixture for a week, rubbing and turning it daily.

When ready to cook the meat, rinse it and soak for 1 hour in cold water. Dry it well, spread the reserved spices over the inside of the beef, roll it up tightly and tie with string.

Put it into a heavy iron casserole which just fits it. Surround it with the bouquet of herbs and the chopped carrots, celery and onion. Pour on the 2 glasses of port and the stock and cover tightly with its lid. Cook for 4–5 hours very, very slowly with the liquid quietly plupping, turning the meat occasionally, or braise it in a very low oven, 150°C, 300°F, Gas Mark 2, for 4–5 hours until very tender. Eat hot or, if wanted cold, allow to cool to lukewarm in the cooking liquid, then take it out and put it between two boards with a 450 g (1 lb) weight on top.

Leave it overnight. The next day eat it plain or coat it with a jelly.

To make the jelly

Remove the fat from the top of the cooled cooking liquid. Strain, skim and taste it. If it tastes too strong and salty dilute it with red wine or weak stock.

Measure 575 ml (1 pint) of the liquid. Put the gelatine in a cup with 3–4 tablespoons of the liquid, heated, and place it in a shallow pan of hot water, over a moderate heat, stirring until it has completely dissolved. Add it and the chopped parsley to the measured amount of cooking liquid, and put it in the refrigerator, stirring it occasionally until it becomes thick and syrupy. Put the beef to chill at the same time.

As soon as the gelatine becomes thick, syrupy and almost set, remove the string from the beef and spoon the glaze over it. Chill and repeat this, giving two more coats so that the beef has a nice thick glaze with green parsley embedded in it.

Pour the rest of the jelly into a shallow dish, allow to set in the fridge (if you are in a hurry, cool it quickly in the ice compartment). Then when the beef is to be served, cut the jelly into dice and pile round the beef on its serving dish.

Serve, sliced, with pickles, and plenty of mustard. Hot baked potatoes can be served on a separate plate.

Boiled beef and carrots with caraway dumplings

TO SERVE SIX

INGREDIENTS
1.2 kg (3 lb) silverside or topside, rolled and tied into a neat shape
2 onions in their skins
1 stick celery
1 small turnip
2 leeks
bunch of parsley, thyme, bayleaf, marjoram (sweet herbs)
$\frac{1}{2}$ tablespoon sea salt
6 peppercorns
900 g (2 lb) carrots
6 pickled walnuts
Caraway dumplings
225 g (8 oz) self-raising flour
100 g (4 oz) prepared suet
1 teaspoon salt
1 egg (size 4), beaten
2 teaspoons caraway seeds
1 tablespoon finely chopped celery
Boiled beef sauce (optional)
1 tablespoon mushroom ketchup
1 glass of port
walnut-sized knob of butter
$\frac{1}{2}$ tablespoon flour
pinch of salt
handful of chopped parsley and chives

Put the beef in a large pan, cover with boiling water and bring very slowly back to simmering point. Simmer for 15–20 minutes, skimming off the scum as it rises. Now add the onions, with roots and outer skins removed but one layer of skin left on – this gives the broth an appetizing colour – the celery, turnip, leeks, herbs and peppercorns. Throw in the salt and simmer very gently, covered, for 2 hours. Add the carefully trimmed and scraped whole carrots and simmer gently for 1 hour longer, 3 hours altogether.

Half an hour before the beef is wanted, make the dumplings. Mix the dry ingredients in a bowl, adding the beaten egg, and enough water (about 8 tablespoons) to make a soft dough. Shape it into little balls the size of small walnuts, with floured hands. When the meat is cooked, remove it from the liquid, put it on a large serving dish and keep it hot. Drop the dumplings into the simmering broth and let them cook for 10 minutes. With a perforated spoon put them on to one end of the serving dish. Spoon out the carrots and place them at the other end. Slice the beef, lay the slices across the dish, decorate with halved walnuts and serve with a jug of very hot strained broth and potatoes.

To make the boiled beef sauce
Strain 275 ml ($\frac{1}{2}$ pint) of the cooking liquid into a small pan, add the mushroom ketchup, port, the walnut of butter worked in with the flour and, if needed, a pinch of salt. Boil it for 5 minutes, add the chopped parsley and chives and serve with the beef.

Any remaining broth, and the vegetables in it, will make the basis of a lovely vegetable soup or can be served, very hot, on its own, enriched with a liqueur glass of white port.

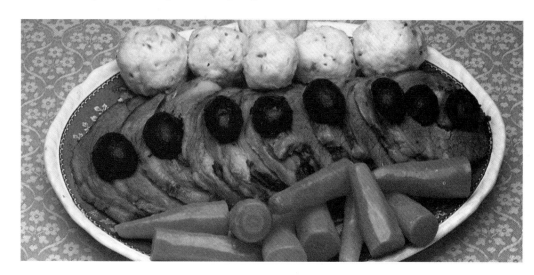

Scotch collops

TO SERVE FOUR

INGREDIENTS
4 onions
100 g (4 oz) mushrooms
50 g (2 oz) butter
1 tablespoon oil
4 1-cm ($\frac{1}{4}$-in) thick slices rump steak – about 150 g (5 oz) each
salt and pepper

This recipe is from the excellent collection of recipes made by Meg Dods in the early 1800s. She ran an inn where she entertained sporting and literary gentlemen, which she knew how to do to perfection.

Slice the onions and chop the mushrooms finely. Heat the butter and oil in a large frying pan and fry the onions until well-browned and cooked through. Remove them to a hot dish and turn up the heat. Brown the steaks in the same butter, allowing 2–3 minutes on each side. Remove them to the same heated dish as the onions, and season with salt and pepper. Muddle them up with the onions and keep hot. Add the mushrooms to the butter in the pan, season with salt and pepper and let them cook gently, until they have given out some of their juice. Pour the mushrooms over the steaks and serve.

Grilled rumpsteak with shallot butter

TO SERVE FOUR

INGREDIENTS

4 rumpsteaks weighing
    about 225 g (8 oz)
a little oil
25 g (1 oz) butter
1 teaspoon wine vinegar
1 tablespoon Worcester
    sauce
4 shallots, finely chopped
salt, freshly ground pepper
2 tablespoons chopped
    parsley

Carpetbag steak

TO SERVE SIX

INGREDIENTS

675 g (1½ lb) skirt steak in
    a piece
1 small glass port
1–2 tablespoons Worcester
    sauce
The stuffing
1 onion
100 g (4 oz) flap
    mushrooms (open flat)
4 rashers bacon
25 g (1 oz) butter
pinch of thyme
salt and pepper
4–5 tablespoons fresh
    breadcrumbs
2 anchovy fillets
1 egg

Ask the butcher to cut a deep pocket in the skirt so that it can be filled with the stuffing. Marinate the steak by leaving it overnight in a china dish with the port and Worcester sauce poured into the pocket and over the meat. Start cooking the dish by making the mushroom stuffing. Chop the onions and mushrooms fairly finely. Cut the bacon into small dice. Melt the butter in a frying pan and fry the bacon gently until the fat starts to run. Add the onions and let them soften for 5 minutes, then add the mushrooms and thyme, season with pepper and a little salt, and cook gently for 15 minutes, stirring occasionally. Allow to cool slightly, then add the breadcrumbs, chopped anchovies and beaten egg and mix well, adding a tablespoon of the port and Worcester sauce marinade.

Pat the skirt dry with kitchen paper and fill it with the stuffing. Skewer the opening together and pat it flat.

Put the steak in a roasting tin and sear it at 220°C, 425°F, Gas Mark 8, for 10 minutes, pour over the marinade and cook for 10–15 minutes more at 180°C, 350°F, Gas Mark 4. Allow to set for 5 minutes, then cut into thick slices. Arrange them on a dish, and pour on the remaining juices. Serve very hot.

The original recipe from a *Housekeeper's Guide* of 1845 recommends 'catsup' instead of Worcester sauce. It is still possible to buy mushroom ketchup which is rather similar and this can be delicious with the shallot butter on any grilled steak.

Rub the steaks on both sides with oil. Heat the grill until it is glowing.

Grill the steaks until cooked to the point that you prefer, turning 2–3 times with a spatula. If using a fork do not prick the meat, but dig it into the fat, or the juices will run out.

Meanwhile just melt the butter in a small frying pan, add the vinegar and Worcester sauce, the shallots, salt and pepper. Heat through, without cooking the shallots, mix in the parsley and keep on one side.

Put the steaks on to a heated dish, and pour some of the shallot butter over each, when it will mingle with the juices. Serve at once, with mashed potatoes.

Left: grilled rumpsteak, carpetbag steak

Beefsteak and kidney pudding

TO SERVE SIX

INGREDIENTS
225 g (8 oz) ox or pig's kidney

875 g (1½ lb) blade or skirt of beef

4 shallots, chopped

25 g (1 oz) flour, seasoned with salt and pepper

100 g (4 oz) tight button mushrooms

salt and pepper

1 tablespoon Worcester sauce

dash of tabasco

1 tablespoon tomato purée

575 ml (1 pint) water

Suet crust

225 g (8 oz) self-raising flour

100 g (4 oz) prepared suet

pinch of salt

This is the dish to present to foreign visitors. It confuses them utterly, it looks so unlike anything else and tastes so unexpectedly superb. In the past it would have contained as well as the kidneys, a dozen or so oysters; with or without these molluscs, it is quite certainly one of our greatest dishes.

Make the suet crust. Mix the flour and suet in a bowl with a good pinch of salt. Add about 8–10 tablespoons of cold water and mix to a soft dough. Roll out two-thirds of the dough on a floured board and use it to line a 1-litre (2-pint) pudding basin, pushing it down with your fist and working it flat round the sides so that it fits snugly. Leave any extra pastry hanging over the sides.

Trim the kidney and cut into pieces the size of a walnut. Cut the beef into cubes, trimming off excess fat and gristle. Chop the shallots. Clean the mushrooms and trim off the stalks.

Roll the steak and kidney in seasoned flour. Fill the basin with layers of meat, shallots and mushrooms. Three-quarter fill with cold water, season with salt, pepper, Worcester sauce, tabasco and tomato purée. Brush the top edge of the pudding with water. Roll out the remaining pastry, lift it carefully on the rolling pin and lay it over the pudding. Press the edges together and trim off extra pastry.

Cover the top with loosely fitting foil, allowing space for the crust to rise. Tie it in place with string. Put into a large pan of boiling water which should come at least half-way up the basin and boil, covered for 4½–5 hours, topping up with boiling water as necessary.

Serve the pudding at the table, removing the kitchen foil and wrapping the outside of the basin in a clean cloth, fastened with a pin. Cut the crust with a spoon and savour the delicious aroma that puffs out with the steam.

Beefsteak and kidney pudding

Beef braised in Guinness

TO SERVE SIX

INGREDIENTS
1.2 kg (2½ lb) boned
  stewing steak
25 g (1 oz) flour
2 large onions
450 g (1 lb) carrots
salt and pepper
2 tablespoons lard or oil
3 bayleaves
275 ml (½ pint) Guinness
2 teaspoons brown sugar
2–3 sprigs thyme
1 teaspoon cider vinegar

Trim the meat of all fat and gristle and cut into pieces. Roll in seasoned flour so that the pieces are lightly coated.

Peel and slice the onions and scrape the carrots, cutting them into thin rounds.

Heat the lard or oil in a casserole and first brown the bayleaves in it to flavour the oil. Remove them and fry the meat, a few pieces at a time, so that it is very well browned on all sides. Transfer the pieces to a dish as they become browned.

When all the meat is a fine colour, brown the onions in the same fat. Then add the carrots and let them cook gently, turning them over with a wooden spoon, to coat them slightly with the fat (this helps to keep them whole during the long cooking). Stir in the remaining flour. Return the meat to the pan, pour on the Guinness, let

it bubble up, season with salt, pepper and brown sugar and a sprig or two of thyme. Bring to a slow simmer on top of the cooker and transfer to a low oven (160°C, 325°F, Gas Mark 2) for 2 hours.

Add the cider vinegar 30 minutes before the end of the cooking time. Serve very hot with dumplings.

Haricot of beef

A savoury, traditional English stew from an early Victorian recipe book

TO SERVE SIX

INGREDIENTS
1.2 kg (3 lb) chuck steak
25 g (1 oz) butter and 1 tablespoon sunflower oil
18 pickling onions or shallots
25 g (1 oz) flour
salt and cayenne pepper
bunch of herbs – thyme, parsley, bayleaf
450 g (1 lb) young or old carrots
1 tablespoon Worcester sauce

Cut the meat into pieces about 2 cm ($\frac{3}{4}$ in) across and fry them in a heavy casserole in the butter and oil until lightly browned. Meanwhile skin the onions, first dipping for 1 minute into boiling water; then boil them in 275 ml ($\frac{1}{2}$ pint) of salted water until they are almost tender. Strain, keeping the liquid, and put the onions on one side.

Sprinkle the flour into the casserole with the meat, and let it brown, then add the cooking liquid from the onions. Season with salt and cayenne pepper, bury a tied bunch of herbs in the centre of the meat and bring to the boil again. Cover the pan and simmer for 1$\frac{1}{2}$ hours, adding a dash of stock if more liquid is needed.

Meanwhile prepare the carrots, either, if they are large, by cutting them in half lengthwise and then cutting them in small pieces, or, if they are small, simply by scrubbing them.

Put them into the stew, add the onions and the Worcester sauce, stir it in and simmer for a further 30 minutes, until the meat and carrots are both tender.

Serve if you like with a sprinkling of capers, parsley, chopped shallot and the chopped yolk of a hard-boiled egg, all sprinkled *very* lightly with the caper vinegar.

This is a traditional English finish to a stew, but if you don't like capers at all, you can leave them out. This stew needs good mashed or baked potatoes to mop up the gravy. Kept until the next day and re-heated it will be more tender and have an even better flavour.

Sanders

TO SERVE FOUR

INGREDIENTS
350 g ($\frac{3}{4}$ lb) leftover rare
   roast beef
2 onions
15 g ($\frac{1}{2}$ oz) flour
salt and pepper
6 sprigs parsley, chopped
15 g ($\frac{1}{2}$ oz) butter
dash of port or sherry
dash of Worcester sauce
dash of wine vinegar
any leftover gravy
1 teaspoon gravy browning
450 g (1 lb) creamy mashed
   potato

This is a recipe specially meant for leftover, underdone beef. It produces something like miniature shepherds' pies, and is very quickly made.

Mince the beef and the onions together, sprinkle with flour and put them in a saucepan with the seasoning, parsley, butter, port or sherry, a dash of Worcester sauce and wine vinegar, and the gravy, together with the gravy browning. Let it simmer for 15 minutes.

Put the mixture into scallop shells or saucers and cover with mashed potato, into which you have stirred a little cream. Dot with butter and cook in the top of the oven at 200°C, 400°F, Gas Mark 6, for 20 minutes, until nicely browned.

Oxtail stew

TO SERVE SIX

INGREDIENTS
2 small onions
2 small turnips
4 leeks
450 g (1 lb) carrots
50 g (2 oz) bacon dripping
    or lard
2 small oxtails, cut up by
    the butcher, sprinkled
    with flour
bunch of thyme, parsley,
    bayleaf (sweet herbs)
½ teaspoon crushed
    peppercorns
1 teaspoon crushed allspice
pinch of celery seed
salt
15 g (½ oz) butter rolled in
    15 g (½ oz) flour, until it
    has absorbed it all

In the past, oxtail and oxcheek were often cooked together in the same pot. This recipe, originated in 1808 by 'A Lady,' is excellent for oxtail (and for those who are prepared to believe that such a thing could be delicious, equally excellent if made with oxcheek or a mixture of both).

Prepare all the vegetables, slice the onions and turnips and cut leeks and carrots into 3-cm (1-in) pieces.

Put the bacon fat or lard in a large casserole and let it get quite hot. Throw in the pieces of oxtail, a few at a time, and brown them slowly but thoroughly on all sides. As they are browned remove them to a side dish, and keep going until even the small end pieces are browned: they will add flavour if not much in the way of meat.

Next fry the onions, allowing them to become very brown, without burning. They will give the stew its rich brown colour. Return the oxtails, add the herbs, spices, and seasoning. Half-cover with cold water and cover. Bring to the boil on top of the cooker, then transfer to a very low oven, 120°C, 300°F, Gas Mark 2, for 2 hours. Add the remaining vegetables and simmer until tender, about 1–1½ hours.

Allow to cool overnight. Take off the fat which has risen to the surface. Heat the stew on the top of the cooker, until it bubbles. Stir in flour and butter in small lumps. These will dissolve and thicken the gravy. Simmer for 10–15 minutes. Serve with baked potatoes.

Corned beef hash

TO SERVE FOUR–SIX

INGREDIENTS
900 g (2 lb) potatoes
a little milk
450 g (1 lb) corned beef
salt and pepper
50 g (2 oz) butter or beef
    dripping
2 onions, sliced
cayenne pepper

When corned beef, previously sold as fresh salt brisket, was first offered to the British in the last century, the sad demise of a little girl called Fanny Adams (due to her eating the contents of a faulty tin) caused a wave of publicity, so corned beef gave us the well-known phrase 'Sweet F.A.'.

Peel the potatoes, boil, drain and mash without any liquid, then add a very little milk, salt and pepper, and mash again. Cut the corned beef into 3-cm (1-in) cubes, and put them in a bowl. Mix with the mashed potatoes. Heat half the butter or dripping in a large frying pan and fry the sliced onions until crisp and brown. Stir them into the corned beef mixture. Heat the remaining butter or dripping, put in the potato and corned beef mixture and spread it out lightly. Cook it fairly fast so that it forms a brown crust underneath, and turn it over in large chunks with a fish slice so that it has brown bits mixed into it. Add a little more fat if necessary. When it is browned and crusty serve it steaming hot.

Top: oxtail stew,
bottom: corned beef hash

Roast loin of veal

INGREDIENTS
1.4 kg (3 lb) rolled and
   tied loin or boned
   shoulder of veal
50 g (2 oz) butter
15 g (½ oz) flour
225 g (½ lb) streaky bacon,
   sliced
2 dozen button onions
1 or 2 tablespoons white
   wine
150 ml (¼ pint) good stock
salt and pepper

Preheat the oven to 160°C, 325°F, Gas Mark 3. Spread the veal with butter and sprinkle it with flour. Place it in a roasting tin and cover the top with rashers of bacon. Put it in the middle of the oven and roast, basting frequently for 35 minutes per 450 g (1 lb). After 1 hour, cover the top loosely with a sheet of foil. Peel the onions and drop them into boiling salted water for 5 minutes. Drain them and put them round the meat for the last 30 minutes of roasting. When the meat is done put it on to a heated dish with the well-drained onions round the sides. Keep it hot and let it rest for 20 minutes to settle and make it easier to carve.

Meanwhile skim the fat from the juices in the roasting tin, add the white wine and let it boil down, stirring and scraping the bottom of the tin. Now add the stock and simmer for a few minutes, season with salt and pepper, and if necessary a squeeze of lemon juice. Serve very hot.

Some white button mushrooms, lightly cooked in butter are a good addition to this dish. Serve it with new potatoes or creamy mashed potatoes, and peas or spinach.

Cornish veal cutlets

TO SERVE SIX

INGREDIENTS
50 g (2 oz) butter
6 large veal cutlets
2 sliced onions
2 sliced carrots
1 stick celery, cut in
   crescents
2 rashers bacon, cut into
   pieces the size of a
   postage stamp
salt and pepper
thyme, marjoram
275 ml (½ pint) chicken
   stock
450 g (1 lb) potatoes
1 egg
3–4 tablespoons double
   cream
a little butter

This recipe is for braised veal cutlets as they were served at a Cambridge college, and is an excellent way of keeping an otherwise dry meat succulent and juicy.

Melt the butter in a large ovenproof casserole. When it starts to darken brown the chops in it on each side and then remove them to a plate. Do not let the butter burn. Put the vegetables and bacon into the same butter and fry them fairly briskly until they start to brown. Now place the chops on top, season with salt and pepper and a scattering of thyme and marjoram.

Heat the stock and pour it over the chops, cover the pan and cook in a moderate oven, 160°C, 325°F, Gas Mark 3 for 45 minutes.

Meanwhile cook the potatoes and mash them with the egg, cream and butter. Put the cutlets and vegetables in a heated serving dish and serve with hot tomato sauce (*see page* 154), served separately, and the creamy mashed potatoes.

Roast loin, Cornish veal cutlets

Stewed veal in a cream and lemon sauce

TO SERVE SIX

INGREDIENTS

1.2 kg (2½ lb) pie veal,
   usually from the scrag
   end
2–3 chopped anchovies
2 sprigs thyme
575 ml (1 pint) chicken
   stock, home-made or
   made with stock cubes
salt and pepper
25 g (1 oz) butter
40 g (1½ oz) flour
150 ml (¼ pint) double
   cream
pinch of nutmeg
grated rind 1 lemon
slices of lemon to garnish
   the dish

This recipe from the *Compleat Housewife*, written in 1729, is remarkably like the well-known French dish *blanquette de veau*, in which veal is simmered in broth and then served in a sauce of egg-yolks, cream and lemon. This is a most satisfying and delicate dish. Serve it with plainly boiled fluffy rice.

Trim the veal of fat and sinews and if the butcher has not already done so, cut it into neat cubes.

Put them into a saucepan with the anchovies and thyme, and cover with stock, season lightly and simmer, covered for 1 hour or so until tender. The veal must cook gently or it will shrink and toughen.

When completely tender, strain the stock into a jug and keep the veal on one side, removing the stalks of thyme. Melt the butter in a saucepan and stir in the flour. When it starts to froth gradually add the veal cooking liquid, stirring it in between each addition so that you have a smooth sauce. Let it simmer for 10 minutes, then stir in the cream, season the sauce with nutmeg and grated lemon rind, and if necessary with salt and pepper. Put the meat back into the sauce and simmer gently until it is heated through. Serve garnished with slices of lemon. 'Green peas are sometimes served in these stews', says the original recipe. 'Their colour is better preserved by boiling separately, and adding to the stew when done.'

Veal and ham pie

TO SERVE FOUR

INGREDIENTS

900 g (2 lb) pie veal
2 tablespoons chopped
   mixed herbs – fresh
   chives, parsley and
   marjoram
¼ teaspoon grated nutmeg
grated rind ½ a lemon
salt, freshly ground pepper
225 g (½ lb) boiled ham or
   gammon, in slices
2 hard-boiled eggs
575 ml (1 pint) good stock,
   home-made white stock
   (*page* 25) or stock made
   with stock cube
225 g (½ lb) home-made
   puff pastry (*see page* 212)
1 beaten egg
15 g (½ oz) gelatine (if
   using stock cube)

This is a good old favourite, less rich than pork pie and quite delicious. It is particularly useful after Christmas for using up leftover ham, and makes a very good lunch or supper dish, sliced and served with baked potatoes and salad.

Trim the veal of fat and sinews and if the butcher has not already done so, cut it into neat cubes.

Put a layer of veal in a 300-ml (1-pint) pie dish and sprinkle with a few herbs, some of the nutmeg and some of the lemon peel. Season with pepper and a very little salt – the ham will be salty. Put in a layer of the sliced ham, then the hard-boiled eggs placed lengthwise in the dish. Fill up with layers of veal, seasonings and herbs and ham, finishing with a layer of ham.

Pour in 275 ml (½ pint) of stock. Brush the edge of the pie dish with a little water and lay a strip of pastry all round the edge. Brush again with water and cover the whole pie with thinly rolled pastry, taking care that it does not stretch. Brush the top

with beaten egg, decorate with leaves cut from the trimmings of pastry and brush again with egg. Make a hole in the centre to let out the steam; you will use it later for filling the pie with jelly so make it large enough to take the end of the funnel. Bake at 220°C, 425°F, Gas Mark 7, for 15 minutes, then at 180°C, 350°F, Gas Mark 4, for 1 hour. When the top is nicely browned cover it with kitchen foil to prevent it from burning.

Dissolve the gelatine in a cup with 3 tablespoons of hot water; if necessary, stand the cup in a shallow pan of simmering water until the gelatine is completely dissolved. When the pie is ready, remove from the oven and pour into it the remaining 275 ml (½ pint) of stock into which you have stirred the gelatine – this is best poured slowly from a jug through a funnel. Stop when you can see that the pie is full of liquid.

Allow to set in the refrigerator overnight before cutting. The flavour improves if the pie is kept 24 hours before serving.

Roast leg of lamb

Also suitable for shoulder of lamb

TO SERVE SIX

INGREDIENTS

1 leg of lamb weighing
   1.4–1.6 kg (3–3½ lb)
1 large onion
3–4 sprigs thyme
50–75 g (2–3 oz) butter,
   softened
1 tablespoon oil
½ glass white wine
   (optional)
275 ml (½ pint) water or
   stock, home-made or
   made with stock cube
salt

Trim away the excess fat at the top of the leg and remove the knuckle.

Heat the oven to 190°C, 375°F, Gas Mark 5. Put the sliced onion and thyme in the roasting tin and put the leg of lamb on top. Spread the butter over the lamb and then pour the oil over this. Put into the middle of the oven and roast, basting frequently for 1½–2 hours. Remove the lamb and put it on a dish, keep it hot, covered with a loose-fitting sheet of foil, and let it rest for 20 minutes and firm up to make carving easier. Meanwhile make the gravy.

Skim most of the fat from the roasting tin. Pour in the wine and let it boil and reduce for 5 minutes while you scrape up the browned juices from the bottom and sides of the tin. They will dissolve in the gravy and give it a wonderful flavour.

When the wine has stopped giving off a winy smell add the water or stock and boil rapidly until it too is somewhat reduced. Taste it for seasoning. Now strain it through a sieve to remove the thyme and onion, and serve boiling hot – all lamb dishes and lamb accompaniments must be boiling hot as the fat becomes granular and hard as it cools.

If the gravy isn't as delicious as it should be, add a teaspoon of wine vinegar and a pinch of sugar, and boil again for a minute or two.

Sprinkle the joint with salt just as it goes to the table and let people put on more salt for themselves when it is carved.

Boiled leg of lamb with onion sauce

TO SERVE SIX

INGREDIENTS
large half leg of lamb,
    shank end preferably
1 turnip
1 leek
3 onions
2 carrots
2 sticks celery
1 tablespoon salt
Onion sauce
25 g (1 oz) butter
25 g (1 oz) flour
4 tablespoons single cream
salt and pepper

By the late autumn, lamb, both imported and home-reared, is on the large side. If you treat it differently from young lamb, taking a leg and boiling it in the old-fashioned way, you will have a most deliciously flavoured dish similar to the excellent mutton that we used to get. Serve it with creamy onion sauce for a really nostalgic, old-fashioned flavour.

Put the lamb in a saucepan and cover with boiling water. Bring it slowly back to the boil, skim it carefully. Let it simmer for 20 minutes, then skim again. Meanwhile clean and peel the vegetables, keeping them whole. Cut the celery into short lengths.

When the scum has stopped rising add the vegetables and salt to the meat, cover the pan, and allow to simmer very slowly and lazily for $1\frac{1}{2}$ hours.

Remove the meat to a plate and keep it hot while you make your onion sauce.

Remove the onions from the broth and chop them coarsely. Melt the butter in a small saucepan and stir in the flour. When it is frothy, slowly add 425 ml ($\frac{3}{4}$ pint) of the strained lamb broth, stirring to a smooth creamy sauce after each addition. Add the chopped onions and the cream, allow to simmer for 10 minutes, taste for seasoning and serve with the lamb carved in the normal way.

Any broth left over can be cooled, skimmed of fat and used to make Scotch broth (*see page* 28) or leek soup.

Guard of honour

TO SERVE FOUR

INGREDIENTS
2 best ends of lamb of
  8 cutlets each
1 onion, sliced
1 tablespoon oil
50 g (2 oz) butter
1 glass of sherry

The stuffing
1 onion
25 g (1 oz) butter
175 g (6 oz) button
  mushrooms
grated rind of $\frac{1}{2}$ a lemon
salt, pepper, cayenne
  pepper
1 teaspoon marjoram,
  thyme and chives,
  chopped
2 tablespoons freshly
  chopped parsley
50 g (2 oz) white bread,
  crusts removed
a little milk

The gravy
1 level dessertspoon flour
275 ml ($\frac{1}{2}$ pint) stock
pinch of sugar
salt and pepper

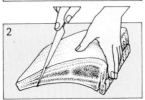

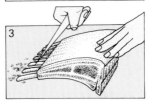

To prepare the guard of
honour: ask your butcher to
chine the best end, completely
removing the backbone; also
to skin it and to trim the
first 2 cm ($\frac{1}{2}$ in) of the end of
the bones (1). Trim the fat
from the top 4 cm ($1\frac{1}{2}$ in) of
the cutlet bones very carefully
with a sharp knife so that they
are neat and bare (2, 3). Score
the outside of the fat diagonally
in both directions to make
diamond shapes. This enables
the fat to cook quickly and
helps it to become crisp.

A guard of honour is a beautiful and traditional dish, made from best ends of lamb,
with bones trimmed and crossed in the air
like swords at a military wedding. It is not a
complicated dish and looks pretty and
festive.

Prepare the guard of honour as in the
diagrams.

Preheat the oven to 200°C, 425°F, Gas
Mark 7. Now stand the best ends on top of
the sliced onion and the chine bones, removed by the butcher, in a roasting tin
with the bone ends upwards and crossed
over at the tips. This forms the guard of
honour. Coat the joints with oil and smear
them with butter. Cover the tops of the
bones with foil to prevent them from
burning. Put into the middle of the oven
and cook for 30 minutes, then baste the
joint and pour the sherry into the roasting
tin. Cook on for a further 20 minutes, basting occasionally. While the lamb is roasting, make the stuffing, which goes in after
the meat is cooked. Chop the onion finely
and soften it in the butter for about 10
minutes without browning.

Now add the finely chopped mushrooms, grated lemon rind and seasoning of
salt, pepper and cayenne. Cook for 5
minutes more. Cut the bread into cubes,
soak in a little milk, squeeze dry and
crumble. Add the mushroom mixture, the
herbs and parsley and mix to a crumbly
soft stuffing. Keep hot.

When the guard of honour is cooked,
remove the protective foil, press the stuffing into the central cavity and place the
meat in position on a heated serving dish.
Keep hot in the oven, turned right down
and with the door slightly open.

To make the gravy, remove the chine
bones from the pan, skim off the fat from
the juices and stir in the flour; let it cook
for a minute, scraping up the caramelized
juices in the bottom of the tin; add the
stock, a small pinch of sugar, and seasoning, and simmer until the gravy is the consistency of thin cream. Serve separately. If
necessary a tiny drop of vinegar can be
added to sharpen the flavour.

Carve the lamb downwards between the
bones, serving two cutlets to each person.
Put them on each plate, crossed over at the
bone end, with a tablespoonful of the
stuffing in between. Lightly cooked French
beans or baby Brussels sprouts tossed in
butter make a good accompaniment to this
dish. Serve with mint sauce or redcurrant
jelly (in the past this was reserved for
mutton, but it is also excellent with lamb).

Reform cutlets with Reform sauce

TO SERVE SIX

INGREDIENTS
12 small lamb cutlets
2 eggs
50 g (2 oz) cooked ham
4 sprigs parsley
100 g (4 oz) fine fresh
   white breadcrumbs
salt and pepper
1 tablespoon oil
25 g (1 oz) butter
Reform sauce
2 carrots
1 onion
1 stick celery
50 g (2 oz) cooked ham or
   bacon
50 g (2 oz) butter
4 cloves
bunch of thyme, parsley,
   bayleaf (sweet herbs)
1 wineglass port or red wine
425 ml (¾ pint) stock made
   with beef stock cubes
2 tablespoons redcurrant
   jelly
1 teaspoon cornflour

Reform cutlets and Reform sauce were invented by the famous Francatelli, head chef of the Royal kitchens until 1852 and then of the Reform Club. His invention made the Club famous, and is still a favourite with London clubs.

The Edward VII chops (*see below*) are a quicker, easier and plainer, but equally good version of Reform cutlets, and are served with a simple mayonnaise instead of Reform sauce.

First make the sauce, which is kept hot while the cutlets are prepared.

Chop all the vegetables finely and cut the ham or bacon into little dice. Melt the butter in a small saucepan and fry the vegetables and ham, together with the cloves and herbs, until nicely browned. Pour on the port or red wine and the stock, bring to the boil, skim carefully and simmer for half an hour. Now add the redcurrant jelly and stir to dissolve it.

Strain the resulting strong brown stock through a wire sieve, pressing it well with a wooden spoon to extract all the juices. Throw out the vegetables and return the stock to the pan.

Mix the cornflour to a cream with a little water and stir it into the stock. Keep stirring as the sauce thickens very slightly and becomes bright and shiny. Keep hot in a bowl over a pan of hot water.

To prepare the chops
Trim the cutlets, leaving the bone quite stripped and only a thin layer of fat on the meat or 'eye' of each cutlet. Beat the eggs. Chop ham and parsley extremely fine and mix with the breadcrumbs.

Season each cutlet with salt and pepper, dip it into the beaten egg, handling it by the trimmed bone, then into the ham and breadcrumb mixture, so that it is well coated. Heat the oil and butter in a frying pan, fry the chops for about 12 minutes, turning them frequently, until they are a beautiful hazelnut brown. Serve piled on a dish with the Reform sauce in a jug. Chips or fried potatoes are usually served with Reform cutlets.

Opposite: Reform cutlets, with Reform sauce

Panfotheram

TO SERVE SIX

INGREDIENTS
6 large lamb chops
salt and pepper
450 g (1 lb) onions
900 g (2 lb) potatoes
575 ml (1 pint) chicken
   stock, freshly made or
   made with chicken stock
   cube

This hefty dish, with its fragrant and delicious layers of vegetables, was the normal dinner eaten at the farmhouse after the shepherd had despatched a sheep.

Trim and season the chops, skin and slice the onions very thinly and peel the potatoes which must also be sliced very fine. Bring the stock to the boil.

Butter a large wide casserole and put in a layer of half the potatoes, then a layer of half the onions. Season well with salt and pepper. Repeat the layers, season again and then lay the chops on top. Pour in the stock, which should come about half-way up the vegetables.

Cover the casserole and bake in a moderate oven 150°C, 350°F, Gas Mark 4, for 2 hours. Have a look during the cooking to see if more liquid is needed. Skim some of the fat off the top and serve very hot.

Left: panfotheram, *right:* Edward VII lamb chops

Edward VII lamb chops

TO SERVE SIX

INGREDIENTS
6 beautiful large lamb
   chops, the bones trimmed
   neatly by the butcher
salt, freshly ground pepper
1 tablespoon flour
2 eggs, beaten
100 g (4 oz) very fine fresh
   white breadcrumbs
150 ml (¼ pint) freshly
   made mayonnaise
   (*page* 156)

Trim the chops of most of their fat with a small sharp knife, scraping the long bone to make a sort of handle. Season them with salt and pepper. Dust them on both sides with flour, and tap them lightly to shake off any that does not stick.

Now dip the chops first into beaten egg and then into fine breadcrumbs, pressing them on so that they form an even coating. Heat the grill to red-hot and grill the chops fast turning them frequently. They will take about 12 minutes altogether.

Serve, with fresh mayonnaise and baked potatoes. A green salad would be refreshing with this.

Bolton hot pot

TO SERVE FOUR

INGREDIENTS
900 g (2 lb) best end of
    lamb
1 onion
4 lamb's kidneys
100 g (4 oz) mushrooms
900 g (2 lb) potatoes
25 g (1 oz) lard or dripping
25 g (1 oz) flour
425 ml ($\frac{3}{4}$ pint) stock
salt, freshly ground pepper
pinch of sugar

Originally this dish, like steak and kidney pudding, had oysters in it, but they have long since become too much of a luxury to spare for a hot pot – anyway the Bolton hot pot is quite as good without.

Ask the butcher to cut the lamb into pieces. When you get it home trim off most of the fat. Peel the onion and slice fairly thickly. Skin the kidneys if not skinned, and slice them into little rounds cutting away the cores. Cut the mushrooms into quarters. Peel the potatoes, slice them into thin rounds and put them in a bowl of cold water. Heat the fat in a frying pan and brown the lamb pieces on all sides. Transfer to a deep casserole using a slotted spoon to drain them of their fat. Now fry the

onions gently to a pale gold, in the same fat. Stir in the flour and let it brown, then add the stock slowly stirring all the time, to make a quantity of smooth gravy. Season with salt and pepper and a pinch of sugar.

Place a layer of kidneys over the chops, then a layer of mushrooms. Season well with pepper and salt between each layer. Pour on the gravy and onions.

Arrange the potatoes on top, overlapping like scales, brush the top with a very little melted butter or dripping to keep the potatoes moist.

Cover the pot and put it into a low oven, 160°C, 325°F, Gas Mark 3, for 2 hours. Remove the lid for the last 30 minutes to brown the potatoes.

114

Shepherd's pie

TO SERVE SIX–EIGHT

INGREDIENTS
1 kg (2¼ lb) potatoes,
    butter, milk
1 onion
2 carrots
1 stick celery
450–675 g (1–1½ lb) cold
    lamb
2 tablespoons tomato
    purée, dissolved in a
    little water
gravy from the lamb
salt, pepper, thyme
dash of Worcester sauce

Peel the potatoes and start them cooking. Mince the onion, carrot and celery and fry them in the butter while you mince the meat. Add it to the vegetables. Add the tomato purée dissolved in a little water, and the gravy, just enough to moisten the whole thing to the consistency of a thick sauce. If you like it thicker, sprinkle a dessertspoon of flour on to the vegetables and meat, and let it fry and thicken for a minute before you add the liquid.

Season with plenty of salt and pepper, thyme and a dash of Worcester sauce. Let the meat simmer while you mash the potatoes with butter, milk, salt and pepper.

Heat the oven to 200°C, 400°F, Gas Mark 6. Put the meat in an oval earthenware baking dish and cover with a nice,

light, peaked layer of mashed potatoes. Fork it into a pattern if you like, and dot with butter. Bake it at the top of the oven for 30 minutes.

Shepherd's pie can be very dreary, but frying the onions and carrots improves the flavour immeasurably.

Roast pork with apples

TO SERVE SIX

INGREDIENTS
half leg of pork, fillet end
  1.4–1.8 kg (3–4 lb) in
  weight, with the skin
  well-scored by the
  butcher
2–3 tablespoons oil
$\frac{1}{2}$ wineglass cider
15 g ($\frac{1}{2}$ oz) flour or 25 g
  (1 oz) if you like the
  gravy very thick
275 ml ($\frac{1}{2}$ pint) water or
  stock
salt and pepper
450 g (1 lb) eating apples,
  peeled, quartered and
  cored

Heat the oven to 190°C, 375°F, Gas Mark 5. Put the pork on a rack in a large roasting tin and rub it all over with oil. Place it in the middle of the oven and roast for 35 minutes per 450 g (1 lb), basting frequently. Half an hour before the end, add the cider to the basting juices in the tin; if the crackling is not quite hard and crisp when tapped with a wooden spoon, turn up the heat to 220°C, 425°F, Gas Mark 7, for the last 10 minutes of cooking. Remove the pork, keep it hot on a large serving dish and let it rest for 20 minutes to allow it to settle and make it easier to carve.

Meanwhile spoon most of the fat from the roasting tin and keep it for frying the apples. Bring the pan juices to the boil and stir in the flour, let it sizzle for a minute or two, stirring with a wooden spoon, then add the water or stock, and simmer, stirring until you have a smooth gravy. Season with salt and pepper, pour it into a gravy boat and keep it hot.

Now heat 2 tablespoons of the pork fat in a frying pan and put in the quarters of apple. Fry them gently to a golden brown and then drain them well of fat and place them round the pork. Serve with the good gravy and with creamy mashed potato.

Shiver of pork

TO SERVE SIX

INGREDIENTS
1.2 kg (3 lb) leg of pork,
  fillet end (top of leg)
oil for rubbing on to
  crackling
6 potatoes
3 medium-sized onions
6 eating apples
salt
½ tablespoon flour
1 wineglass cider
275 ml (½ pint) stock

Ask the butcher to score the crackling in narrow strips all over. Rub with oil. Place the pork in a roasting tin and roast at 190°C, 375°F, Gas Mark 5, for 30 minutes.

Meanwhile peel the potatoes and drop them into boiling salted water. Let them cook for 10 minutes. Drain them well and put them into the roasting tin with the peeled and quartered onions and peeled, quartered and cored apples. Baste vegetables and pork with the hot pork drippings and cook for a further 1½–2 hours altogether.

To serve the shiver; put it on a heated serving dish and arrange the vegetables and apples, well-drained of fat, all round. Keep it hot. Spoon most of the fat from the roasting tin – this dripping is excellent for fried potatoes. Heat the remaining juices in the tin and stir in the flour. Pour the cider into the pan drippings and stir round, loosening the caramelized juices from the edges of the tin. Now add the stock, boil until reduced by one third and taste for seasoning. Strain into the gravy boat and serve very hot.

Left: roast pork with apples, *right:* shiver of pork

Roast sucking pig

INGREDIENTS
1 sucking pig weighing
   about 7 kg (15 lb)
100 g (4 oz) butter
75 ml (3 fl oz) oil
150 ml (¼ pint) double
   cream
Herb stuffing
1 teaspoon fresh chopped
   herbs – sage, basil and
   thyme
2 teaspoons salt
½ teaspoon powdered
   cinnamon
6 peppercorns, pounded
75 g (3 oz) butter
12 thin slices of bread with
   crusts removed
Sausage farce
2 small onions
675 g (1½ lb) fresh blade of
   pork
1 teaspoon finely chopped
   sage
generous grating of nutmeg
salt and pepper
The gravy
25 g (1 oz) flour
800 ml (1½ pints) good
   beef or chicken stock,
   home-made or made with
   stock cubes
juice of ½ a lemon
salt and pepper
**Old spiced
currant sauce**
275 ml (½ pint) red wine
225 g (8 oz) currants
100 g (4 oz) sugar
12 cloves
2 5-cm (2-in) cinnamon
   sticks

Meg Dods, proprietress of the Border Inn at Howgate, famous favourite haunt of Sir Walter Scott, wrote in 1829: 'A sucking pig, *un cochon de lait*. France and England, natural enemies on the relative merits of ragouts and roast beef, are in brotherhood here. The age on which every gourmand, whether insular or continental, sets his seal, is from 10 days to double that number.'

Should you wish to try a celebratory sucking pig, order it well in advance from your butcher, and make sure you have a roasting tin large enough to hold it, and that it will go into your oven. If not, ask the butcher to divide it in half; cook the two halves in two tins and reassemble them afterwards. It must be served very hot – 'in the crispness of its beauty'; it is a most unusual and quite delicious dish. If you think it looks a little sad, carve it in the kitchen before serving. The spiced currant sauce should be made the day before if possible.

Preparing the herb stuffing
Mix the herbs, salt, cinnamon and pepper with the butter. Butter the thinly sliced bread generously with the mixture, pressing it in well. Stack the slices one on top of the other and cut into 3-cm (1-in) squares.

Preparing the sausage farce
Boil the onions in salted water for 15 minutes and chop. Mince the pork with the sage, nutmeg, and the onions, putting it twice through the finest blade of the mincer. Season with salt and pepper and then mix well.

Stuffing the pig
Lay the pig on its back. Dry the inside with a piece of kitchen paper.

Put the squares of bread inside the pig, then place a layer of sausagemeat over the top. Skewer or sew up the belly of the pig with a poultry needle and thread. Do not overstuff it or it may cause a catastrophe by bursting as the stuffing expands. Protect the ears and nose with foil to prevent them from burning.

Place the pig on a roasting rack. Brush it all over with liberal quantities of oil, and put it into a hot oven: 200°C, 425°F, Gas Mark 7. Baste it frequently with melted butter and let it cook for 30 minutes. Turn down the oven to 180°C, 350°F, Gas Mark 4, then cover loosely with foil and allow to cook for a further 3 hours altogether – lift the foil and baste from time to time. After 2½ hours remove the paper and brush the skin all over with double cream, so that it can become beautifully golden and crisp.

When the pig is cooked remove it from the pan and put it on a dish to keep hot in

the oven, with the heat turned right down and the door open a little way to keep the crackling crisp. Take off the protective foil.

Make the gravy: spoon most of the fat from the roasting tin, sprinkle in the flour, let it cook for 2 minutes, then add the stock, lemon juice, and seasoning. Simmer for 10 minutes.

Put the pig on a splendid, heated dish, decorate it handsomely with leaves and flowers and show it to your guests. Then, since it can be rather a messy business, do your carving out of sight. Put the carved pieces on a large dish, with the crackling in manageable pieces all round the edge and hand it round.

Old spiced currant sauce

Make this the day before if possible to allow the currants to swell and imbibe the wine.

Put all ingredients in a saucepan and cook for 15–20 minutes, until the wine has reduced by about half. Remove from the heat and pour the mixture into an earthenware or china basin. Let it cool and leave to steep in its own juice for at least 6 hours. Reheat before serving.

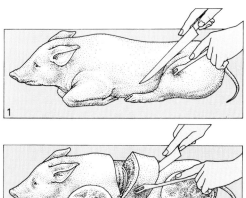

When you carve a sucking pig, do not aim for thin slices but for thick juicy pieces. Remove the shoulder and leg from the side nearest to you (1). These are carved separately, and shared out with the other meat and the crackling. Cut away a piece of the 'saddle', exposing some of the ribs (2). These are pulled out so that you can spoon out the stuffing. Cut all the meat from one side before starting on the other.

Pork cutlets with tomato sauce

TO SERVE SIX

INGREDIENTS
6 thin pork chops, with
  bones trimmed
100 g (4 oz) butter
75–100 g (3–4 oz) dried
  breadcrumbs, home-
  made for preference
½ teaspoon dried marjoram
  or ¼ teaspoon dried sage
pinch of salt, freshly
  ground pepper
The sauce
12 fresh tomatoes or
  1 × 500 g (1 × 1 lb) tin of
  tomatoes
25 g (1 oz) butter
salt and pepper
squeeze of lemon juice

Pork chops or cutlets were often served fried or broiled or grilled in a crisp coating of breadcrumbs. This serves the purpose of preventing the chops from becoming dry and adds a delicious crispness to meat and fat alike.

Cut away the rind and some of the fat from the chops. Melt the butter in a small saucepan and pour half into a warm soup plate. Dip the well-trimmed chops into the butter, so that it coats them on all sides, then into the breadcrumbs mixed with herbs, salt and pepper, so that they are encrusted with a nice even layer of crumbs. Now start the tomato sauce. Put all the tomatoes into a medium saucepan with a nut of butter, and season lightly with salt and pepper. Place the pan on a medium heat and let the tomatoes simmer down to a moist purée.

Meanwhile pour the remaining melted butter into a large frying pan and heat through. When the butter is light brown put in the chops and fry them over a medium heat, turning them once or twice until they are crisp and brown. They will take about 20 minutes. Any crumbs that come off can be scooped up and put on the top of the chops at the end.

When they are done, drain the chops on kitchen paper for a minute, put them into a heated dish and keep them hot. Finish the tomato sauce; sieve it if using fresh tomatoes, otherwise whisk it with a fork, add a squeeze of lemon juice and serve in a heated bowl, with the pork chops.

To make breadcrumbs
Cut stale bread into 3 cm (1 in) cubes and put them into the food processor or liquidizer to reduce to fine breadcrumbs. Shake them through a sieve into a roasting tin. Put back any that will not go through and grind again. Put the roasting tin in a very low oven until the crumbs are dry, crisp and a warm, golden brown.

Left : pork cutlets with tomato sauce,
top right : Dublin pork sparerib with apples,
bottom right : braised pork chops with sherry

Braised pork chops with sherry

TO SERVE FOUR

INGREDIENTS
4 pork chops, well-trimmed
1 tablespoon oil
15 g (½ oz) butter
2 carrots, 2 onions, 1 stick
  of celery, 1 leek, all
  trimmed and sliced
225 g (¼ lb) mushrooms,
  trimmed and sliced
6 pounded allspice
grating of nutmeg
1 strip lemon peel
salt and pepper
275 ml (½ pint) chicken
  stock, home-made or
  made with stock cubes
1 wineglass sherry
2–3 tablespoons double
  cream

Trim a good deal of the fat off the chops. Heat the oil and butter in a fireproof casserole the right size to hold all the chops side by side. Fry them on each side until a nice brown, then remove to a plate, leaving the fat in the casserole. Brown the vegetables, except for the mushrooms, in the same fat. When they start to turn brown add the mushrooms. Place the chops on top of this bed of vegetables, season them with allspice and nutmeg, add the lemon peel, salt and pepper. Pour on the stock and half the sherry, cover the pan, bring it to the boil and then transfer it to a moderate oven, 190°C, 325°F, Gas Mark 3. Let it cook for 1 hour quite slowly.

Take out the chops and put them on a dish. With a slotted spoon take out the vegetables and cover the chops with them. Keep them hot.

Boil the juices to reduce them, when they are getting slightly thick and no more than 275 ml (½ pint) is left (the juices from the vegetables will have increased the cooking liquid considerably), add the cream, boil for 3 minutes, pour over the chops and vegetables and serve.

Dublin pork sparerib with apples

TO SERVE SIX

INGREDIENTS
6 slices of sparerib
4 sharp cooking apples
3 onions
salt, freshly ground pepper
1 level tablespoon brown
  sugar
bunch of herbs – parsley,
  thyme, bayleaf (sweet
  herbs)
1 wineglass dry, still cider

In country households until the turn of the nineteenth century or even later, the pig was 'the gentleman that pays the rent' and was a very prized possession. He met his end in the autumn, when the main part of the pork would have been pickled or turned into hams to see the family through the winter, but a few dishes for fresh pork survive and this is one of them.

Cut the outside fat and rind from the sparerib chops and cut it into thin strips. Peel, core and slice the apples thinly and cut the onions into thin slices. Season the chops with salt and pepper.

Butter a wide casserole, put in a layer of apple slices, sprinkle them with half the sugar and spread half the onions over the top. Season with salt and pepper and place the chops on top. Place the herbs in the centre.

Now cover with more onions, more apples and the remaining sugar. Place the pieces of pork fat criss-crossed in a lattice over the top, pour in the cider, cover the pot and bake at 180°C, 350°F, Gas Mark 3, for 1 hour, lower the heat and cook a further hour at 150°C, 300°F, Gas Mark 2. Skim off the excess fat from the top and turn up the heat to 220°C, 425°F, Gas Mark 7 to crisp the crackling and lightly brown the apples to a pale golden colour.

Ham

Fresh pork, because of its doubtful keeping qualities, in the days before refrigeration used to be largely ignored by middle-class families who relied more heavily than we do now on the charms of veal to give them variety. However, no gentleman's table was complete without a great ham with a large paper frill round its bone. The niceties of curing and dressing hams were known to every good housewife – she had to rub the ham with salt and brown sugar, and lay it in an earthen crock with more salt, black treacle, saltpetre (which gives it its lovely pink colour) spices and sometimes ale or cider. It had to be turned and inspected and finally hung up to dry and smoke inside the big kitchen chimney, then stored, wrapped in a cloth,

Stout nails, hammered into rafters, beams and any other woodwork, used to support the great home-cured hams that needed plenty of air to keep them 'sweet'.

until it was needed. When the time came to cook the ham it had to be soaked for up to a week to relieve it of its preserving salt. Then it had to be cooked, skinned, crumbed, cooled, and at last was ready for slicing.

Although few people cure ham at home today, there are still a number of different cures going strong in this country. Of the more traditional there are York hams, famous all over the world, firm, mild, pink and succulent, Bradenham, black-skinned and deep red in colour, cured in black treacle and full of flavour, and Wiltshire which is cured with bacon and is therefore, strictly speaking, gammon. This keeps less well and is milder than other hams.

Of course there was and is more to a bacon pig than a couple of hams and since nowadays even the hams are cut into small joints after curing, it is as well to know what the mysterious names of such cuts as corner gammon and gammon slipper actually mean. Although the names and cuts vary slightly from district to district, it is as well to know which cuts are most suited to different cooking methods.

Frying and grilling ham or gammon
If the slices of uncooked ham or gammon are salt (you will find out by asking the grocer or assistant but nowadays with light commercial cures and brine-injections this is becoming increasingly rare) soak them briefly in cold running water; 15 minutes will be enough.

Dry the slices, by patting them with folded kitchen paper, and cut off the rinds, with kitchen scissors. Nick the edge of the fat here and there to keep it flat. Now fry or brush with oil and grill; a thick rasher of gammon or ham will take about 5 minutes on each side. Take care not to overcook it or it will be come dry.

Serve with mustard and cider sauce, or with parsley sauce and mashed potatoes.

Braising or stewing gammon
Although not strictly suited to braising, gammon joints or pickled pork from the fattest parts of the pig are essential to the long slow process of turning beans or lentils into a creamy and delicious mass. They absorb the fat gradually and lose their stringent dryness of texture.

Soak flank, belly or hock in cold water for a couple of hours before placing in the middle of the pot of beans or lentils, previously soaked, cover with water, complete the flavouring by adding an onion stuck with cloves and a bayleaf or two and cook slowly, 160°C, 325°F, Gas Mark 3 for several hours.

Boiling gammon or ham joints
All gammon joints should be boiled for at least part of their cooking time. They will first need soaking, then boiling for 15 minutes per 450 g (1 lb) and only then, minus their rind and coated with a lovely rich glaze, are they ready to go into the oven.

As the joints increase in size, so they need fewer minutes in the pot for every 450 g (1 lb); the chart will help whatever the size of your joint, and these can vary from 450 g (1 lb) or so up to 9 kg (20 lb) or even more for a whole gammon:

450 g (1 lb)	allow 45 minutes
450 g–1.2 kg (1–3 lb)	allow 1–1½ hours
1.2–2.7 kg (3–6 lb)	allow 30 minutes per 450 g (1 lb)
2.7–4.5 kg (6–10 lb)	allow 3–3½ hours
4.5–6.3 kg (10–14 lb)	allow 3½–3¾ hours
6.3–8.1 kg (14–18 lb)	allow 3¾–4¼ hours
8.1–9.5 kg (18–21 lb)	allow 4¼–4½ hours

Once boiled they can, if being eaten cold, be allowed to cool in their liquid which helps to keep the meat moist. If you want a delicious hot boiled joint allow to set in the liquid for at least 10 minutes with the heat turned off before removing, skinning and slicing.

For a glazed joint remove and skin 30 minutes before the end of the cooking time and place in the oven, covered with a spicy sweet-sharp glaze (see page 124) for the last 30 minutes.

Frying bacon
The best bacon for frying is undoubtedly smoked bacon; look for the rich russet brown of the rind and a more rosy pink to the meat than in green bacon.

Choose back or streaky cut thick or thin, but always take bacon with fresh-looking white fat – buy not more than a week's supply at once and keep it in a plastic container in the refrigerator.

When you decide to fry your bacon take up the kitchen scissors and cut off the rinds: not the fat which provides the lubrication, just the rinds.

Put a teaspoon or two of oil or a nut of lard in the frying pan, heat it through, then put in the bacon rashers and fry fairly briskly, turning once or twice until the fat is an appetizing brown.

Glazed gammon and cider sauce

TO SERVE SIX

INGREDIENTS

1 piece gammon weighing 1.8 kg (3 lb) or more, soaked overnight if necessary to remove excess salt
1 onion, stuck with a clove
1 bunch parsley, thyme, bayleaf
2–3 tablespoons brown sugar
1 tablespoon Dijon mustard
1 teaspoon grated orange rind
several whole cloves
275 ml ($\frac{1}{2}$ pint) dry cider
1 tablespoon dry English mustard

Put the soaked gammon into a large saucepan of cold water together with the onion stuck with a clove and the bunch of herbs.

Bring it rather slowly to the boil, skimming off the froth that rises, and then cover the pan and simmer steadily but gently for 2 hours – 30 minutes per 450 g (1 lb) plus 30 minutes. Remove the gammon from the cooking liquid and cut away the skin, leaving the pale fat looking quite naked.

Now, with a small sharp knife, score the fat across at 3-cm (1-in) intervals, then do it again across the first cuts so that the fat opens slightly into diamond shapes. Stick a clove into each interstice of the lattice pattern. Mix the brown sugar, mustard and orange rind in a bowl and coat the fat thickly with the mixture. Put the gammon in the roasting tin with the cider, and the English mustard, mixed to a cream with a little water, and roast in a hot oven (220°C, 425°F, Gas Mark 7) until nicely browned and glazed, basting it with the cider 2–3 times. It will take about 20 minutes to brown nicely. Then let it rest 20 minutes before carving. Serve it with its own pan juices. If it tastes too salty add more cider to the sauce. Cumberland sauce (*see page 155*) is also traditional with glazed gammon, which can be served hot or cold, and sliced very thinly.

Opposite : glazed gammon

Cambridge cabbage and bacon

TO SERVE FOUR

INGREDIENTS

1 large crisp white cabbage
4 rashers back bacon (or more)
4 rashers streaky bacon (or more)
knob of butter
salt, pepper, pinch of ground allspice

Trim and quarter the cabbage and wash it well. Bring a large pan of salted water to the boil and throw in the cabbage. While it is cooking, cut the bacon into small pieces, and fry in butter in a hot frying pan.

When it is tender, after about 10 minutes, drain the cabbage thoroughly, cut it into shreds with a knife and press lightly to strain off the water.

Place it in a mound on a deep dish and throw the bacon and its hot fat over the top. Season with pepper and a pinch of allspice and serve large helpings.

Top : Cambridge cabbage and bacon, *bottom :* gammon steaks with dry cider sauce

Gammon steaks with dry cider sauce

TO SERVE FOUR

INGREDIENTS

4 thick gammon steaks weighing 175–225 g (6–8 oz) each with rinds removed
3 teaspoons Dijon mustard
2 level teaspoons brown sugar
275 ml ($\frac{1}{2}$ pint) dry cider
1 level teaspoon cornflour
2 tablespoons double cream
salt and pepper

Soak the gammon steaks in water for 1 hour. Remove them and pat them dry with kitchen paper. Make a paste with the mustard, sugar and a little cider, and spread the gammon steaks with the mixture, allowing them to soak up the flavour for 20 minutes.

Put the steaks, coated with the mixture, in the bottom of a casserole and pour on the cider. Bake in a hot oven, 200°C, 400°F, Gas Mark 6, for 20 minutes. When the gammon steaks are cooked, strain off the liquid into a small saucepan. Add the cornflour dissolved in 2 tablespoons of water and stir while you bring the mixture to the boil and let it simmer gently for 5 minutes. When the cornflour is cooked stir the cream into the sauce, taste for seasoning and add salt and pepper.

Pour the sauce over the gammon steaks, garnish with parsley and serve hot.

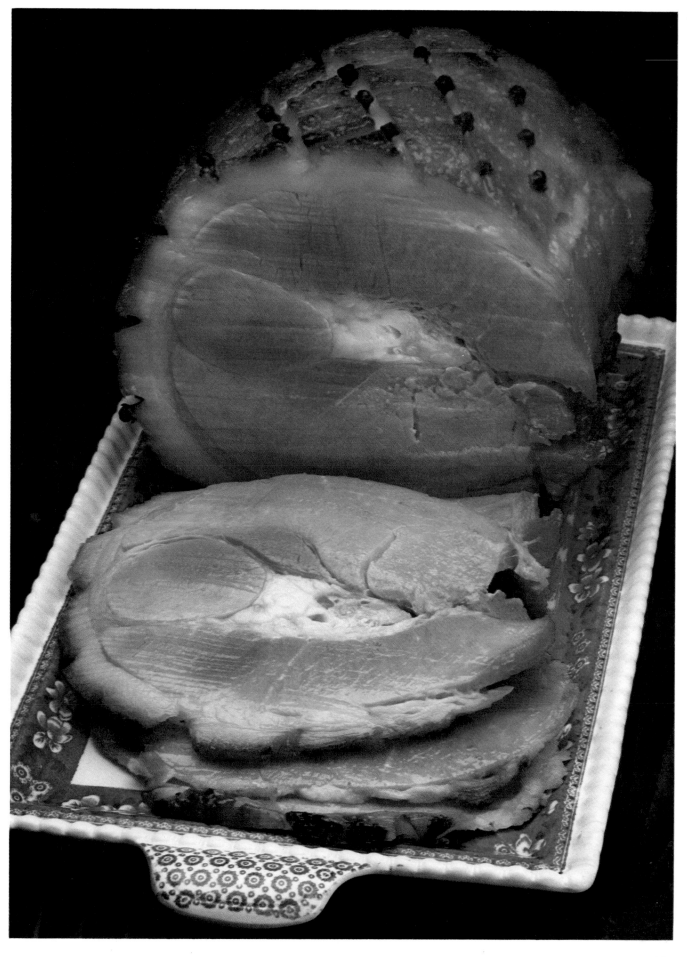

Beans and bacon

TO SERVE SIX–EIGHT

INGREDIENTS
450 g (1 lb) small white
  pearl beans, soaked
  overnight
50 g (2 oz) butter
225 g ($\frac{1}{2}$ lb) salt pork or
  green streaky bacon, with
  rind removed
1 onion
2 tablespoons black treacle
1 teaspoon salt
2 teaspoons dry mustard
3 tablespoons tomato
  ketchup

Beans and bacon is an old British favourite.
George III dined on it *al fresco* with the
workmen at Woolwich Arsenal, and enjoyed their beans and bacon so thoroughly
that he instituted an annual beanfeast in
memory of the occasion.

Put the beans in a saucepan, cover by 3 cm
(1 in) with cold water and bring slowly to
the boil. Simmer for 1–1$\frac{1}{2}$ hours until
almost tender.
    Put 25 g (1 oz) of butter in a frying pan,
slice the pork or bacon into six–eight slices
and fry them for 3–4 minutes, turning
them over once or twice.
    Transfer the bacon and their fat to a

deep casserole. Drain the beans and save
the liquid. Pour the beans into the casserole
and push the onion into the middle. Mix
the treacle, remaining butter, salt, dry
mustard and tomato ketchup with the bean
liquid and pour over the beans.
    Cover the pot and cook in a very slow
oven, 150°C, 300°F, Gas Mark 2, for 2–3
hours, adding more water if necessary.
Remove the lid for the last 30 minutes to
brown the top.
    The bacon fat will permeate the beans
and give them a delicious melting quality.

Ham knuckle with pease pudding

TO SERVE FOUR

INGREDIENTS
450 g (1 lb) split yellow
  peas
2 onions, finely chopped
1 smoked shank or knuckle
  of ham 850 g (about
  1$\frac{3}{4}$ lb) or ham bone
freshly ground pepper
1 bayleaf
knob of butter

'Pease pudding hot, pease pudding cold,
pease pudding in the pot nine days old!'
    In fact pease pudding is very good cold;
when it has been cooked with a shank or
knuckle of gammon or ham it sets to a
beautiful jelly; 9 days old might not be so
good, though it will keep at least 3–4 days
in a cool place, and can be reheated by
steaming.

Soak the peas overnight. If using an uncooked shank or knuckle ask the butcher if
it needs soaking; if necessary, soak it overnight.
    The following day strain the soaked peas
and put them into a muslin bag or tie them
loosely in a cloth (or clean table napkin)
together with the onions. Place them in a
large saucepan with the ham, pepper and
bayleaf and cover with water. Simmer
gently for 2–2$\frac{1}{2}$ hours, covered. Take out
the mushy peas, let them drain for a
minute, then turn them into a basin.

Season with salt if necessary, and beat in a
knob of butter with a wooden spoon or
fork. Keep the ham simmering in its
liquid and place the basin over a separate
pan of boiling salted water. Cover it well
and steam for 45 minutes.
    This pease pudding can now be turned
out and sliced. Serve it with slices of meat
from the knuckle and some of the cooking
liquid, which is already thickened by
starch from the peas. It is delicious and
filling.

Hot scarlet tongue and caper sauce

TO SERVE FOUR

INGREDIENTS
1 scarlet tongue, soaked
  overnight if necessary
25 g (1 oz) butter
25 g (1 oz) flour
425 ml ($\frac{3}{4}$ pint) milk
1 tablespoon double cream
2–3 tablespoons capers
1 tablespoon of vinegar
  from the capers
salt and pepper

A scarlet tongue is a salted tongue, the brine turns it an appetizing red. Choose one that is on the small side and ask the butcher how long it will need soaking: if it is correctly pickled, it will need little if any; but if you are not certain, let it soak overnight.

Let the tongue soak in a large bowl of cold water for the appropriate length of time.

Now put it into a large casserole and cover with fresh cold water. Put the lid on the pan, bring it slowly to the boil and simmer for $2\frac{1}{2}$–$3\frac{1}{2}$ hours until the tongue can be very easily pierced with a skewer; it should feel very tender and soft. Remove it from the heat and let it sit in its hot stock while you make the sauce.

Melt the butter in a small pan, stir in the flour and when it foams start adding the milk slowly, a little at a time, stirring after each addition. When you have a smooth creamy sauce let it simmer gently for 10 minutes, then add the cream, capers and caper vinegar. Season with salt and pepper and keep hot.

Remove the tongue from its liquid and skin it; do this with your fingers. Although it is hot work, this is the best method. You will find, if the tongue is cooked, that the skin peels off in satisfying strips. Slip out the bones underneath the tongue, slice it fairly thickly and lay the slices round and over a heated serving dish. Put a sprinkling of capers over the top and serve very hot with the caper sauce and mashed potatoes.

If the tongue cooking liquid is not too salty it can be used to make a golden pea-soup (see page 34).

Fricassée of sweetbreads

TO SERVE THREE-FOUR

INGREDIENTS
675 g (1½ lb) lambs' or calves' sweetbreads
275 ml (½ pint) stock
1 carrot, peeled and sliced
1 small onion, peeled and sliced
1 stick celery
bouquet of parsley, thyme and bayleaf
50 g (2 oz) butter
3 tablespoons brandy
squeeze of lemon juice
150 ml (¼ pint) double cream
1 teaspoon mild Dijon mustard
salt and pepper
1 tablespoon finely chopped parsley

Soak the sweetbreads in cold water for 2 hours to remove the impurities, changing the water from time to time. Drain and put into a pan of cold water, bring to the boil and simmer for 2 minutes, skim well, then drain and plunge into cold water. Skin them, removing any thick layers of connective tissue.

Put them into the cleaned saucepan again with the stock, peeled and sliced carrot and onion, the celery cut into 5-cm (2-in) pieces, and the bunch of herbs. Bring to the boil again and poach the sweetbreads at a gentle simmer for 10 minutes. Drain, and if they are large, slice them into small slices, reserving the stock. Take out the vegetables, and herbs. Melt the butter and return the sweetbreads to

the pan, let them stew gently for about 10 minutes, stirring round to coat them well with butter. Add the brandy and let it bubble for 1 minute, then add 3 tablespoons of the sweetbread cooking liquid, the squeeze of lemon juice and the cream. Stir in the mustard, and season lightly with salt and pepper. Simmer until the sauce is thick, about 8–10 minutes, and serve in a shallow dish, sprinkled with finely chopped parsley. Spinach and boiled potatoes are excellent with this rich dish.

The sweetbread cooking liquid and vegetables can be used later to make soup.

Grilled kidneys with parsley butter

TO SERVE FOUR

INGREDIENTS
1 bunch watercress with large leaves for garnish
8–12 lamb's or 4 pig's kidneys
salt, pepper, cayenne pepper
25 g (1 oz) butter, melted
Parsley butter
50 g (2 oz) butter
2 tablespoons parsley
juice of ½ a lemon
salt and pepper

To make the parsley butter chop the parsley finely. Then allow the butter to soften to room temperature in a bowl. Mash it with a fork, add the parsley, lemon juice, salt and pepper and mix until smooth. Allow to set in a cold place.

Wash and pick over the watercress, and shake it dry in a cloth. Now skin the kidneys if they have not already been skinned. Split them down the rounded side, and trim the central core but do not quite divide them. Run a skewer through the back of each so that the kidneys stay flat during cooking. Season them highly with salt, pepper and cayenne and brush with melted butter.

Heat the grill, and grill the kidneys for 5

minutes on each side, brushing with more butter if they seem dry.

Serve sizzling hot with a walnut of the parsley butter melting on top of each kidney, and a small neat bunch of watercress on each plate to dip into the juices.

Mixed grill

TO SERVE FOUR

INGREDIENTS
4 lamb cutlets, 2 cm (3 in) thick
4 lamb's kidneys
4 pork sausages
oil or melted butter
4 rashers smoked back bacon
4 rashers smoked streaky bacon
4 large flap mushrooms
4 small tomatoes, cut in half
salt, freshly ground pepper
1 bunch watercress

Nothing could be more English or more delicious. As far back as the seventeenth century, if you wanted to eat a quick lunch in the City of London you would undoubtedly have gone to a chophouse or, later, a grill room. Here in a dark and smoky room you would have seated yourself on a high-backed wooden bench with sawdust under your feet and eaten a quick meal grilled over charcoal. This is where the mixed grill had its origins.

The mixed grill is composed of a crisp lamb chop, kidney still pink within, a glistening brown sausage, a thick curl of bacon, pink and gold, a large, black juicy mushroom and a tomato red-gold and tender. It *must* be hot and accompanied if possible by two or three sprigs of watercress and nothing else.

Heat the grill. Take out the grill pan and line it with kitchen foil, if you want to make the washing-up less of a chore. Trim

the excess fat off the chops. Skin and halve the kidneys, removing the central core. Brush the chops, kidneys and sausages with oil or melted butter. Trim the rinds off the bacon and nick the fat to stop it from crinkling. Brush the undersides of the mushroom caps and the cut sides of the tomatoes with oil or melted butter, and season with salt and pepper. Place the chops and sausages on the grill pan and start them grilling. They take 6–8 minutes on each side. Keep them hot on a dish in the oven with the door slightly open. Next place the kidneys, bacon, mushrooms and tomatoes on the grill and grill for 10 minutes, turning the kidneys after 5 minutes.

When everything is cooked share out between four heated plates and place a small bunch of watercress on each plate. Serve at once; many people like bottled fruit sauce with a mixed grill.

Liver and bacon

TO SERVE FOUR

INGREDIENTS
450 g (1 lb) lambs' liver or (even better) calves' liver in 4 slices 2 cm (½ in) thick
4 large rashers or 8 smaller rashers of back bacon
25 g (1 oz) butter
flour for dusting
salt
Staffordshire frying herbs
450 g (1 lb) fresh spinach or spinach beet
2 bunches spring onions
2 good handfuls parsley
50 g (2 oz) butter
salt and pepper

Trim the edges of the liver to remove the fine membrane round it – this shrinks in cooking and makes the liver curl up. If you want to take the trouble it can be peeled off like a skin without wasting any meat. Cut the rinds off the bacon (but not the fat). Heat the butter in a large frying pan and fry the bacon until the fat loses its transparent look. Push the bacon to the side of the pan.

Dust the slices of liver lightly with flour and put them into the sizzling bacon fat. Cook them very briefly and reasonably fast – overcooking makes liver hard and dry.

They will need no more than 3–4 minutes on each side. Put them round a heated dish, season with a sprinkling of salt, put the bacon in the middle and pour the juices

from the pan over the top. Serve at once with lovely creamy mashed potatoes and, if you like, with traditional Staffordshire frying herbs.

Staffordshire frying herbs
Wash the spinach or spinach beet. Trim and chop the spring onions and chop the parsley coarsely. Melt the butter in a thick pan (this is important as no water is used in the cooking except that clinging to the spinach).

Shake the spinach, put it in the pan with the onions, parsley and a seasoning of salt and pepper. Stir it for a minute until it wilts down and cook gently in a covered pan for 15 minutes, stirring occasionally. Drain if necessary and serve with liver and bacon.

Left: grilled kidneys with parsley butter, *centre:* mixed grill, *right:* liver and bacon

Vegetables

The British and their vegetables have always been something of a puzzle. How is it that at flower shows and country fêtes you can marvel at the delicate tints and perfect flesh of rosy carrots, silvery leeks, snow-white cauliflowers, tomatoes glowing with health, green peas in matchless pods, broad beans and lettuces, radishes and cabbages all bursting with freshness and variety, and then find, all too often, in British kitchens, particularly those of restaurants, the saddest sorriest apologies for vegetables that can be seen anywhere in the world.

For centuries British vegetables have been the subject of ridicule amongst the better-educated of other nations. An eighteenth-century foreign visitor observed that the Englishman's meat was normally accompanied by 'a few cabbage leaves boiled in plain water over which they pour a sauce made of flour and butter; the usual method of dressing vegetables in England', and another remarked that the excessive eating of these uninspiring greens 'made the Englishman a dull animal'.

However not all early writers despised vegetables. It was in 1808 that 'A Lady' – Maria Rundell – gave the following advice for boiling vegetables green in her *Book of Cooking for Private Families*: 'Be sure the water boils when you put them in. Make them boil fast. Don't cover, but watch them and if the water has not slackened you may be sure they are done when they begin to sink. Then take them out immediately or the colour will change. If overboiled they lose their beauty and their crispness.' Good advice and still well worth following especially if you also remember to add plenty of salt and to drain the vegetables very thoroughly and then toss them with a nut of butter before serving.

Fresh or frozen, there is one sure way of serving wretched vegetables and that is to overcook them. Basically, they should only be cooked until just tender – their own heat will continue to cook them even after they are drained.

When you choose fresh vegetables, take those that have a just-gathered freshness about them, as their fine flavour is gradually lost with the passing of the hours; just picked vegetables have a very special creaminess of texture too, which is even more quickly lost.

To preserve their freshness, once picked or brought home from the shop, it was once advised to lay vegetables out of the draught on to a stone flagged floor. Now they go into the compartment designed for their storage in the refrigerator, or, if this is full, can be wrapped in polythene and placed on the lowest shelf.

When it comes to the cooking, Countess Morphy, one of Britain's more distinguished cookery writers, remarks rather chillingly, 'There are no distinctive ways of preparing vegetables in England', but most lovers of good food now recognize that really young tender summer vegetables need very little more than butter or cream to enhance them.

However, in the winter certain of the root vegetables can be dressed up to make more interesting alternatives to the eternal boiled cabbage to which, in the past, the British have been inclined. (One foreign writer observed in the nineteenth century that 'the English have but three vegetables, of which two are cabbage'.) It is a moot point perhaps today as to whether it is cabbage – which can be splendid if cooked correctly – or the frozen pea that takes pride of place after the potato as the English favourite in the vegetable stakes, but winter or summer, we can take the potato as favourite vegetable number one – so it might be as well to offer a few suggestions for dealing with it.

Firstly, unblemished potatoes are quite delicious, old or new, when boiled in their skins and this also retains all their nutritious elements, which are evidently most highly concentrated just under their skins, in the bit that is normally peeled off and thrown in the bin.

Secondly, mashed potatoes are best made by mashing well-drained boiled potatoes, dry, until they are light and fluffy before the addition of butter (use plenty), milk, salt and freshly ground pepper.

They are not good made with waxy potatoes as they became sticky – choose floury varieties such as Duke of York, King Edward and Golden Wonder for perfect mashed potatoes. Waxy potatoes, however, make the best salads.

Salads have always played quite a large part in English diet. In the sixteenth century it was thought that the best salads had the most ingredients, and a typical Salamagundy would include cold roast chicken, anchovies and many kinds of meat in the centre, and ring upon ring of different coloured flowers, seeds, fruits, herbs and nuts lapping outwards towards the edges of the dish. You might find capers, pickled broom buds, olives, pickled oysters, lemon, orange, almonds, blue figs and sweet potatoes, the whole thing dressed with chopped onion and tarragon, and of course with parsley and chives which are useful for enhancing all our vegetables, hot or cold.

London's famous vegetable and flower market at Covent Garden as it looked early in this century.

Pan haggerty

TO SERVE FOUR

INGREDIENTS
675 g (1½ lb) potatoes
2 onions
50 g (2 oz) bacon fat or
    lard (or a mixture of oil
    and butter)
75 g (3 oz) grated Cheddar
salt, freshly ground pepper

This traditional Scots recipe is either a good filling supper on its own or a rich accompaniment to a plainly boiled piece of gammon or bacon.

Slice the potatoes finely and grate the onions. Heat the bacon fat or lard in a large, heavy and reliable frying pan.
    Put in the sliced potatoes, onions and cheese in layers, seasoning with salt and pepper as you go. Cook slowly on the top of the cooker for about 30 minutes until tender all the way through; test by sticking a skewer or knife into the centre. When cooked through, brown the top under the grill.

Herb champ

TO SERVE FOUR

INGREDIENTS
675 g (1½ lb) old potatoes
275 ml (½ pint) milk
3 tablespoons chopped
    chives and parsley
salt and pepper
50 g (2 oz) butter (or more)

Champ is the name of mashed potatoes as eaten in Scotland; they are often mixed with other vegetables such as spring onions or even mashed beetroot when they acquire different regional names. If you add mashed turnips, you have clapshot, if puréed cooked greens or cabbage and cream, your champ is called Kailkenny. But the great thing about all champ is to pile it up steaming hot on individual plates and make a little crater in the centre which is filled with melted butter. Each forkful is then dipped into this molten golden pool.

Peel and halve the potatoes and boil them in salted water for 25 minutes. Drain and return to a low heat to lose some of their moisture. Then mash them thoroughly before adding the heated milk, which is added a little at a time and beaten in well between each addition.
    Stir in the finely chopped herbs so that you have a nicely flecked green purée. Taste for seasoning, pile on individual plates, make a well in the centre of each mound and slip in a nut of butter. Serve straight away.

Punchnep

TO SERVE FOUR

INGREDIENTS
450 g (1 lb) potatoes
450 g (1 lb) young turnips
50 g (2 oz) butter
salt, freshly ground pepper
4 tablespoons cream

This is a Welsh dish combining potatoes and turnips to make a lovely buttery purée dotted with pools of hot cream.

Boil the peeled potatoes and turnips in separate saucepans – this is essential to obtain the authentic flavour. Drain and mash each vegetable separately with 25 g (1 oz) of butter. Now combine the two purées, season with salt and freshly ground pepper and beat thoroughly until you have a light soft mixture. Pile it up into a heated dish, stick the handle of a wooden spoon or a finger into the purée to make 6 or 8 holes. Fill each with cream and serve hot.

Top : Scottish nep purry,
bottom : Herb champ, punchnep

Scottish nep purry or bashed neeps

TO SERVE SIX

INGREDIENTS
1 kg (2 lb) young swedes
salt, freshly ground pepper
ground ginger
50 g (2 oz) butter

As in all Scottish recipes the neps or neeps referred to are not turnips but swedes – and purry is of course purée. This dish of mashed swedes is a good alternative to mashed potato and excellent with sausages (or, in Scotland, with haggis).

Bring a pan of salted water to the boil. Peel, trim and dice the swedes, and boil them until they are tender, about 30 minutes –

the younger they are the shorter the cooking time.

Drain the swedes and blend to a fine mush in the liquidizer with a little of their cooking liquid. Reheat the purée, season with salt, pepper and ginger and stir in the butter. Pile up in a dish and serve very hot with a pool of melted butter on the top.

Game chips

INGREDIENTS
2 or 3 large potatoes
oil for frying

Game chips are traditionally served with roast game birds – pheasant, partridge and grouse – but they also go very well with drinks and are in fact the most delicious home-made crisps. To make them you need a mandoline, a special kind of vegetable cutter – with a wavy blade, or 'teeth'.

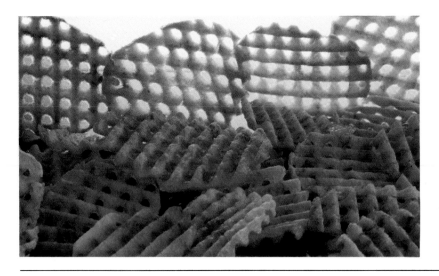

Peel the potatoes. Hold the potato with the palm of the hand against the teeth of the wavy blade (1), and cut straight down. Turn the potato 90°, your fingers are now facing the other direction (2). Cut straight down. Turn the potato 90° for the next slice – you are criss-crossing the slices. Wash the slices, pat them dry and fry in hot oil from which a blue haze (not smoke) is rising – 190°C (375°F) – until golden. Drain on kitchen paper. Serve hot.

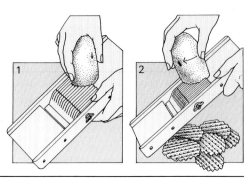

Suffolk red cabbage

TO SERVE FOUR

INGREDIENTS
red cabbage
50 g (2 oz) butter
1 slice ham, thickly cut – weighing about 100 g (4 oz)
2 tablespoons vinegar
1 tablespoon sugar
salt and pepper

A dish with a delicious sharp-sweet flavour that goes extremely well with game, roast pork or sausages.

Cut the red cabbage into quarters with a stainless steel knife; remove the cores, then slice fairly thin. Melt the butter in an oven-proof casserole and add the ham cut in little sticks about 3 cm (1 in) long. Let it simmer gently in the butter without browning for five minutes, then stir in the sliced cabbage and turn it over in the butter until it is all coated and glistening. Cover the pan and allow to sweat for 10 minutes. Now stir in the vinegar and sugar, season with salt and pepper and cover the pan. Put in a very low oven, 160°C, 325°F, Gas Mark 3, and let it cook very gently for 2 hours, stirring occasionally. This reheats well.

Mild cabbage in milk

TO SERVE FOUR

INGREDIENTS
1 large cabbage or 2 small
cabbages – it shrinks
considerably
150 ml (¼ pint) milk
25 g (1 oz) butter
salt, freshly ground pepper

This is a delicious melting cabbage dish which has a particularly English flavour.

Bring a large pan of salted water to the boil. Roughly chop the cabbage, discarding the stalk and coarse bits of rib. Wash and put into the boiling water for 2 minutes to remove strong flavours. Drain and return the cabbage to the pan with the milk and nut of butter. Season lightly, cover the pan and simmer gently for 20 minutes, taking

care it does not burn. Remove the pan from the heat and stir in the remaining butter. Pile the cabbage in a heated dish and serve hot and juicy.

Perfect buttered cabbage

INGREDIENTS
1 cabbage (any size)
50 g (2 oz) butter
salt, freshly ground pepper

Bring a large pan of well-salted water to the boil. Cut the cabbage in quarters, wash well, and remove the stems with a sharp knife. Plunge the cabbage into the boiling water, cover the pan *only until the water returns to the boil*, which must be as fast as possible.

Now remove the lid and let the cabbage cook gently until just tender and still a vibrant green.

Drain in a large colander, slicing through the chunks with a knife until all the water

has drained away and the pieces are a manageable size, about 3 cm (1 in) or so across. Return to the pan. Smother with at least 50 g (2 oz) of butter, season with salt and plenty of freshly ground pepper and stir over a very low heat for 5 minutes. Serve piping hot.

Suffolk red cabbage, mild cabbage in milk, perfect buttered cabbage

137

Good cauliflower cheese

TO SERVE FOUR

INGREDIENTS
1 good sized fresh white or
  creamy yellow cauliflower
575 ml (1 pint) creamy
  milk
1 bayleaf
1 small onion
50 g (2 oz) butter
50 g (2 oz) flour
salt and pepper
grated nutmeg
100 g (4 oz) grated, sharp
  Cheddar cheese
50 g (2 oz) toasted
  breadcrumbs
25 g (1 oz) butter

This brown, speckled, creamy dish is a far cry from the heavily blanketed cauliflower cheese of school memories. Served with a fresh green salad, it makes a wonderful lunch or supper.

First make a really good cheese sauce. Heat the milk to boiling point with the bayleaf and sliced onion and let it infuse over a very low heat for 5 minutes before straining it into a measuring jug.

Wipe out the pan, and in it melt the butter. Stir in the flour and let this pale *roux* cook very gently for 2 minutes. Remove it from the heat and allow to cool slightly before adding the hot milk a little at a time, to make a cream sauce. Allow to cook for 15 minutes. Bring a pan of salted water to the boil for the cauliflower.

Season the sauce with salt, pepper and nutmeg and stir in the grated cheese. Cook the cauliflower for 15 minutes until just tender. Remove it carefully to a colander. Fry the toasted crumbs in melted butter, until crisp and golden.

Place the cauliflower on a heated dish, pour the creamy cheese sauce over the top, sprinkle with fried crumbs and place under the grill for a few minutes until bubbling and brown on top.

Good cauliflower cheese, purple sprouting broccoli

Purple sprouting broccoli

INGREDIENTS
any quantity of purple
  sprouting broccoli
25–50 g (1–2 oz) butter or
  more
salt

To cook purple sprouting broccoli to perfection, bring a large pan of salted water to the boil. Drop in the trimmed and well washed broccoli and cook uncovered for 10 minutes until just tender.

Drain thoroughly, return the broccoli to the pan and add a good nut of butter. Allow to simmer very gently in the butter, stirring all the time, until any excess moisture has evaporated and the broccoli is melting and buttery, after about 5 minutes. Serve very hot.

Brussels sprouts with chestnuts

TO SERVE SIX-EIGHT

INGREDIENTS
450 g (1 lb) fresh chestnuts
450 g (1 lb) Brussels
  sprouts (fresh or frozen)
salt
50 g (2 oz) butter

This is the dish that Christmas turkey cries out for; it is beautiful, a fresh colour, and has just the right combination of crunch and softness, sweet and rich, that the bland meat of the turkey needs. Use fresh or frozen sprouts but always make the effort to use fresh chestnuts.

Deal with the chestnuts first. Make a cut on the flat side with a small sharp knife then drop them into a pan of boiling, salted water and let them boil for 5 minutes. Now remove them two or three at a time (they must be peeled hot) and remove both shells and bitter inner skins. Time and patience are needed to do this job properly. Now simmer them in a fresh pan of salted water for 10–15 minutes or until they are tender; do not overcook or they will fall to pieces. Drain and keep them hot.

Meanwhile trim the sprouts if using fresh ones, and remove the loose outside leaves; if they are large, cut a small cross in the base of each to speed up the cooking of the stalk.

Wash in a basin of cold, salted water and shake dry; now plunge them into a large pan of fast boiling water and cook them, uncovered, until just tender, about 12 minutes. Drain them very thoroughly and add the chestnuts and the butter and toss them over the heat for a few seconds to coat with butter before serving.

If you are making this for Christmas, when making the gravy needs your last-minute attention, pre-cook the chestnuts and sprouts and reheat both in butter in a wide pan, giving them an occasional shake to prevent them from browning.

Brussels sprouts with chestnuts, hot spiced chestnuts with prunes

Hot spiced chestnuts and prunes

TO SERVE SIX

INGREDIENTS
350 g ($\frac{3}{4}$ lb) prunes
450 g (1 lb) chestnuts
575 ml (1 pint) chicken
  stock
1 tablespoon castor sugar
1 teaspoon ground
  cinnamon
pinch salt
1 teaspoon lemon juice
1 wineglass sherry

As an accompaniment to Christmas roast turkey, this traditional spicy combination of two well-known stuffing ingredients for Christmas birds is well worth reviving.

Soak the prunes in water overnight. Slit the chestnuts on the flat side with a sharp vegetable knife. Drop them into a pan of boiling water, boil 5 minutes and then remove a few at a time and shell and skin them – a job best shared with someone else if at all possible as it is very tedious. Now put them back into a saucepan with the chicken stock and let them simmer until tender, for 30 minutes. In the meantime poach the prunes in their soaking water,

sweetened with a tablespoon of castor sugar and spiced with cinnamon. After 15–20 minutes, when they are plump and just tender, drain them, reserving the juice.

Mix the prunes with the chestnuts and moisten with a wineglass of the prune juice, the lemon juice and the wineglass of sherry. Heat through and serve. It also makes a good accompaniment to roast pork.

Celery in cheese sauce with ham

TO SERVE FOUR

INGREDIENTS
2 heads of celery
25 g (1 oz) butter
25 g (1 oz) flour
425 ml ($\frac{3}{4}$ pint) milk
50 g (2 oz) Cheddar,
  Cheshire or Leicester
  cheese
4 slices ham
salt, pepper, nutmeg
3 tablespoons double
  cream
2 tablespoons browned
  breadcrumbs – make
  them by toasting fresh
  breadcrumbs very slowly
  to a golden brown
a little butter

Celery and cheese makes a very proper combination. This particular recipe makes a good first course for a dinner party since it can be prepared well beforehand and can then be put in the oven, 20 minutes before the meal starts, to heat through.

Trim away the celery leaves, including the inner ones, but keep heads whole. Bring a large pan of salted water to the boil and plunge in the celery heads; let them cook for about 15 minutes, until they are tender but not too soft. Drain carefully.

Meanwhile melt the butter in a smaller saucepan, stir in the flour and let it cook gently for a minute or two without burning. Now add the milk gradually, stirring until smooth after each addition so that

the sauce is free of lumps. Let it cook gently for 15 minutes. Add the cheese and let it melt into the sauce, stirring so that it is smooth and velvety. Season with salt, pepper and a grating of nutmeg. Cut the celery heads in half, wrap each half round with a slice of ham and lay them in an oval ovenproof dish. The dish is now prepared, except for the last and final stage. At least 20 minutes before you are ready to serve it, spoon the cheese sauce over the celery. Pour the cream over the top, sprinkle with breadcrumbs and dot with butter. Bake in a hot oven, 220°C, 425°F, Gas Mark 7 for 20 minutes, and serve brown and bubbling.

Clockwise: Celery with cheese sauce in ham, leeks with brown butter, broad beans with ham

Broad beans with ham

TO SERVE FOUR

INGREDIENTS
1 kg fresh or 350 g frozen
  (2 lb or $\frac{3}{4}$ lb) broad beans
1 small onion
50 g (2 oz) butter
25 g (1 oz) flour
1 glass white wine or stock
50 g (2 oz) chopped ham
salt, freshly ground pepper
1 tablespoon chopped
  parsley
1 teaspoon sugar

Shell and wash the beans, if using fresh ones, and blanch them in boiling salted water for 2 minutes. Then drain them. Chop the onion and soften it in the butter. When it is pale golden brown, stir in the flour and let it simmer in the butter for 2 minutes. Stir in the wine or stock and add the beans and ham, and a little salt and pepper. Stew the mixture for 15 minutes, until the beans are tender. Add the sugar,

and chopped parsley and raise the heat so that it boils rapidly for a few seconds – do not leave it longer as broad beans harden if cooked too long.

Serve with sausages or as a lunch dish on its own.

Leeks with brown butter

TO SERVE FOUR

INGREDIENTS
900 g (2 lb) leeks
salt
50 g (2 oz) butter
2 teaspoons toasted
   breadcrumbs
squeeze of fresh lemon
   juice

Leeks are among the most ancient of our vegetables, but surprisingly were, for centuries, used mainly as flavouring rather than as a vegetable in their own right. In time they reached proper vegetable status, and were often served with a white sauce poured over them. However, even the nicest sauce tends to mask their delicate flavour, so try them with butter only.

Clean the leeks by washing in two waters, cutting away the dark green part which can be saved for flavourings in the old tradition. If the leeks are fat, cut them in rings otherwise leave them whole. Drop them into a large pan of boiling salted water for 15 minutes. Test for tenderness with a pointed knife. Drain thoroughly and keep hot. In a separate small pan melt the butter and cook until a nice golden brown, the colour of hazelnuts. Toss in the crumbs, stir them in, add the lemon juice and pour over the leeks.

Scrape any remaining crumbs from the pan and scatter them over the steaming, buttery, silver leeks.

Glazed whole onions

TO SERVE FOUR

INGREDIENTS
350 g (¾ lb) small onions
25 g (1 oz) butter
50 g (2 oz) castor sugar
150 ml (¼ pint) chicken
   stock
salt, pepper, nutmeg

This is the perfect combined garnish and vegetable for any plainly roasted meat, but most particularly veal.

Trim the onions and remove the brown papery skins. Melt the butter in a heavy-based saucepan, and when it sizzles add the onions, tossing them about, so that they become slightly browned. Sprinkle the sugar over them and continue turning and tossing the onions over a very low heat until they are covered with a sticky brown glaze.

Add the stock, and, still shaking the saucepan from time to time, let them simmer, until the liquid has evaporated and the juices have formed a syrupy glaze. Roll the onions about in this so that each one is bronzed and shining, and serve very hot.

Glazed young carrots

TO SERVE FOUR

INGREDIENTS
2 bunches carrots – 1 kg
 (2 lb)
50 g (2 oz) butter
1 teaspoon sugar
a little salt, freshly ground
 pepper
chopped parsley

This recipe is for the pale gold early summer carrots sold in bunches complete with their lacy green tops. They look most springlike if the tiniest bit of top is left on each and the pointed ends of the roots barely trimmed.

Remove the green tops and scrape but do not peel the carrots. Toss them into a saucepan of fast-boiling lightly salted water and cook gently for about 10 minutes after the water has come back to the boil – very small carrots need even less. They should still be slightly firm. Drain, reserving a few tablespoons of the cooking liquid.

Clean out the saucepan and melt the butter and sugar over a gentle heat. When you have a pale blonde mixture, put in the carrots and shake them well to coat them with the glaze and cook over a gentle heat for 10 minutes, shaking and turning them frequently. Add the seasoning.

Serve sprinkled with chopped parsley; they are delicious with pale delicate meat – chicken or veal – or with grilled sole.

Mange-tout or sugar peas

TO SERVE FOUR

INGREDIENTS
450 g (1 lb) peas (they are
 very light)
salt
25 g (1 oz) butter

These are peas with tender, pale green pods which are eaten whole before the peas have had time to form. The pods, which are topped and tailed like French beans, have a very delicate flavour which comes through best if they are plainly boiled.

Top and tail the sugar peas and wash them. Bring a large pan of well-salted water to the boil. Plunge the peas into the water and let them return to the boil as rapidly as possible. Reduce the heat and cook gently for 8–10 minutes, drain, return to the pan and shake with the butter until all the peas are coated and glistening.

Bright green beans

TO SERVE FOUR

INGREDIENTS
450 g (1 lb) green beans
salt
butter

There are two schools of thought about the cooking of beans – many home-cooks, particularly the older generation, think that they should be cooked until they are really tender and soft, by which time they taste delicious but are also the colour of a murky pond.

But a more recent approach is to cook the beans until they are tender but haven't softened and lost their firm texture, and are still a brilliant and beautiful green.

Bring a very large pan of water to the boil and put in double the usual quantity of salt – say, two teaspoons. This will help the beans to keep their colour. Plunge in the topped and tailed beans, sliced if they are runner beans, broken into manageable lengths if they are French, wax, snap or bobby beans.

Let them boil uncovered for 10 minutes, then test – keep testing every 3 minutes and when they are tender – but still with a bit of bite to them – drain them immedi-

ately and return them to the pan with a good knob of butter. Put them over the lowest possible heat, shake until each bean is glistening with butter, then put them in a heated serving dish and place a nut of butter on top.

Glazed young carrots, mange-tout peas, bright green beans

Green peas and lettuce

TO SERVE FOUR

INGREDIENTS
6 small silver onions
salt
1 kg (2 lb) or more of fresh
  green peas in their pods
  or 350 g (¾ lb) frozen peas
the good outer leaves of a
  lettuce (save the heart for
  a salad)
25 g (1 oz) butter
1 sugar lump

The combination of peas, button onions and lettuce gives one of the most delicious traditional summer flavours. The peas will not be their usual bright green but will have a melting succulence.

Boil the skinned onions in salted water for 10 minutes to blanch them. Shell the peas if fresh. Wash the lettuce leaves but do not dry them, and use them all except two to line the inside of a small saucepan, just large enough to hold the peas. Put in the peas and onions, the butter and sugar and a

little pinch of salt. Put the pan over a very low heat and keep an eye on it as the lettuce leaves wilt and start to give out their moisture. When you hear liquid starting to bubble, lay the two remaining lettuce leaves over the top and simmer gently for 10 minutes. Serve at once, complete with lettuce leaves.

Old peas can be cooked to a nice creamy consistency by using the same method and cooking the peas for three-quarters of an hour.

Green peas and lettuce, creamed spinach

Creamed spinach

TO SERVE FOUR

INGREDIENTS
450 g (1 lb) fresh spinach
  or 225 g (½ lb) frozen
  spinach
50 g (2 oz) butter
1 tablespoon flour
3–4 tablespoons single
  cream
salt, pepper, nutmeg

Succulent spinach to accompany boiled gammon should be cooked in the old-fashioned way with plenty of butter and cream.

Wash the spinach and push the leaves into a large pan of boiling salted water. Let it boil for 10 minutes, then drain it thoroughly in a large colander. Chop slightly and press it lightly with a wooden spoon to get rid of excess moisture. If using frozen spinach, cook and drain it in the usual way. Melt

the butter in the cleaned saucepan, put back the spinach and stir it round. Sprinkle with a tablespoon of flour and stir over a gentle heat until the spinach juices are absorbed, about 5 minutes. Now add the cream and season the spinach with salt, pepper and nutmeg. Stir 3 minutes longer. Serve in a mound in a hot dish.

Upside-down mushrooms in cream

TO SERVE FOUR

INGREDIENTS
8 fine large mushrooms
a drop or two of fresh
  lemon juice
150 ml (¼ pint) single
  cream
salt, freshly ground pepper
8 slices of hot freshly
  buttered toast

An old farmhouse recipe for cooking field mushrooms. Although these open umbrellas are hard to find unless you live in the country and know what to look for and where, free-ranging field mushrooms do sometimes find their way into the shops: alternatively, use the wonderful *champignons de Paris*, large and pinker than our usual button mushrooms, which are too small for this dish.

Preheat the oven to 190°C, 375°F, Gas Mark 5. Wipe the mushrooms clean, trim but do not remove the stalks.

Dip the tops one by one into a bowl of water acidulated with a little lemon juice to prevent them from discolouring. Shake them dry and place them stems upwards in an ovenproof dish large enough to accommodate them comfortably.

Pour the cream over the mushrooms and let it run down into the dish. Season with salt and freshly ground pepper.

Cook for 20 minutes on the middle shelf of the oven. Meanwhile make the toast. Then place the mushrooms on the toast, spoon the cream over the top, and eat at once before the toast becomes soggy.

Asparagus in crisp rolls

TO SERVE SIX

INGREDIENTS
6 white rolls, preferably
  oval shaped
350 g ($\frac{3}{4}$ lb) thin asparagus
150 ml ($\frac{1}{4}$ pint) cream
2 egg yolks
salt, freshly ground pepper,
  grating of nutmeg
50 g (2 oz) butter

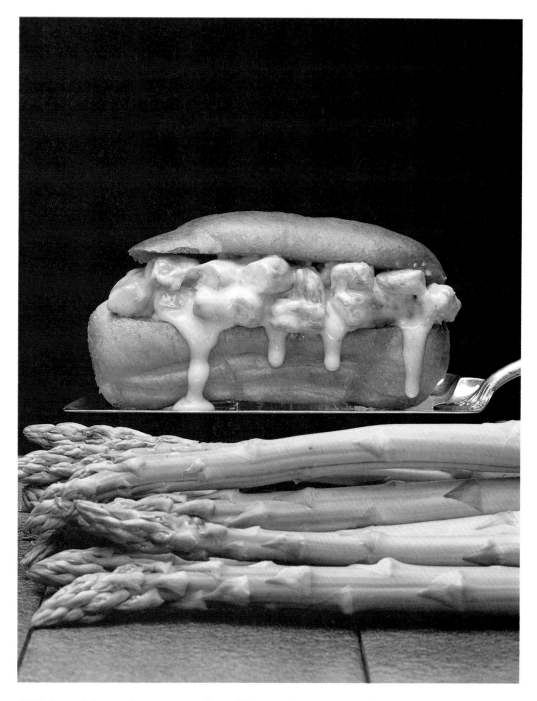

This is an eighteenth-century recipe which is still as delicious today as it ever was. In the old days the recipe called for 'a hundred or so of grass' so it is safe to say that their asparagus were the merest whisps compared with what we now eat. Use this recipe when there are not quite enough asparagus to go round.

Slice the rolls straight across the top, removing an oval slice of crust which will form lids for the rolls. Pull out the crumbs so that you have six crusty shells. Put them aside. Trim the asparagus to remove all the woody parts, and wash thoroughly.

Chop the asparagus into short pieces and cook in boiling, salted water until tender,

about 12–15 minutes. Drain, catching the cooking liquid in a bowl, and reserve it. Now heat the cream in the pan with 4 tablespoons of the asparagus liquid. Beat the egg yolks, pour on the hot but not boiling cream and whisk together, until the mixture thickens to a velvety sauce. Add the asparagus pieces and keep warm without allowing it to boil or it will curdle. Season.

Fry the rolls and lids in butter until they are crisp and golden brown, and place them on a heated serving dish. Spoon the asparagus mixture into the rolls, replace the lids and serve.

Fried parsley

INGREDIENTS
bunch of parsley
oil for frying

Fried parsley draining on kitchen paper

Fried parsley is one of the prettiest garnishes, lacy and green, crisp and delicate. It is particularly good with fried whitebait or trout.

Pick over the parsley, removing the large stalks so that neat sprigs remain. Wash it clean and shake dry in a cloth. Heat the oil in a deep pan until a blue haze rises – 190°C (375°F). Put the parsley in the frying basket and hold it in the fat for 2 minutes. Drain well and place in a low oven until quite dry, crisp and brittle.

Farmhouse salad

TO SERVE FOUR

INGREDIENTS
For the salad
1 cos lettuce
1 iceberg lettuce
1 bunch spring onions
1 cucumber
6 radishes
For the dressing
1 tablespoon lemon juice
pinch of sugar
pinch of salt
1 teaspoon made mustard
4 tablespoons oil

Take the lettuces apart, discarding the tougher outside leaves. Wash and shake the lettuce leaves so that they are perfectly dry. A clean tea-towel makes a good salad shaker; swing it outside if possible as there will be a good spray of water. Put the lettuce in a large salad bowl.

Discard the hollow tops of the onions, and cut the white parts in half lengthwise. Throw them on top of the lettuce together with the cucumber, peeled and cut in thick slices. Slice the radishes very thinly and scatter the little ice-white rounds with their scarlet edges over the top of the salad.

Make the dressing by placing all the ingredients except the oil in a basin, stirring them together and then gradually beating in the oil to give a smooth mixture.

To keep the salad crisp and fresh and green, do not mix it with the dressing until you are ready to eat it.

Miss Berry's herb salad

TO SERVE FOUR

INGREDIENTS
2 hard-boiled eggs
2 heads of chicory
1 lettuce
box of mixed mustard
  and cress
4–5 sprigs each of the
  following herbs as
  available – parsley,
  tarragon, chervil and
  chives
1 tablespoon finely
  chopped onion
4 tablespoons single cream
1 tablespoon wine vinegar –
  preferably tarragon
  vinegar
1 teaspoon made mustard
salt, freshly ground pepper

This wonderfully varied, refreshing green salad can be strewn with whatever herbs are available, and if you live in the country, a few wild leaves can be added for good measure – wild sorrel, herb burnet, and a few sprigs of watercress would all be good additions.

Peel the hard-boiled eggs and chop coarsely. Wash the chicory, dry it, and break off each leaf separately. Place these all round the sides of a salad bowl. Wash and shake the lettuce and pile it up in the middle. Strew on the mustard and cress, chop the chives and break up the herbs into leaves and sprigs – sprinkle them over the greenery in the bowl. In a small bowl, combine the onion, cream, wine vinegar, mustard, and seasoning and stir well. Pour the mixture over and around the salad just before bringing it to the table, and scatter the hard-boiled eggs over the top.

Opposite : Farmhouse salad,
Miss Berry's herb salad

146

Sauces

British sauces are as good as the cook who makes them; they can be, and have been in the past, as fine and interesting as any. They may not have been as renowned perhaps as French sauces, or as subtle, but do they deserve their wretched reputation?

Everybody has heard the famous French quip 'The English have sixty religions but only one sauce'. Ambrose Heath, in his *Book of Sauces*, wondered which one they meant. Unfortunately we know the answer all too well. Thick white sauce, that heavy blanket, now so out of fashion, was the butt of many rude remarks. One joker excelled himself with his statement that the English kitchen has three taps: hot water, cold water and white sauce.

It is true that a properly made white sauce or better still, its delicate cousin, butter sauce, is a very frequent point of departure for quite a number of British sauces, but was he not forgetting our delicious greenish-gold apple sauce, sweet-sharp Cumberland sauce, tomato sauce, mint sauce, traditional mustard sauce and creamy thick puréed onion sauce? There are so many splendid recipes, some dating back hundreds of years, that are so much a part of our tradition, that we almost forget to be proud of them.

In medieval days, when the ubiquitous white sauce had not yet even been invented, the favourite was green sauce, a piquant mixture of bread, vinegar, mint, garlic, parsley and thyme, very similar to the splendid *salsa verde* eaten in Italy with boiled meat.

A white version, almond sauce, was made with almonds, eggs and cream; white flour was a little known luxury then. Geese were eaten with a thick sauce of pounded, cooked garlic or with dark prune sauce, while lamb was served with russet rowan-berry jelly. Anchovies were used a great deal, particularly with fish, an inheritance perhaps from Roman times.

But when French chefs began to be imported into England by those who could afford such luxuries, an eighteenth-century journal looked back sadly on those days 'when our cookery was plain and simple . . . now all the earth must be ransacked for spices, pickles . . . spoiling a wholesome diet by costly, pernicious sauces'.

By the end of the eighteenth century the medical profession was getting worried – they felt that the heavily spiced dishes were 'inflaming' and a society for the suppression of vice, having considered 'the inflammatory nature of rich sauces', pressed the government to lay a heavy duty on pepper, salt and wine, in the hope that by making these exciting ingredients less available, morals would be restored.

All that happened, of course, was that higher prices were paid, 'another instance' stated Ignotus, a doctor himself and author of a well-known eighteenth-century cookery book, 'of the obstinacy and depravity of mankind'.

But simplicity did return, and nowadays returning British travellers, having eaten splendidly in France, come home happily to good, plain British cooking. It is even the case now that the French themselves have suddenly realized that much of their beloved, and in all fairness it must be added, delicious, *haute cuisine* is over-sauced and over-rich.

That does not, however, mean that sauces must be abandoned, but only adapted, on both sides of the Channel. It takes very little practice to be able to make a pure, light, simple sauce that reveals and points up the flavour of a dish rather than disguises it. It is really a question of mastering a few simple techniques, to give that final loving touch to all dishes.

No eggs or rich fruit in our pudding you'll find
But our sauce is the best, contentment of mind:

White sauce

INGREDIENTS
With cold milk
25 g (1 oz) butter
25 g (1 oz) flour
425 ml (¾ pint) cold milk
salt and pepper
With hot milk
25 g (1 oz) butter
25 g (1 oz) flour
425 ml (¾ pint) milk
   heated to boiling point
salt and pepper

This plain, easily made, delicious and altogether useful sauce has given rise to a good deal of derisive comment over the years. Below are two ways of making the same sauce – one with cold milk which economizes on saucepans and a quicker way with hot milk.

Poor white sauce, it is unfair that it should have such a bad name, since properly made it is light and velvety and extremely versatile. Take care when you make it to cook it long enough – at least 15 minutes – and all will be well.

White sauce with cold milk
Melt the butter in a small, thick, extremely clean saucepan. Stir in the flour and let it cook gently for 1 minute, until it is bubbling. Keep the pan on a moderate heat and gradually add the milk a few tablespoons at a time, stirring well after each addition until the milk has been absorbed, before adding more. As the sauce becomes smooth and creamy, add the milk in larger quantities. When it is all in, cover the pan with a lid and simmer for 15–20 minutes, to cook the flour thoroughly, stirring from time to time.

Now season well and whisk with a wire whisk to obtain a smooth and glossy sauce. A few dabs of butter stirred in at the end give a velvety texture.

White sauce with hot milk
Melt the butter in a small, thick, extremely clean saucepan. Stir in the flour with a wooden spoon and let it cook for 1 minute. Now remove the pan from the heat and allow this roux to cool. Heat the milk to boiling point and pour it on to the cool roux, whisking with a small wire whisk. Don't be alarmed if it does not look smooth at this point. Bring it back to the boil, whisk once or twice and all the soft lumps will disappear. Cover and cook for 15–20 minutes, whisking occasionally and season well with salt and pepper. A few slips of butter whisked in at the end will make the sauce velvety in texture.

The following sauces can also be made from the basic white sauce:

Egg sauce (*for croquettes and fishcakes*)
Hardboil 2 eggs for 12 minutes, cool them under the cold tap, shell them and chop into very small dice. Stir into your white sauce and heat through.

Cheese sauce (*for all sorts of fish and vegetable dishes*)
Grate 50 g (2 oz) of cheese – the ideal mixture is 25 g (1 oz) Parmesan, 25 g (1 oz) Cheddar, but any well-flavoured, dryish cheese will do. Stir the grated cheese into the sauce and beat it well until it melts. Season with cayenne pepper and a touch of nutmeg, but don't put in too much salt as the cheese is salty already.

Caper sauce (*for boiled leg of lamb and fish*)
Make the white sauce; when it is cooked, stir in a tablespoon of caper vinegar from the bottle of capers and 2 tablespoons of whole capers. Simmer for 5 minutes, stir in 2 tablespoons of cream and serve very hot. This is thinner than most of the white-sauce based sauces, and is intended to be so.

Basic white sauce with the ingredients for egg, cheese and caper variations

Onion sauce
For boiled lamb and goose

INGREDIENTS
2 large onions
1 bayleaf
2 blades mace
salt
25 g (1 oz) flour
25 g (1 oz) butter
275 ml ($\frac{1}{2}$ pint) milk
salt, white pepper, nutmeg
2 tablespoons cream

This is a variation of white sauce, but some of the onion cooking liquid is used to replace some of the milk, to give added flavour.

Put the onions into a pan of water, together with the bayleaf, mace and a good pinch of salt. Boil them for 30 minutes, covered, until they are tender. Take out the onions and drain them, keeping 150 ml ($\frac{1}{4}$ pint) of their cooking liquid, and allow them to cool. While they are cooling make a sauce by melting the butter in a small pan, stirring in the flour, letting it cook for 1 minute and then adding the milk gradually, stirring after each addition. When you have a smooth mixture add the onion cooking liquid.

Chop the onions fairly fine and put them into the sauce. Season it with salt, white pepper (black pepper looks gritty in this pale sauce) and nutmeg, and simmer for 15–20 minutes, covered, stirring occasionally. Lastly stir in the cream.

Parsley sauce

INGREDIENTS
150 ml ($\frac{1}{4}$ pint) chicken
    stock
275 ml ($\frac{1}{2}$ pint) creamy
    milk
2 sticks celery, chopped
1 onion, sliced
large bunch parsley
25 g (1 oz) butter
25 g (1 oz) flour
walnut-sized knob of butter
salt, freshly ground pepper

Heat the chicken stock and the milk together with the chopped celery and sliced onion, over a very gentle heat, until it reaches simmering point.

While the liquid is absorbing the flavours of celery and onion, pick over the parsley, removing the thick stalks. Wash it well and dry it before chopping it finely. Now strain the liquid through a sieve. Make a white roux by heating the butter in a small thick saucepan and stirring in the flour. When it starts to bubble and foam, gradually add the strained stock and milk mixture, stirring after each addition, to obtain a smooth, creamy sauce. Let it cook gently for 10 minutes, covered, then taste for seasoning, stir in the parsley and cook for a further 5 minutes, uncovered, keeping the sauce well stirred. Add the knob of butter, cut into small pieces, and beat the sauce with a wooden spoon to make it shine. Serve very hot.

Shrimp sauce

INGREDIENTS
575 ml (1 pint) fresh
    shrimps
1 onion, sliced
25 g (1 oz) butter
25 g (1 oz) flour
275 ml ($\frac{1}{2}$ pint) milk
150 ml ($\frac{1}{4}$ pint) of the fish
    stock, made with the
    shells of the shrimps
cayenne pepper
pinch of nutmeg
salt if necessary
walnut-sized knob of butter

Shell the shrimps and put the shells in a saucepan with the water and the onion. Bring to the boil and simmer for 30 minutes. Strain the liquid.

Melt the butter in a small saucepan, stir in the flour, let it cook for 1 minute, then add the milk gradually, stirring after each addition until you have a smooth sauce. Now add 150 ml ($\frac{1}{4}$ pint) of the shell cooking liquid. Season with cayenne and nutmeg.

Simmer the sauce gently for 15–20 minutes. Now stir in the shrimps and heat them through, but be careful not to allow the sauce to boil or the shrimps will toughen. Taste for seasoning, add salt if needed, stir in the knob of butter in little slips and serve very hot.

Mushroom sauce
For fish and chicken

INGREDIENTS
1 shallot
25 g (1 oz) butter
100 g (4 oz) hard white
    button mushrooms
juice of $\frac{1}{2}$ a lemon
25 g (1 oz) flour
425 ml ($\frac{3}{4}$ pint) milk
salt, pepper, nutmeg
2 tablespoons cream

Chop the shallot very finely, melt the butter in a saucepan and soften the shallot, without letting it brown, over a low heat.

Meanwhile trim the mushrooms and wash them briefly in a bowl of cold water with a dash of the lemon juice in it. Drain them well and cut them into little dice about $\frac{1}{2}$ cm ($\frac{1}{4}$ in) across. Add them to the pan with the shallot, stir them round for a minute, then add the flour. When this mixture has started to sizzle, add the milk gradually, a little at a time, stirring after each addition. When you have a smooth creamy sauce, season it with salt, freshly ground pepper and nutmeg and allow to simmer gently for 15 minutes, covered, stirring occasionally to prevent the sauce catching.

Stir in the cream and remaining lemon juice at the end and serve very hot.

Bread sauce

INGREDIENTS
275 ml ($\frac{1}{2}$ pint) milk
1 small onion, sliced
4 cloves
12 peppercorns
$\frac{1}{4}$ teaspoon grated nutmeg
1 bayleaf
hazelnut of butter
salt
100 g (4 oz) fresh white
   breadcrumbs
1 tablespoon single cream

Hanover sauce

For roast chicken

INGREDIENTS
1 chicken liver from the
   chicken being cooked
150 ml ($\frac{1}{4}$ pint) double
   cream
juice of $\frac{1}{2}$ a lemon
1 anchovy fillet, washed in
   milk
salt and pepper

Put the milk in a saucepan with the onion, cloves, peppercorns, nutmeg, bayleaf and butter. Bring the milk slowly to the boil and then turn the heat right down to just below simmering point, so that the milk is kept very hot but does not rise in the pan. Let it 'draw' for 10 minutes to absorb all the flavours. Now strain and return the milk to the pan, bring it back to the boil, add a pinch of salt and stir in the breadcrumbs. Remove from the heat, stir in the cream, beat well with a fork and serve hot.

This must have been hard work to make in Victorian days when all the pounding was done by hand, but is easily done in a liquidizer. It is a smooth, pale-beige sauce with a rich and interesting flavour.

Trim off strings and any yellow parts and boil the chicken liver with the rest of the giblets to make a little stock. This will take about 30 minutes. Put it into the liquidizer with the rest of the ingredients, but use very little salt as the anchovy is a little salty. Liquidize, pour into a saucepan and heat through.

Sauces for roast chicken – *top:* bread sauce, *bottom:* Hanover sauce

Drawn butter sauce

INGREDIENTS
100 g (4 oz) fresh butter –
   good quality Cornish
   butter makes the best
   sauce
15 g ($\frac{1}{2}$ oz) flour
150 ml ($\frac{1}{4}$ pint) milk
1 tablespoon lemon juice
salt if necessary

This rich light sauce was used very extensively in Britain in the eighteenth and nineteenth centuries, and is as delicate a sauce as you can find. If you want to give it a little more substance, and to use it where a French cook would use an Hollandaise sauce, simply stir in an egg yolk at the end of the cooking (*see* green sauce). With or without egg yolk it makes a perfect accompaniment to asparagus, leeks, sea kale or any other fresh vegetables. It can also be used, like white sauce but with a lighter result, as a base for many different sauces.

Let the butter soften to room temperature. Cut it into 8 pieces and roll them in the flour so that it is all absorbed.
   Put the pieces into a saucepan and place it over a very low heat, stirring and beating with a wire whisk until you have a pale, creamy mixture. Gradually add the milk, whisking after each addition. Don't worry if it looks strangely rubbery at this point, it will turn back into a creamy sauce as you add more milk. When all the milk has been incorporated, add the lemon juice and cook the sauce very gently for 5 minutes, whisking all the time. Serve very hot.

The following sauces can also be made from the basic drawn butter sauce:

Fennel sauce *(for grey mullet, halibut or John Dory)*
Stir a tablespoon of chopped fennel herb (the green wispy part) into your drawn butter sauce, heat through and serve with your plainly cooked fish.

Light parsley sauce *(for fish or ham)*
Stir a tablespoon of finely chopped parsley into your melted butter sauce, and heat through.

Crab sauce *(for fish)*
Stir 3 tablespoons crab meat, both brown and white, into your drawn butter sauce. Season well with cayenne pepper and powdered mace, heat through and serve.

Green sauce *(for salmon, turbot, halibut or cod)*
Stir a tablespoon of finely chopped parsley and half a tablespoon of finely chopped chives into the sauce, add 2 tablespoons of cream and one beaten egg yolk and heat gently without boiling. Serve hot.

Egg and butter sauce *(for croquettes, fishcakes and fried fish)*
Hardboil 2 eggs for 12 minutes, run them under the cold tap to cool, then chop them finely into very tiny dice. Stir them into the drawn butter sauce and heat through.

153

Buttered crumbs

INGREDIENTS
25 g (1 oz) butter
75 g (3 oz) fresh white
  crumbs
finely chopped parsley

This very good dish of fried breadcrumbs was popular in the eighteenth century with game birds and venison and is still just as good and popular today.

Heat the butter in a frying pan and when it bubbles slowly add the crumbs, a sprinkle at a time, until they have covered the bottom of the pan. Stir them round with a fork until they are all crisp and golden, then tip them quickly on to a double sheet of kitchen paper to drain. Pile them into a bowl and serve swiftly, sprinkled with finely chopped parsley if liked.

Eliza Acton's brown butter sauce
For poached skate and eggs

INGREDIENTS
75 g (3 oz) butter
2 tablespoons white wine
  vinegar
pepper and salt

Have the cooked fish or eggs ready on a heated dish. Also have the vinegar ready in a cup.
  Melt the butter in a small frying pan and let it darken to a nut-brown colour. Immediately take the pan off the heat and dash in the vinegar, season it with a little salt and pepper and pour it sizzling hot over the fish or eggs. This is also delicious with a few capers added.

Fresh tomato sauce
For fish, grills and pasta

INGREDIENTS
450 g (1 lb) fresh tomatoes
1 carrot
1 stick celery
1 onion
1 tablespoon oil
pinch thyme
pinch sugar
salt, freshly ground pepper
15 g (½ oz) butter

Put the fresh tomatoes in a bowl, pour boiling water over and skin them at once.
  Chop the carrot, celery and onion very finely and put them in a saucepan with the oil. Let them cook gently, covered, for 15 minutes, giving them an occasional stir to make sure they do not stick or brown.
  Chop the tomatoes coarsely and put them into the saucepan with the thyme, sugar, salt and pepper.
  Cook the sauce over a medium heat, uncovered, for 15–20 minutes, then purée it either in the liquidizer or with a mouli-légumes. Return to the cleaned saucepan and heat through. Stir in the butter in little pieces and serve.

Top : tomato sauce, *centre :* apple sauce, *bottom :* mint sauce

Apple sauce
For roast pork or goose

INGREDIENTS
450 g (1 lb) cooking apples
  (Bramleys are best)
1 tablespoon water
25–50 g (1–2 oz) sugar
  according to how sweet
  you like it
25 g (1 oz) butter
pinch of salt

Peel, core and quarter the apples and put them in a saucepan with the water. Cover the pan, and heat very slowly until all the apples have softened and fluffed. Beat in the sugar, cook a few minutes longer, beat in the butter and a pinch of salt and serve very hot.
  It should be a soft moist purée. If it seems too wet, cook, uncovered, until most of the liquid has evaporated.

Mint sauce
For lamb and mutton

INGREDIENTS
3 tablespoons finely
  chopped fresh mint
1 tablespoon castor sugar
3 tablespoons vinegar

Simply mix the ingredients an hour or so before the meal to allow the flavour to develop.
  The following method gives you fresh-tasting mint sauce in the winter; in the summer when there is plenty of mint, half fill a clean glass jam jar with golden syrup. Chop enough mint to fill the jar, stir it into the syrup and cover the jar. When you need mint sauce put some of this mixture into a bowl and add the required amount of vinegar.

154

Wow-wow sauce
For bubble and squeak or hot boiled beef

INGREDIENTS
25 g (1 oz) butter
just under 25 g (1 oz) flour
275 ml (½ pint) beef stock from boiled beef or made with stock cubes
1 tablespoon wine vinegar
1 tablespoon Worcester sauce
1 tablespoon mustard
salt and pepper
2–3 tablespoons chopped parsley
2 pickled cucumbers

Wow-wow, being an exclamation of surprise and admiration, is presumably what the eighteenth-century guests of Dr Kitchiner, who invented this sauce, were heard to say when they first tried it.

Melt the butter in a small pan and make a white roux by stirring in the flour and letting it cook a little. Gradually add the beef stock, stirring after each addition, to make a smooth sauce. Season with the wine vinegar, Worcester sauce and mustard and cook gently, covered, for 20 minutes. Taste for seasoning, stir in the chopped parsley, cut the pickled cucumbers into small dice and stir these in carefully.
    Heat through and serve – 'send up in a sauce tureen' was the original instruction.

Benton horseradish sauce
For hot or cold roast beef

INGREDIENTS
2 tablespoons grated horseradish
1 tablespoon wine vinegar
blob of mustard
pinch of salt
pinch of sugar
4 tablespoons double cream

Mix all the ingredients together in a bowl. Fresh horseradish can be so very hot, much hotter than the bottled variety, that it can rather overpower the vinegar, so taste a tiny shred to see if you need more vinegar. Keep at room temperature, until needed, but it is best made the morning it is to be used.

Wow-wow sauce

Hot orange sauce
For duck or wildfowl

INGREDIENTS
2 carrots
1 onion
1 stick celery
25 g (1 oz) butter
1 teaspoon sugar
275 ml (½ pint) good beef stock
2 oranges
juice of 1 lemon
1 teaspoon cornflour
salt and pepper
3 teaspoons brandy

Chop the vegetables and put them in a thick saucepan with the butter. Sprinkle them with sugar and fry to a deep brown. Add the stock and bring the sauce to the boil. Skim and simmer for 2 minutes.
    Meanwhile, peel the oranges with a potato peeler and cut the peel, which should have no pith on it, into small, even shreds. Drop these into a pan of boiling salted water and let them boil for 5 minutes to get rid of their bitter taste. Strain them through a large wire sieve and keep them on one side on a plate.
    Now strain the sauce through the same wire sieve, pressing the vegetables with a wooden spoon to extract all their juice.
    Return the strained sauce to the saucepan, add the orange and lemon juice, the cornflour stirred into a tablespoon or two of water, season with salt and pepper and simmer for 5 minutes, stirring all the time.
    Now the sauce is almost ready. Keep it hot until the birds are cooked.
    Remove them from the oven and put them on a dish. Skim almost all the fat from the roasting tin, pour in the brandy, let it bubble, then pour in the sauce and stir it round until it boils quite fast. Add the shreds of orange peel, pour the sauce into a gravy boat and serve at once.

Cumberland sauce

INGREDIENTS
rind and juice of 2 oranges
rind and juice of 1 small lemon
225 g (½ lb) redcurrant jelly
2 wineglasses port
½ teaspoon powdered ginger
large pinch cayenne pepper
salt

Some very good recipes come from Cumberland – Cumberland sausages are excellent and Cumberland butter, a rum-based version of brandy butter, is delicious with Christmas pudding. But perhaps best known is Cumberland sauce, a rich sharp mixture which is the very best accompaniment to hot or cold ham or venison.

Pare the rind of the oranges and lemon very thinly with a potato peeler, cut into thin matchstick strips, and blanch in a small pan of boiling water for 5 minutes. Drain and keep the peel on one side.
    Melt the redcurrant jelly in a small pan, add the port, orange and lemon juice, spices and salt and boil for 15 minutes. Add the blanched peel and either heat through and serve, or eat cold.

Salad sauce

For all sorts of green or cooked vegetable salads

INGREDIENTS
2 hard-boiled eggs
1 dessertspoon Dijon mustard
3 dessertspoons oil – arachide, sunflower or olive
pinch of sugar
salt, pepper, cayenne pepper
1 tablespoon tarragon vinegar
4 tablespoons double cream
1 tablespoon chopped parsley

This salad sauce, made very easily from hard-boiled egg yolks, is a less rich and less temperamental cousin of mayonnaise. It is delicious with fish, cold meat, salads of all kinds, hard-boiled eggs and potato salad, so much nicer than the bottled salad cream that has generally replaced it today.

You can make this sauce in the liquidizer – or you can rub the yolks of the hard-boiled eggs to a smooth paste in a bowl with a wooden spoon. Then stir in the mustard and then, little by little, the oil. Mix (or whisk) until you have a smooth sauce, then add the seasoning, vinegar and lastly the cream. Sprinkle in the chopped parsley, and serve with the salad. If any sauce is left over, it will keep for a few days in a cool place, but do not keep it in the refrigerator.

Lord Marcus Hill's sauce

For cold meats

INGREDIENTS
2 sprigs mint
1 handful parsley
3 shallots
1 tablespoon wine vinegar
4 tablespoons olive oil
salt and pepper

This is a sort of salad dressing that used to be eaten with cold meat; it would be equally at home on a potato salad.

Chop the herbs and the shallots finely, and put them in a bowl. Pour on the vinegar, add the oil and beat well. Season with salt and pepper.

Top: salad sauce,
bottom: Lord Marcus Hill's sauce

Mayonnaise

INGREDIENTS
2 egg yolks
1 teaspoon made mustard
salt and pepper
275 ml ($\frac{1}{2}$ pint) sunflower and olive oil, mixed together
1–2 tablespoons cider vinegar or lemon juice
Mayonnaise made in a liquidizer
1 whole egg (size 2)
$\frac{1}{2}$ teaspoon made mustard
1 tablespoon cider vinegar
salt and pepper
275 ml ($\frac{1}{2}$ pint) sunflower and olive oil, mixed together

Mayonnaise, said to be the invention of the French doctor of Mary Queen of Scots, must in fact have been introduced to this country by her Court, but is a far older sauce. *Moyen* or *mayon* was the medieval French for egg yolks, and a mixture of oil, vinegar and egg was already known in those early times, although it may not have been quite the same sauce as the mayonnaise we know today.

All the ingredients must be at the same temperature – room temperature – or you may have trouble.

Put the egg yolks in a bowl and stand the bowl on a damp cloth, so that it doesn't slide about while you are stirring. Mix the egg yolks thoroughly with the mustard, salt and pepper. This first mixing is important.

Now start adding the oil, a few drops at a time, stirring with a slow steady rhythm. As the oil is incorporated add a little more, but go very cautiously as the mayonnaise will curdle at this point if the oil is added too fast.

As you add more oil the mixture thickens considerably; thin it with a teaspoon or two of vinegar or lemon juice, and then continue to add more oil, in slightly larger amounts now, but still stirring after each addition until the oil is absorbed, before adding more. Add more vinegar or lemon when the mixture becomes too thick to stir. When all the oil is added, taste for seasoning and add more salt or vinegar.

The mayonnaise can be eaten as it is, thick and jelly-like, or if you prefer it thinner, thinned with single cream.

To rescue curdled mayonnaise
Put another egg yolk and half a teaspoon of mustard into a clean bowl, beat it well, then gradually, little by little, stir in the curdled mayonnaise – it will come back together again, like magic.

To make mayonnaise in a liquidizer
Put the egg, mustard, vinegar and salt in the liquidizer and blend for 1 minute.

With the liquidizer open and at high speed pour in the oil in a very thin stream, and continue to add it very slowly until it is all mixed in.

Tartar sauce

INGREDIENTS
275 ml ($\frac{1}{2}$ pint) mayonnaise
1 tablespoon each parsley
   and capers
1 shallot, finely chopped
1 hard-boiled egg
1 teaspoon each wine
   vinegar and freshly
   made mustard
pinch of salt

Mayonnaise can also be transformed into tartar sauce to eat with fried fish of all kinds. Finely chop the parsley, capers, shallot and hard-boiled egg. Mix all the ingredients into the mayonnaise in a bowl. Taste for sharpness and seasoning and add more vinegar and salt if necessary.

To make a salad

By the Rev. Sydney Smith, an early nineteenth-century wit and 'bon viveur'

INGREDIENTS
2 small boiled potatoes
1 teaspoon made mustard
2 pinches salt
4 tablespoons olive oil
2 tablespoons vinegar
2 pounded yolks of hard-
   boiled eggs
1 small onion pounded to
   a paste
1 teaspoon anchovy sauce

Follow the 'Smith of Smiths' poetic instructions by puréeing the ingredients in a liquidizer to make a heavenly dressing for any salad, or simply use it for cooked vegetables or hard-boiled eggs.

Two boiled potatoes strained through a
   kitchen sieve
Softness and smoothness to the salad
   give;
Of mordant mustard take a single spoon,
Distrust the condiment that bites too
   soon;
Yet deem it not, thou man of taste, a
   fault,
To add a double quantity of salt.
Four times the spoon with oil of Lucca
   crown,
And twice with vinegar, procured from
   town;
True paste requires it, and your poet
   begs,
The pounded yellow of two well-boiled
   eggs.
Let onions' atoms link within the bowl,
And, scarce suspected, animate the
   whole;
And lastly, in the flavoured compound
   toss,
A magic spoonful of anchovy sauce.
O great and glorious! O herbaceous meat!
T'would tempt the dying anchoret to eat;
Back to the world he'd turn his weary
   soul,
And dip his finger in the salad bowl.

High teas and suppers

Most of the dishes in this chapter are movable feasts. Some of them, like macaroni cheese, may feature at lunchtime as well as at supper. Alternatively, they may be the main feature of that most British of meals, high tea. High tea, which forms such an essential part of British life wherever there are children in the house, is something of a puzzle to foreigners.

'In England little boys don't have dinner,' explains Sigi, the small hero of Nancy Mitford's book *The Blessing* to a baffled Frenchman. 'No dinner?' he enquires. 'No, supper, and sometimes high tea.' 'What is this, high tea?' 'Yes, well, it's tea, you know, with cocoa and scones . . .' *The Blessing* then enumerates such savoury dishes as kippers and sausages '. . . and you have it rather late for tea, about six.' 'How terrible this must be,' says the Frenchman, aghast at such an alien notion.

'Oh no,' says Sigi. 'High tea is absolutely smashing. Until you come to supper-time and then I must say you do rather long for supper.'

Mrs Beeton herself had to go to some trouble to explain high tea to her readers. 'There is tea and there is tea . . . The substantial family repast (high tea) in the home of the early diner, and the cosy chatty affair that late diners have instituted. The family tea-meal is very much like breakfast, only more cakes and knick-knackery should be provided. A high-tea where meat plays a prominent part, is really a tea-dinner.'

Afternoon tea, she says, 'signifies very little more than bread and butter and a few elegant trifles by way of cake and fruit'.

In this chapter we concentrate on fairly substantial and for the most part savoury dishes, such as might be eaten around sixish, with a cup of tea and a good deal of cosy chat. We have also included the useful sandwich; although the credit for that splendid invention goes to the fashionable John Montagu, Earl of Sandwich, 'sandwiches' were known earlier – his great innovation was that the filling was enclosed by two pieces of bread so that 'it need not be touched with the fingers of the most elegant lady'.

Recipes for the delicious curranty teabreads, scones and cakes that are offered at the end of a proper high tea are given in the baking chapter.

'A Yorkshire high tea'

An omelet, known in old English as an *amulet*, is a friendly dish, and as Dorothy Hartley points out in her wonderful book on English cooking, should never be started by the cook until the eater is sitting at the table. It must never be overdone and is best when soft and almost liquid inside. It can be varied enormously, made simple or rich and extravagant, by varying the filling. Generally speaking it will take less time to cook than a boiled egg – if you like it just done allow 3–3½ minutes or up to 4 for well-done, but no longer.

Allow 2–3 eggs per person, 5 eggs for two people, but never try and make an omelet for more than two people.

Top : the Dowager Lady Buckinghamshire's mushroom omelet, *bottom :* omelet Arnold Bennett

The Dowager Lady Buckinghamshire's mushroom omelet

TO SERVE TWO

INGREDIENTS
100 g (4 oz) mushrooms
squeeze of lemon juice
40 g (1½ oz) butter
1 teaspoon very finely chopped onion
salt
1 teaspoon very finely chopped parsley
5 eggs

This recipe dates from 1757, and even then the stress was on undercooking rather than overcooking your omelet. The original author says twice in as many sentences 'be sure to fry your omelet very tender'.

Clean and cut the mushrooms in ½-cm (¼-in) dice, sprinkle them with lemon juice. Melt 25 g (1 oz) of the butter in a small saucepan and soften the onion for several minutes without letting it brown. Stir in the mushrooms and let them stew gently for 5 minutes, covered. Season with salt and stir in the chopped parsley; keep the mixture hot.

Break the eggs into a bowl and season with a little salt. Beat briefly with a fork until well mixed, but do not overbeat as this will make the omelet tough.

Heat half the remaining butter in an omelet pan; at the moment when it starts to brown, pour in half the eggs, let them fry, moving them round briskly with a fork for a minute and lifting the edges to allow the uncooked mixture to run underneath. When *just* set put half the mushrooms across the middle and slide the omelet on to a heated plate, folding it over to make a half-moon shape as you do so. Fry the second omelet in the same way.

Omelet Arnold Bennett

TO SERVE FOUR

INGREDIENTS
6 eggs
25 g (1 oz) *gruyère* cheese cut in ½-cm (¼-in) cubes
100 g (4 oz) cooked smoked haddock, flaked into small pieces
salt, freshly ground pepper
25 g (1 oz) butter for cooking the omelet
Cheese sauce
15 g (½ oz) butter
15 g (½ oz) flour
275 ml (½ pint) milk
50 g (2 oz) grated *gruyère* cheese

This dish was created for Arnold Bennett by the chef of the Savoy Grill in 1937. Bennett lunched in the Grill regularly when he was working in Fleet Street as columnist and book reviewer of the *Evening Standard*, and later wrote about the hotel in his famous novel *Imperial Palace*. (Another recipe, this time a soufflé, using his favourite combination of ingredients, can be found on *page 52.*)

Make the cheese sauce; melt the butter in a very small pan, stir in the flour, let it cook for a minute then gradually add the milk, stirring well after each addition. Add more milk, enough to make a smooth sauce, let it cook for 15 minutes, very gently, stirring from time to time. Now add the grated cheese and let it melt. Keep the sauce on one side.

Beat the eggs in a bowl. Add the cubes of *gruyère* cheese and the smoked haddock and season with pepper and a very little salt. Beat with a fork.

Heat the butter in an omelet pan. Fry half the omelet mixture but be sure it remains rather fluid. Slide it on to a dish, cover with cheese sauce and put under a hot grill until the top is nicely browned. Make a second omelet in the same way. Serve straight away; half an omelet per person is quite enough as they are rather rich and filling.

161

Curried eggs

TO SERVE FOUR

INGREDIENTS
8–12 eggs
1 onion
25 g (1 oz) butter
2 dessertspoons of mild
  Madras curry powder
15 g (½ oz) flour
275 ml (½ pint) good
  chicken stock
150 ml (¼ pint) double
  cream
salt and pepper
juice of ½ a lemon
1 teaspoon curry paste
  (optional)
paprika

The nineteenth century saw a great vogue for all things Indian, particularly when Queen Victoria became Empress, an event with which she was inordinately satisfied. Paisley shawls, Benares brass and ivory work flooded in, and of course curry became immensely popular.

Although the dishes served as curry were often entirely free of a single authentic ingredient, they were rather good, and curried eggs is an excellent example.

Chop the onion finely and fry it lightly in the butter without letting it brown. Add the curry powder and fry it gently for a further minute, stirring well. Curry powder should always be fried gently before any liquid is added, so that there is no taste of raw turmeric, which is unpleasant. Stir in the flour, add the stock slowly and the cream and simmer for 15 minutes, covered. Meanwhile hardboil the eggs for 10–12 minutes, peel and keep them warm.

Halve the eggs, put them in a heated dish, season the curry sauce with salt, pepper, lemon juice and a teaspoon of curry paste if you have it, and pour it over the eggs. Sprinkle with paprika and serve with plain boiled rice.

Ramekins, egg with anchovies

Ramekins

TO SERVE FOUR

INGREDIENTS
2 eggs
1 teaspoon flour
50 g (2 oz) melted butter
50 g (2 oz) grated cheese
2 tablespoons single cream
salt and cayenne pepper
½ teaspoon ginger
2 teaspoons chives

Delicately 'baked eggs' used to be a great favourite for tea. They also make a very good first course for dinner.

Heat the oven to 190°C, 375°F, Gas Mark 5.
Butter four little fireproof ramekins. Mix the beaten eggs with the flour, melted butter, cheese and cream. Now season with salt, cayenne pepper and ginger and mix in the finely chopped chives. Pour the golden, speckled mixture into the buttered pots and bake for 15 minutes.

Eggs with anchovies

TO SERVE FOUR

INGREDIENTS
2 small tins anchovies
50 g (2 oz) softened butter
4 large slices fresh white
  bread
vinegar
4 eggs
oil for frying
cayenne pepper

Make the anchovy butter by pounding half the anchovies using a pestle and mortar and then mixing with the butter, or by blending the two together in a liquidizer. Bring a wide pan of water to the boil on top of the cooker.

Cut the crusts off the bread and toast it. Keep it hot. Add a teaspoon of vinegar to the water in the wide pan, but no salt. Slip the eggs into the simmering water and poach gently for 5 minutes.

Meanwhile spread the toast generously with the anchovy butter.

Drain the eggs well on a slotted spoon and put one on each piece of toast. Put a cross of anchovy fillets on each one, sprinkle with cayenne pepper and serve.

Scotch eggs

TO SERVE FOUR

INGREDIENTS
6 hard-boiled eggs
225 g (8 oz) sausagemeat
6 crushed allspice
good grating nutmeg
1 tablespoon chopped
    parsley
pinch thyme
25 g (1 oz) seasoned flour
salt, freshly ground pepper
1 beaten egg
75 g (3 oz) home-made
    dried breadcrumbs
deep fat for frying

Scotch eggs are an old way of making a simple egg into a filling and delicious dish. In the past the coating was grated ham, chopped anchovies and breadcrumbs, but sausagemeat is easier to handle and tastes excellent if a few extra spices and herbs are added to it.

The eggs should be boiled for 10–12 minutes, not longer. Cool and shell them carefully. Mix the sausagemeat with the herbs and spices. Divide it into six even portions.

Season the flour with a little salt and pepper. Dust the eggs with seasoned flour, and coat them with a thin layer of sausagemeat with floured hands, using the palm of one hand to cup the sausage layer and the egg while you work the meat round the egg with the other hand.

Brush with beaten egg, roll in crumbs and fry in deep fat until a golden brown. Drain on absorbent kitchen paper and serve hot or cold.

Egg croquettes

This makes an excellent lunch, with a green salad

TO SERVE FOUR

INGREDIENTS
275 ml (½ pint) milk
flavouring of blade mace,
    1 small peeled onion,
    bayleaf and sprig of
    parsley
40 g (1½ oz) butter
40 g (1½ oz) flour
25 g (1 oz) grated
    Parmesan
salt and pepper
4 hard-boiled eggs,
    separated
1 beaten egg
dried breadcrumbs
    (*page* 120)

Infuse the milk with the mace, onion, bayleaf and parsley. Make a stiff white sauce (*see page* 151) with 25 g (1 oz) of butter, all the flour and the strained flavoured milk. Add the cheese, season it with salt and pepper and beat in the remaining butter bit by bit. Sieve in the egg yolks and mix them thoroughly into the sauce. Add the chopped whites and stir them in.

Spread the mixture out on a lightly oiled plate and allow it to cool completely before making it into little cork shapes with floured hands. Chill these until they are needed, overnight if possible, then dip them in flour, beaten egg and breadcrumbs and deep-fry to a golden brown.

Curried egg croquettes
Fry a teaspoon of curry powder and a small grated onion in the butter before adding the flour and making the sauce. Leave out the Parmesan cheese.

Croquettes with tarragon
Add a teaspoon of chopped tarragon or 2 pinches dried tarragon to the sauce before adding the egg yolks. This is much tastier than adding chopped parsley.

Ham and egg croquettes
Add 2–3 slices of ham and some parsley, both finely chopped, to the sauce before adding the egg yolks.

Egg croquettes, parsnip cakes

Parsnip cakes

TO SERVE FOUR

INGREDIENTS
900 g (2 lb) parsnips
1 tablespoon double
    cream
25 g (1 oz) butter
salt and pepper
good pinch curry powder
1 beaten egg
50 g (2 oz) home-made
    dried breadcrumbs
    (*page* 120)
3 tablespoons sunflower oil

When fried into little golden cakes, parsnips have a most delicate and interesting flavour, and make a nice winter supper.

Peel the parsnips and put them into a pan of cold salted water. Bring them to the boil and boil until tender, about 20–25 minutes depending on their size and age. When they are soft, drain thoroughly and mash them to a soft pale yellow purée with the cream and butter, salt, pepper and curry powder. Let them cool, then form them into little cakes about 5 cm (2 in) across and 2 cm (1 in) high. Brush with beaten egg, dip into dried breadcrumbs and fry in hot oil until golden on both sides.

Cheese pie

INGREDIENTS
3 eggs
150 ml (¼ pint) single
  cream
175 g (6 oz) Cheddar
  cheese or Emmenthal
salt, pepper, and cayenne
275 g (10 oz) shortcrust
  pastry (*page 212*)
1 teaspoon cool melted
  butter

Beat together the eggs and cream and strain them through a sieve into a bowl. Stir in the grated cheese and seasoning, shaking in a good quantity of cayenne pepper.

Line a buttered 20-cm (8-in) pie plate with half the pastry. Brush the bottom of the pie with cool melted butter to prevent the egg mixture from making the pastry soggy. Add the mixture. Brush the outside rim of pastry with water. Cover with a second layer of pastry in which you have cut a 3-cm (1-in) slit to act as a steamhole. Pinch the edges together (*see page 212*). Brush the top carefully with any remaining beaten egg, and bake at 220°C, 425°F, Gas Mark 7 for 12 minutes, then at 160°C, 325°F, Gas Mark 3 for 20 minutes more. Cover the top with slightly crumpled foil if it should start to get too brown. Allow to cool for 5–10 minutes before serving. This creamy pie is also excellent cold.

Top : cheese pie, *bottom :* egg and bacon pie

Egg and bacon pie

INGREDIENTS
100 g (4 oz) thinly sliced
  bacon, streaky or back
1 teaspoon oil
3 eggs
150 ml (¼ pint) single cream
salt, pepper, nutmeg
1 tablespoon chives
275 g (10 oz) shortcrust
  pastry (*page 212*)

Cut the rinds off the bacon rashers, and fry them briefly in a very little oil without browning. Remove and allow to cool.

Beat the eggs with the cream and seasonings, strain through a sieve into a bowl and stir in the chopped chives.

Line the bottom of a buttered 20-cm (8-in) pie plate with half the pastry, brush it with the cool bacon fat and then lay the bacon rashers over the bottom – the bacon fat acts as a buffer between pastry and egg mixture and prevents the pie from becoming soggy. Pour in the egg mixture, lightly brush the outside pastry rim with water, cover with a second layer of pastry, pinch the edges (*see page 212*), brush with any beaten egg mixture remaining in the basin, cut a slit in the centre to act as a steamhole and bake for 12 minutes at 220°C, 425°F, Gas Mark 7, and a further 20 minutes at 160°C, 325°F, Gas Mark 3, covering the top with slightly crumpled foil if it starts to get too brown. Allow to cool for 5–10 minutes before serving. This egg and bacon pie is excellent cold and makes very good picnic food.

Macaroni cheese

TO SERVE FOUR–SIX

INGREDIENTS

425 ml ($\frac{3}{4}$ pint) white sauce
  (*page* 151)
salt, cayenne pepper, mace
225 g (8 oz) cheese, a
  mixture of Cheddar and
  Stilton
50 g (2 oz) fresh white
  breadcrumbs
50 g (2 oz) butter
275 g (10 oz) macaroni
6 generous tablespoons
  single cream

Few people realize what a venerable dish macaroni cheese is; macaroni with grated cheese and butter, known then as macrows, was eaten at the court of Richard II, and by the early nineteenth century it was served bathed in a cheese sauce, with a lovely tomato sauce handed separately to eat with it. This is an adaptation of Eliza Acton's recipe.

First make the white sauce in a large saucepan, seasoning it with a little salt and plenty of cayenne pepper and ground mace. Stir in the cheese and keep stirring until it has completely melted into the sauce.

Keep the sauce hot over a gentle heat.

Fry the breadcrumbs to a pale golden colour in the butter. Tip them on to kitchen paper to dry.

Meanwhile drop the macaroni into a large pan of boiling salted water and let it cook for 10 minutes until tender. Drain it thoroughly and toss gently in the sauce, add the cream and stir it in. Pour the mixture into a fireproof earthenware dish, soufflé dish or pie dish, and sprinkle the crumbs over the top. Set the dish briefly under a medium grill until it is bubbling hot and golden, and serve at once.

Gloucester cheese stew

TO SERVE FOUR

INGREDIENTS

450 g (1 lb) potatoes
275 ml ($\frac{1}{2}$ pint) milk
salt, freshly ground pepper
3 medium-sized onions
225 g ($\frac{1}{2}$ lb) Double
  Gloucester cheese

Peel the potatoes and slice them thinly. Put them in a saucepan with the milk, season with salt and pepper and simmer gently for 10–15 minutes until almost tender, but still whole and unbroken. Scoop them out of the milk and keep the milk on one side. Peel the onions and chop them fairly finely. Grate the cheese.

Butter a medium-sized earthenware casserole and put in layers of potato, onion and cheese in that order, seasoning as you go and ending with a layer of cheese. Pour on the milk and bake, uncovered, at 180°C, 350°F, Gas Mark 4 for 1 hour until the top is golden brown.

From left to right : macaroni cheese, Scotch rarebit, Gloucester cheese stew

Scotch rarebit

TO SERVE TWO

INGREDIENTS

100 g (4 oz) grated cheese
1 liqueur glass of real ale
1 teaspoon made English
  mustard
$\frac{1}{2}$ teaspoon freshly ground
  pepper
2 pieces freshly made
  buttered toast

This recipe is called a knick-knack, and its original nineteenth-century author recommends that it should be served on a double dish with hot water under, in order to keep it hot. It is salutary to remember that when food had to be carried long distances from kitchen to parlour or dining-room, and there was no such thing as central heating, it must have got cold extremely quickly.

Melt the cheese in a small pan with the beer, mustard and pepper, stirring vigor-

ously all the time. Pour the mixture over the pieces of buttered toast and put under a hot grill to brown.

Cornish pasties

TO SERVE FOUR

INGREDIENTS
The pastry
225 g (8 oz) plain flour
100 g (4 oz) lard or half
  lard, half butter
salt
a little cold water
The filling
350 g (¾ lb) chuck steak
1 small onion
2–3 potatoes
plenty of salt
plenty of pepper
1 beaten egg

This particularly portable lunch is as popular today as it ever was. Purists say that Cornish pasties should not be made with mince, but with good chuck steak cut by hand into tiny pieces, and this is certainly the way to get the best results.

Make the pastry, rubbing the fat into the flour and salt and then adding a little very cold water. Let it rest in the refrigerator while you prepare the filling.

Cut the meat into tiny pieces. Slice the onion into the finest slices possible, then chop it coarsely.

Peel the potatoes and cut into little thin pieces, not cubes. This can be done by slicing the potato thinly and then cutting up the slices, or by cutting the corners off the peeled potato, turning it round and round in your hand – according to one account, this is called 'shripping'. Put the 'shripped' potatoes in a bowl of cold water so that they will not discolour.

Roll out the pastry and cut four 15-cm (6-in) discs. Pile wet potato in the centre of each, then onions, then meat; season with salt and pepper and then add more potato shreds, with their drops of water. Brush the edges of the pastry lightly with water, and draw them up, in the familiar fat pasty shape. Pinch together firmly and flute with the fingers. Brush with beaten egg and place on a greased baking sheet.

Bake at 220°C, 425°F, Gas Mark 7 for 10–15 minutes to cook the pastry. Then turn the oven down to 150°C, 300°F, Gas Mark 2 and bake for 30–40 minutes, more if the steak was tough. To reheat, put them back in a moderate oven, 180°C, 350°F, Gas Mark 4, for 10–15 minutes.

Kromeskies
Stuffed bacon rolls

TO SERVE FOUR

INGREDIENTS
1 medium-sized onion
100 g (4 oz) mushrooms
25 g (1 oz) butter
100 g (4 oz) fresh
  breadcrumbs
2 egg yolks (the whites are
  used in the exquisite
  light batter)
2 tablespoons double cream
salt, pepper, and grating of
  nutmeg
225 g (8 oz) chopped
  cooked chicken, turkey,
  ham or tongue
16 rashers of thinly cut
  streaky bacon
oil for frying
The batter
175 g (6 oz) flour
pinch of salt
1 dessertspoon oil
275 ml (½ pint) tepid water
2 egg whites (*see above*)

Kromeskies, or cromesquis, are found frequently in early nineteenth-century cookery books, and appear to be strange hybrids, part-French, part-Polish, part-sausage, part-croquette. In any case they are wholly delicious: this version was the one favoured by the South Kensington School of Cookery in its heyday, one hundred years ago.

Chop the onion and mushrooms finely and cook them gently in butter for a few minutes. When they are soft, but not browned, mix them with the breadcrumbs, egg yolk, cream, salt, pepper and nutmeg. Stir in the chopped chicken, turkey or ham.

Stretch the rashers of bacon and flatten them with the blade of a knife. Cut each one in half, spread it thickly with the mixture and roll it up. Put in the refrigerator to become firm.

To make the batter
Put the flour and salt in a bowl, pour the oil into the centre, gradually add the water, stirring it well with a wooden spoon to make a creamy batter.

Beat the egg white to a stiff foam, and fold it lightly into the batter. Dip the bacon rolls into the mixture and deep-fry them to a golden brown (about 5 minutes). Drain on kitchen paper and serve very hot.

From top to bottom: kromeskies, white devil, dunelm of chicken

White devil

*A splendid way of using up
leftover turkey, chicken or
game*

TO SERVE FOUR

INGREDIENTS
15 g ($\frac{1}{2}$ oz) butter
225 g ($\frac{1}{2}$ lb) thinly sliced
   cold cooked turkey,
   chicken or game
150 ml ($\frac{1}{4}$ pint) double cream
1 tablespoon Worcester
   sauce
4 anchovy fillets, finely
   chopped
dash of anchovy essence
salt and cayenne pepper
2 egg whites (optional)

Melt the butter in an oval ovenproof dish
and lay the slices of cold meat in it. Place it
in a moderate oven 180°C, 350°F, Gas
Mark 4, for 10 minutes, covered with a
sheet of foil, to heat through. Meanwhile
whip the cream in a bowl until it is thick
and velvety but soft.

Stir in the Worcester sauce, anchovies,
anchovy essence, salt and cayenne pepper.
If using egg whites – it is a good way of
using them up if you have made mayonnaise – whisk them until stiff and then fold
into the cream mixture.

Pour the mixture over the hot chicken
and return to the oven to heat through,
about 10 minutes. If egg whites have been
included in the sauce it will be brown and
soufflé-like, if they have been omitted it
will be creamy and rich.

Dunelm of chicken

TO SERVE TWO

INGREDIENTS
225 g (8 oz) breast of cold
   roast chicken
100 g (4 oz) small white
   button mushrooms
50 g (2 oz) butter
150 ml ($\frac{1}{4}$ pint) chicken
   stock, home-made or
   made with stock cube
salt, freshly ground pepper
juice of $\frac{1}{2}$ a lemon
4–5 sprigs tarragon,
   chopped
3 tablespoons double cream
8 freshly made small
   triangular pieces of fried
   bread

A dunelm is a Scottish hash that can be
made of chicken or veal, usually in con-
junction with mushrooms and cream.

Cut the chicken into tiny slices the size of a
50 pence piece.

Slice the mushrooms thinly and soften
them gently in the butter until they are
limp. Add the chicken stock, salt and pepper, lemon juice and chopped tarragon and
bring to the boil. Boil until the liquid has
reduced by half, then add the cream and
boil for 4 minutes. Put in the chicken, turn
down the heat, and let it heat right through
very thoroughly without boiling, as this
would dry up the meat.

Serve at once on a heated plate with the
sippets of fried bread placed round the
edge of the plate.

167

Spatchcock

'Indian mode and sea fashion' adds the Victorian colonel's wife from whose cookbook this particular recipe comes.

TO SERVE FOUR

INGREDIENTS
1 small chicken or
  2 poussins
salt and pepper
75 g (3 oz) butter
1 teaspoon curry powder

The word spatchcock comes from the dish – a happy rooster one minute and a rather flat-looking grilled chicken the next – all done with great despatch. This simple recipe was a favourite with army officers sent to India by sea, which used to entail several weeks' long voyage. Coops of chickens were kept on board and were a great treat for the bored passengers when despatched and cooked in this way.

With a large sharp knife, split the chicken or poussins through the back, close to the backbone and beat flat with a steak beater. Season with pepper and salt, and rub both sides with butter. Sprinkle lightly with curry powder.

Heat the grill to red hot, grill the flat-tened chicken for 20 minutes, turning frequently and turning down the grill after the first 5 minutes.

Heat a serving dish and put a lump of butter, about 25 g (1 oz) to melt in it.

As soon as the chicken is cooked, when a clear bead of liquid appears as the thigh is pricked with a skewer, season with salt and pepper and put it in the heated dish. Serve very hot.

A good addition to this dish: sauté two chicken livers in a little butter and then pound it or purée it in the liquidizer with some cream, salt and pepper, and a few drops of sherry. This paste is spread on rounds of fried bread or toast and placed round the dish when it is served.

Spatchcock, real Indian pilau

A real Indian pilau

From a late nineteenth-century British cookbook

TO SERVE SIX

INGREDIENTS
3 onions
3 hard-boiled eggs
50 g (2 oz) butter
15 cloves
3-cm (1-in) piece of
  cinnamon
350 g (12 oz) rice
850 ml (1½ pints) chicken
  stock, home-made or
  made with stock cubes
350 g (12 oz) cold chicken
  or cold lamb
50 g (2 oz) each almonds
  and raisins, lightly fried
  in butter
salt and pepper

Slice the onions very finely. Boil the eggs for 10–12 minutes but do not shell them yet, as you want to keep them hot. Melt the butter and soften the onions together with the cloves and cinnamon.

Add the rice and stir it in the butter for 3 minutes without letting it brown. Now add half the stock and let the rice cook gently, stirring. When it has absorbed the stock, add the chicken or lamb cut in pieces, the fried almonds and raisins, salt and pepper and some more stock.

Keep adding more stock as it is absorbed by the rice, until it is quite tender and has absorbed all the liquid.

Pile the pilau on a dish, decorate it with the shelled, quartered eggs and serve.

Faggots or poor man's goose

Also known as savoury ducks

TO SERVE FOUR

INGREDIENTS
350 g (¾ lb) minced pig's liver
225 g (½ lb) minced belly of pork or salt pork
2 medium-sized onions, finely chopped or minced
1 teaspoon marjoram or sage
good pinch ground nutmeg
salt and freshly ground pepper
1 egg
100 g (4 oz) freshly made breadcrumbs (*page* 120)
milk to moisten the mixture
caul fat (traditional but not essential)
150 ml (¼ pint) gravy or rich home-made stock

These savoury parcels, much liked in the West Country and the Midlands, taste very much like a robust pâté but are eaten hot. They can be bought ready made, but are much richer and more flavoursome if made at home. Some farm households eat them for breakfast, but they are best served as a high tea or supper dish with mushy peas.

Mix together the liver, pork and onion. Put in a pan over a low heat, with the seasoning, herbs and nutmeg and cover the pan, so that they cook very gently in their own juice; let them simmer for 30 minutes.

Drain off the fat and juices and keep them on one side. Add the beaten egg and breadcrumbs, and enough milk to make a

firm mixture. Cool slightly and shape into rounds about the size of golf balls.

If you use caul fat, soak it in warm water for a few minutes to soften it, cut it into 10 cm (4 in) squares and wrap each faggot round with it, making a small round parcel. If caul fat is not available the faggots can be moulded and put into the tin as they are.

Set the faggots close together in a baking dish, and add the gravy or stock. Bake at 160°C, 325°F, Gas Mark 3 for 30 minutes, until nicely browned. The juices in the dish can be mixed into the gravy.

Faggots, toad in the hole

Toad in the hole

TO SERVE FOUR

INGREDIENTS
450 g (1 lb) sausages
The batter
175 g (6 oz) plain flour
pinch salt
2 eggs
575 ml (1 pint) milk and water mixed
15 g (½ oz) lard or dripping

Traditionally the friendly sounding toad was another good, filling recipe for using up leftover meat, but is now always made with bangers. For the best results use really good sausages with plenty of character to make this dish.

Make the batter 1 hour before you start to cook the dish. Put the flour into a bowl with the salt, make a well in the centre and break in the eggs. Beat them into the flour, gradually adding milk and water to make a smooth creamy batter. Beat it well and allow to stand for 1 hour. (This can be quickly made in the liquidizer.)

Heat the oven to 220°C, 425°F, Gas Mark 7.

Melt the lard or dripping in a frying pan and brown the sausages nicely all over – they look and taste better if they are fried, rather than browned in the oven, at the start of the recipe.

Pour fat and sausages into a 30-cm (12-in) roasting tin, put it into the oven to heat through, pour in the batter and put back in the oven. Turn down the heat to 190°C, 375°F, Gas Mark 5 when the batter is nicely puffed and golden brown, and cook for 35–40 minutes altogether.

169

Haggis

TO SERVE FOUR

INGREDIENTS
1 sheep's paunch and
    pluck (the pluck is lights,
    heart and liver in one
    piece with the wind pipe
    attached)
275 ml (½ pint) oatmeal
450 g (1 lb) finely chopped
    beef suet
2 Spanish onions
2 tablespoons salt
1 teaspoon pepper
½ teaspoon grated nutmeg
juice of 1 lemon
850 ml (1½ pints) good
    stock or gravy

For those brave enough to attempt it, here is Sir Harry Luke's recipe, given to him by the courtesy of Lt Colonel A. Murray of the King's Own Scottish Borderers, on St Andrew's night in 1935. (From *The Tenth Muse*, his entertaining collection of recipes published in 1954.)

Queen Victoria, guest of the Duchess of Atholl at Blair Castle, said in *Leaves of a Highland Journal*: 'There were several Scottish dishes, two soups and the celebrated haggis, which I tried and really liked very much. The Duchess was delighted with me for taking it.'

Although the making of a haggis is not something to be lightly contemplated by the ordinary housewife, who, if she wanted to serve one on St Andrew's night or Burns' night might go to the shops and buy one, it is fascinating to unravel the origins of this extremely ancient Celtic sausage.

In fact the habit of using an animal's stomach as a container goes back, beyond Celts, Romans and ancient Greeks, to days when there were no man-made containers to cook food in; it is a survival of a pre-historic method of cooking.

A modern haggis, just like its ancestor, is a roundish grey-brown sausage with, according to Burns, an 'honest, sonsie [homely] face, Great chieftain o' the puddin' race!' It is served, with ceremony, at Scottish functions and piped in by a fully-kitted Heelander playing a tune on another animal's stomach – this time made into a bagpipe. The traditional accompaniment is mashed potatoes, and neat whisky is drunk – a good idea to counteract the fat in the haggis. It is scooped from a cross-shaped cut with a spoon, each person helping himself. The flavour is delicious, nutty and rich, but is really only at its best when it is piping hot.

Soak the paunch for 6 hours in cold water and salt, then turn it inside out and wash thoroughly in several waters. Wash the pluck, cover the liver with cold water, boil it for 1½ hours and at the end of ¾ hour add to it the heart and lights. Chop half the liver coarsely, the rest with the heart and lights, more finely, mix all together and add the oatmeal, suet, finely chopped onions, salt, pepper, nutmeg, lemon juice and stock. Turn these ingredients into the paunch, sew up the opening, taking care that sufficient space is left for the oatmeal to swell, for if the paunch is overfull it may burst. Put the haggis into boiling water and boil gently for 3 hours; during the first hour it should be pricked occasionally with a needle to allow the air to escape.

As a rule neither sauce nor gravy is served with haggis, but dish up on a foundation of mashed potatoes, as the haggis is very slippery which makes for difficulty in serving.

The above amount is sufficient for 8–9 persons. If a lesser quantity is required, use a lamb's paunch and pluck which should suffice for 4–5 people according to the age of the lamb. The ingredients must not be chopped too finely and, above all, must never be minced as this tends to make the haggis 'saggy'.

To cook a bought haggis, steam it for at least 1 hour until it is heated all through.

Top to bottom : haggis, Mrs Collecott's brawn, tripe and onions

Mrs Collecott's brawn

TO FILL THREE 600-ML (1-PINT) BASINS

INGREDIENTS
3 salted pig's trotters: if you
  cannot obtain trotters
  ready salted add a piece
  of collar-bacon weighing
  225 g (8 oz) together with
  the fresh trotters
625 g (1½ lb) lean belly of
  pork
450 g (1 lb) boned rabbit
1 teaspoon wine vinegar or
  lemon juice
½ teaspoon dry mustard
4 cloves
¼ grated nutmeg
salt, freshly ground pepper

Brawn, popular in the Middle Ages, was part of the everyday diet of the Elizabethans, being served at the very beginning of every meal with lavish quantities of mustard. In those days it was seasoned with galingale, a spicy root similar to ginger, and from this sprang the name galantine. Other seasonings used included grated lemon peel, mace, allspice, cloves, and cayenne pepper.

Very often the brawn was wrapped up like a parcel in a great piece of tripe and pressed.

Now, brawn has become a much simpler dish and you don't need a pig's head and a cow heel to make it. This recipe is easily made and a great summertime dish.

Wash the trotters and let them soak for at least 3 hours, together with the bacon if you are including it.

Put trotters and bacon in a pan, cover with cold water and bring slowly to the boil. Skim and simmer gently for 2 hours. Add the belly of pork and rabbit and cover with more boiling water. Simmer for 2 hours or more, until the meat is tender enough to leave the bones. Allow to get cold and skim off the fat.

Take out the meat with a slotted spoon, strain the liquid into a saucepan, let it boil for about 1½–2 hours to reduce to an almost syrupy consistency. Meanwhile trim and chop the meat, while it is still hot, into small pieces – about 2 cm (½ in) or less across, having first removed any bones.

Return the chopped meat to the liquid, add the vinegar, spices, more salt if needed, and pepper, and simmer for a further 15 minutes.

Rinse out three 600-ml (1-pint) moulds or basins with cold water and fill them with the brawn mixture (or allow to cool slightly, and put into containers ready to freeze).

Allow to set overnight and serve sliced. Delicious in the summer with green salad and home-made bread.

Tripe and onions

TO SERVE FOUR–SIX

INGREDIENTS
4 large onions
425 ml (¾ pint) milk
275 ml (½ pint) water
2 bayleaves
4 blades mace
12 peppercorns
salt
900 g (2 lb) best prepared
  or dressed tripe
15 g (½ oz) butter
15 g (½ oz) flour

Tripe is considered a vulgar dish, but, if it helps people to overcome their aversion to it, was enjoyed by the Prince of Wales in 1933. It is in fact, for those who have decided to like it, a very good dish indeed and succulent in texture. Choose different parts of the tripe for your dish; a piece of honeycomb and a piece of double tripe, nice and white.

Cut the onions into quarters and then cut the quarters across. Put them in a pan with the milk, water, bayleaves, mace and peppercorns. Season with salt and simmer for 30 minutes. Cut the tripe into small oblong pieces, about 3 × 5 cm (1 × 2 in),

put them into the milk and let it simmer on for about 2 hours.

Melt the butter in a separate pan, stir in the flour and then spoon in the liquid from the tripe to make a smooth sauce. Return it to the tripe and onions, cook for 15 minutes, season it well and serve very hot.

Potted kipper

TO SERVE FOUR

INGREDIENTS
2 mild-smoked kippers
1 slice white bread
a little milk
1 clove garlic
75 g (3 oz) softened butter
juice of ½ a lemon
freshly ground pepper

Cook the kippers gently in water for 5 minutes or until tender. Remove the flesh, taking out as many bones as you can. Soak the bread in milk and squeeze fairly dry. Pound first the garlic and then the bread in a pestle and mortar or liquidizer. Add the fish and pound thoroughly, removing any little bones you have missed. Add the butter, pound while you incorporate this and the lemon juice. Add pepper, taste for seasoning, put into pots and chill. This keeps for about a week in the refrigerator.

Sandwiches

Sandwiches were brought into polite society in the eighteenth century by the gambling Earl of Sandwich – he couldn't bear to leave the gaming-table for proper cooked meals. 'The sandwich', said Wyvern, a gentleman cook and author, 'is invaluable when time is of the essence.' Since he was writing in about 1900 when cooks and parlourmaids abounded, he was presumably not talking about the sandwich-maker's time. Certainly a plate of his favourite sandwiches filled with herb butter would take time to prepare, but would make a delicious snack before the theatre or when time, for the eater, was short.

The bread for making sandwiches

Although harder to cut, very fresh bread is best and makes the nicest sandwiches. Use an extremely sharp carving knife and try to cut the bread very thin. In the early days of sandwich-making they were eaten with a fork, so had to be cut very small, but today sandwiches are usually halved or quartered.

Wyvern's Edwardian sandwiches

TO SERVE FOUR

INGREDIENTS
8 slices extremely fresh
  bread
100 g (4 oz) each of cooked
  chicken and cooked
  tongue, cut in thin
  matchstick strips
Ravigote butter
generous handful of parsley
  or parsley and chervil
  mixed, chives, and
  tarragon
100 g (4 oz) butter,
  softened to room
  temperature
salt and pepper

Bring a small saucepan of salted water to the boil, and throw in the herbs. Let them boil for 1 minute, drain, pat dry with kitchen paper and chop extremely finely. Mix them into the butter, seasoning it with salt and pepper. Spread the bread with this mixture. Cover half the slices with a generous quantity of chicken and tongue and cover with the remaining slices of bread. Cut off the crusts.

Top : Adelaide sandwiches, *centre :* Wyvern's
Edwardian sandwiches, egg sandwiches,
sandwiches for hunters, *bottom :* cinnamon toast

Adelaide sandwiches from Tyttenhanger

Called after the hostess of this great house

INGREDIENTS
100 g (4 oz) bacon
oil for frying
4 anchovy fillets, finely chopped
2 tablespoons grated Parmesan cheese
2 tablespoons double cream
½ beaten egg
8 very thin slices of bread

These sandwiches were originally made with chicken or pheasant but bacon is nicer.

Cut the bacon rashers in half and fry them. Keep them crisp.

Mix the anchovies, Parmesan, cream and egg to a paste, beat to a firm consistency and keep aside. Cut 16 small rounds out of the bread and fry them to a bright yellow colour in oil. Spread half with the cheese mixture, place half a slice of bacon on top, cover with a second round of fried bread, skewer each sandwich with a cocktail stick, and heat through in a hot oven. Serve very hot.

Egg sandwiches

TO SERVE FOUR

INGREDIENTS
2 hard-boiled eggs
1 teaspoon chopped parsley
50 g (2 oz) butter
8 slices of bread
100 g (4 oz) cold chicken, finely sliced
1 dessertspoon mango or other fruit chutney
the heart of a lettuce, shredded

The following recipe is from Lady Sarah Lindsay. Her well-filled egg sandwiches are made juicy and interesting with a little chutney and a layer of chicken and lettuce.

Use the yolks only of the hard-boiled eggs. Chop them up extremely finely and mix them to a paste with parsley and the butter, softened to room temperature. Spread the bread with this mixture, cover half the slices with 2–3 layers of finely sliced chicken, spread with chutney. Cover with lettuce and then put the tops on to the sandwiches. Cut off the crusts.

Sandwiches for hunters

INGREDIENTS
For each sandwich
2 slices of bread, toasted on one side
3 slices chicken
1 or 2 slices York ham
½ teaspoon curry paste
piece of Cheddar cheese, cut into wafer-thin slices
butter

'Toast the outsides of the bread slightly to prevent their getting into crumbs from the shaking in the pockets,' read the old instructions; but nowadays when wrapping is no problem, the toasting still adds character to the sandwiches.

The filling is made from cold chicken, a little ham, a little curry paste, a little Cheddar cheese and some butter.

Cinnamon toast

TO SERVE FOUR

INGREDIENTS
1 dessertspoon sugar or more according to taste
1 teaspoon powdered cinnamon
4 slices bread
2 tablespoons butter

Mix the sugar and cinnamon. Toast the bread gently, butter it lavishly (this is easier if you have softened the butter to room temperature first). Sprinkle with cinnamon sugar and put back under the grill for 1 minute.

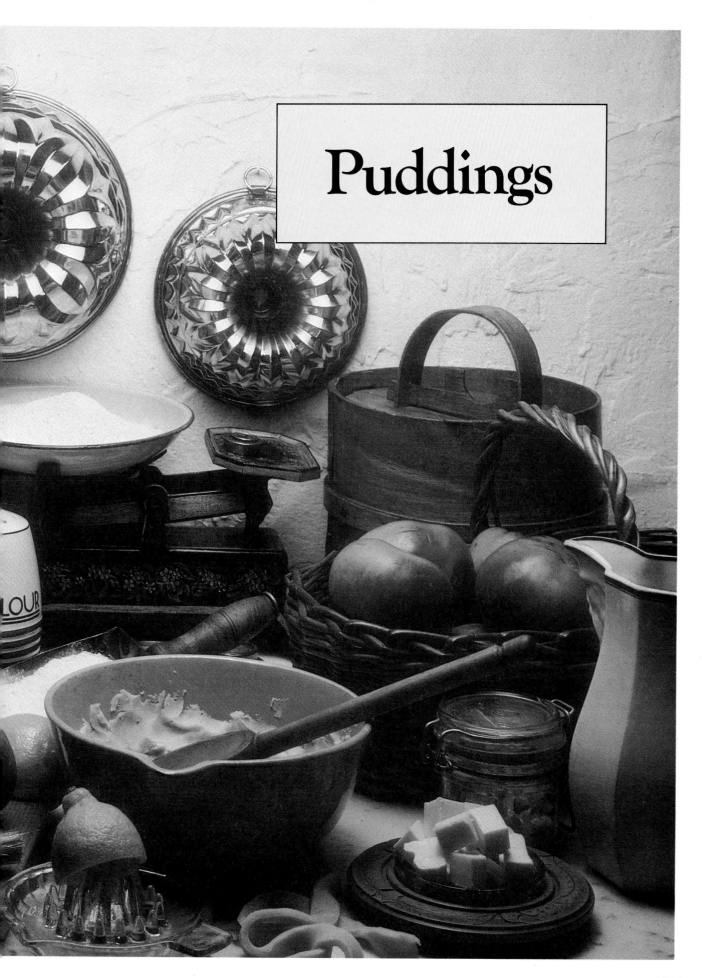

Puddings

The British repertoire of puddings – the steamed puds, pies, tarts, trifles, flans, flummeries and fools – is unequalled anywhere. From early times it seems the English nation had a sweet tooth and today even French gastronomes, normally so unfairly critical of British food, admit that our 'variety of puddings is probably greater than in any part of the world'; and visitors to English homes always hope to get, for pudding at least a crisp treacle tart or apple pie with a dollop of incomparable English cream.

British puddings have a long and honourable pedigree. Almost all have descended from two ancient confections, 'the stately pye' or pudding, filled with dates and raisins, currants, flour, suet, nuts and almonds plus meat or fish finely shredded or minced, and a festival dish, called frumenty – a soft jellied milk pudding made of wheat or barley cooked very gently and long and then eaten with milk and honey – a sort of early breakfast cereal.

In time eggs, cream and then sugar – this last more slowly because it was scarce and expensive – came to join the other ingredients. The puddings at this stage were often contained in a bag, an animal's stomach (haggis still is) – or in a great thick pastry crust or 'coffyn'.

This led to custard pies and custard pie jokes followed quickly after – Good Queen Bess was one of the first to laugh when, after the 'coffyn' containing the custard had been brought on and her assembled guests had been served, her jester flew into the room and, leaping over the heads of the company, dived straight into the gooey mess, splattering the courtiers' velvets.

The Queen's taste for sugary comfits and confections had a notable effect on her teeth. These were remarkably black – according to one observer, who added that this seemed to be 'a defect to which all the English seemed subject, owing to their too great use of sugar'.

Robust Elizabethan amusements included a good deal of leaping. Ladies and gentlemen, including Her Majesty (seen here with Lord Leicester) leapt on the dance floor whilst the Court fool leapt into the custard.

176

It was certainly true that puddings were served grandly in those days. There were on great occasions huge numbers of puddings on the table with a vast cloved and gilded pippin-pie in the centre breathing its scented steam. 'Your breath is like the steam of apple-pie' was a nice compliment in those days, although in fact the surreptitious chewing of cloves, which sweetened the breath, was also a remedy for toothache.

The grander the occasion, the grander the sweetmeat course. In the sixteenth and seventeenth centuries a banquet was not the feast, but the sweet course that followed it, and was designed to provide entertainment as much as an opportunity to eat wonderful confections. Pies would be opened to release the well-known four-and-twenty blackbirds or even frogs which 'made the ladies skip and shreek'.

All good things have to come to an end, and by the end of the seventeenth century, fat pink Venuses were no longer required to appear from very large pies, and the fountains of wine were still. But the good old country dishes were still enjoyed throughout the countryside; the batter puddings and plate pies and steamed puddings such as Granny's Leg – a currant-speckled pastry roly poly object boiled in a cloth. There is hardly a town in Britain that doesn't boast of a local pudding – or at least of a dish sold at local fairs, or junkets as they were called – thus giving the name to yet another pudding which could be made on the spot with milk warm from the cow.

The pudding is still a favourite in Britain, and a freshly made rhubarb tart or Brown Betty is certainly hard to beat.

Let's hope the fashion of slimness will not lead to giving up our wonderful puddings, too much maybe for an ordinary working day, but tremendous at week-ends when for once at least everybody can sit down and dedicate themselves to the business of eating, and a pudding can have its day.

The medieval junket, which was to give its name to any pleasurable expedition, in time made way for ice cream, which used to be sold at fairs from the turn of the century by itinerant Italians.

Queen of puddings

TO SERVE FOUR

INGREDIENTS
275 ml ($\frac{1}{2}$ pint) milk
25 g (1 oz) butter
grated rind of $\frac{1}{2}$ a lemon
75 g (3 oz) fresh
   breadcrumbs
2 whole eggs plus 1 extra
   white
50 g (2 oz) sugar
100 g ($\frac{1}{4}$ lb) raspberry or
   strawberry jam

Canary pudding with lemon sauce

TO SERVE FOUR

INGREDIENTS
100 g (4 oz) butter or
   margarine
100 g (4 oz) sugar
2 eggs
50 g (2 oz) self-raising
   flour
50 g (2 oz) fresh white
   breadcrumbs
grated rind of 1 lemon
1 tablespoon Madeira or
   sweet sherry (optional)
Lemon sauce
2 egg yolks
25 g (1 oz) castor sugar
1 lemon
150 ml ($\frac{1}{4}$ pint) water

Put the milk, butter and grated lemon rind into a saucepan and bring the mixture to the boil. Pour it, boiling, over the breadcrumbs and let it cool and soak to a creamy mush.

Separate the eggs and beat the yolks into the breadcrumb mixture, together with the sugar. Pour the mixture into a buttered 1-litre (2-pint) pie dish, stand it in a roasting tin of hot water and put in the centre of the oven at 180°C, 350°F, Gas Mark 4 for 20 minutes. When it has just set, spread the jam over the top – if it is very stiff jam, heat it with a teaspoon of water to thin it a bit.

This light pudding was originally made with a flavouring of Madeira, the sweet and somewhat sherry-like fortified wine from the Canary Islands. However, it is delicious without any such luxuries.

Remember that this pudding needs room to expand as it cooks if it is to be light, so do not overfill the bowl.

Cream together the butter and sugar until they are light and fluffy. This can be done with an electric beater or by hand. Beat in one egg, then half the flour, then another egg and the remaining flour. Do not beat more than necessary once the flour starts to go in, as this toughens the mixture. Add the breadcrumbs, grated lemon rind and lemon juice and the wine and mix. Spoon the mixture into a greased 1-litre (2-pint) pudding basin, cover the top with greased kitchen foil and tie it in place with string, making a string handle to lift it out of the pan.

Bring a large pan half-filled with water to the boil, put an inverted saucer or small piece of wood in the bottom; put in the pudding, cover the pan and allow to simmer for $2\frac{1}{2}$ hours, topping up with more boiling water as necessary.

When you are ready to serve the pudding remove the foil and string, hold a heated plate over the basin, turn it quickly over and give it a little shake. Then let it slide out gently on to the plate.

Lemon sauce
Put the egg yolks, sugar, grated lemon rind in the top half of a double boiler and whisk over a gentle heat until the mixture starts to foam. Now add the lemon juice and whisk again. Finally, add the water, a little at a time, whisking in between each addition until you have a light and fluffy sauce. Keep it warm over the hot water but do not let it get any hotter. Just before serving, add 1 tablespoon hot water and give the sauce a last energetic whisk.

Beat the egg whites to a firm snow. Add 1 tablespoon of sugar and whip again. Spoon them over the jam to cover it. Sprinkle with a little sugar and bake at 180°C, 350°F, Gas Mark 4 for a further 10 minutes until the meringue is a pretty pale fawn colour.

Castle puddings

TO SERVE SIX

INGREDIENTS
100 g (4 oz) butter
100 g (4 oz) castor sugar
3 small eggs
100 g (4 oz) self-raising
  flour
grated rind of 1 lemon
Castle pudding sauce
2 eggs
2 tablespoons sherry
2 teaspoons sugar

Cream the butter and sugar together to a light soft fluff. Beat in the eggs one at a time, adding a heaped tablespoon of flour after each egg to help prevent curdling. Stir in the grated lemon rind.

Butter 12 small castle-pudding or dariole moulds and spoon in the mixture, so that they are half-filled.

Bake in a moderate oven 190°C, 375°F, Gas Mark 5, for 20 minutes until golden and light.

Serve with castle pudding sauce or a sauce made of half a pot of jam, heated with one tablespoon of water.

Castle pudding sauce
In the top of a double boiler, over a pan of hot – but never boiling – water, whisk the eggs with a wire whisk and gradually whisk in the sherry a teaspoon at a time. Lastly, still whisking, add the sugar. The eggs will rise in an amber-coloured froth which is very delicious with any plain sponge pudding.

Back: Queen of puddings, *front:* Canary pudding, castle puddings

Rice pudding

TO SERVE SIX

INGREDIENTS
50 g (2 oz) rice – this must
  be the round-grained
  Carolina variety
575 ml (1 pint) milk
pinch of salt
100 g (4 oz) castor sugar
split vanilla pod, 5 cm
  (2 in) long
15 g (½ oz) butter
grating of nutmeg

Where rice pudding is concerned, long and gentle cooking is the order of the day. In the days of kitchen ranges, the tradition was to leave the pudding in overnight with the fires banked down. Nowadays, three or four hours in a very slow oven will do the trick, turning the rice and milk gradually into a rich caramel-coloured cream.

Butter a 1-litre (2-pint) pie dish. Put the rice in the bottom. Heat the milk, with the pinch of salt, sugar, and vanilla pod, stir-ring to dissolve the sugar. When it reaches simmering point, remove the vanilla pod and pour it over the rice.

Dot the top all over with little slips of butter, grate a sprinkling of nutmeg over the top and set the dish on the middle shelf of a very low oven, 130°C, 275°F, Gas Mark 1. After 30 minutes stir the pudding. Repeat the stirring every 30 minutes or so until the rice is soft and the milk creamy. Move the pudding to a higher shelf. Bake until a rich brown – it takes 3 hours in all.

Jam roly poly

TO SERVE FOUR

INGREDIENTS
100 g (4 oz) self-raising
  flour
50 g (2 oz) suet
pinch of salt
225 g (½ lb) raspberry,
  plum or strawberry jam

This is one of those comfortable old English recipes that have gone completely out of fashion today, but are still much loved by many, partly for childhood associations and partly because they are so good and warming.

Mix the flour, suet and salt in a bowl, and then stir in, with the blade of a knife, just enough water to bind the mixture to a light dough. Roll it out to an oblong shape. Make it fairly thin, about ½ cm (¼ in), and then spread the centre lavishly with jam leaving a 3-cm (1-in) margin all the way down each side and at one end. Roll it up loosely starting from the other end, and enclose it in a loose parcel of kitchen foil – it should have pleats in it so that it can expand with the roly poly; this helps to keep the pudding light.

Fill the bottom half of a large steamer or fish kettle with water and bring it to the boil. Put the pudding roll in the top over the boiling water, cover the pan and steam for 2 hours, topping up with more boiling water as necessary.

Serve the roly poly with custard sauce (*see opposite*).

Treacle pudding

TO SERVE SIX–EIGHT

INGREDIENTS
100 g (4 oz) softened butter
100 g (4 oz) castor sugar
2 eggs
100 g (4 oz) self-raising
  flour
pinch salt
4 tablespoons golden syrup
The sauce
4 tablespoons golden syrup
2 tablespoons water

This pudding, a rich golden mound, and perfectly delicious, would in the past have been made of suet and boiled for three hours in water – the result was a real rib-sticking pudding, heavy as lead and de-signed to stay with you during cold hours of work in the fields. Today we like our puddings lighter, but the treacle pud is far too excellent to be lost, so it has been adapted to make a dish which is as good as ever, but easily digested.

Butter a ½-litre (1-pint) pudding basin. Cream the butter and sugar in a bowl until they are soft and fluffy. Add the eggs one at a time, stirring in a tablespoon of flour with the second egg to prevent it from curdling.

Fold in the flour and salt, mixing it thoroughly but lightly. If the mixture seems dry add a teaspoon or two of milk – this rather depends on the size of the eggs.

Spoon 4 generous tablespoons of golden syrup into the buttered basin, then put the sponge mixture on top. Cover with a sheet of buttered foil and bake at 190°C, 375°F, Gas Mark 5 for 35–40 minutes.

Meanwhile heat the remaining 4 table-spoons of syrup, diluted with 2 table-spoons of water, in a small pan. When the pudding is cooked turn it out on to a hot dish and serve with the hot syrup in a small heated jug.

Spotted Dick

TO SERVE FOUR

INGREDIENTS
75 g (3 oz) self-raising flour
75 g (3 oz) chopped suet
50 g (2 oz) fresh white
  breadcrumbs
75 g (3 oz) raisins
75 g (3 oz) currants
50 g (2 oz) sugar
pinch of salt
½ teaspoon mixed spice
150 ml (¼ pint) milk

Put all the dry ingredients into a bowl and mix them together well. Now add the milk and mix to a fairly soft dough.

Put the mixture in a greased 1-litre (2-pint) pudding basin and cover with kitchen foil, making a pleat across the centre to allow the pudding to rise. Tie the foil firmly in place with string, forming a handle across the top so that you can lift the pudding easily.

Bring a large pan of water to the boil and place an inverted saucer or piece of wood in the bottom. Lower in the pudding basin and let it boil, covered, for 2 hours, filling the pan with more boiling water as the level falls.

Remove from the pan by the string handle, unwrap, turn out on to a heated dish and serve with custard sauce (*see opposite*).

Back : Rice pudding, custard sauce, treacle pudding; *front :* jam roly poly, spotted Dick

Custard sauce

INGREDIENTS
425 ml (¾ pint) milk
2 level tablespoons castor
 sugar
1 strip lemon peel and
 grating of nutmeg, or
 1 teaspoon vanilla sugar
2 eggs
2 teaspoons cornflour
 mixed with 4 tablespoons
 milk

Heat the milk and sugar in a saucepan together with the lemon rind and nutmeg or the vanilla sugar. Stir in the cornflour dissolved in milk. When the milk comes to the boil simmer for 1 minute, stirring. Remove it from the heat and allow it to cool for 30 seconds.

Pour it slowly on to the egg mixture whisking all the time. Pour it back into the saucepan through a sieve, to catch the lemon peel and bits of egg.

Place this pan in another larger pan with 2 cm (½ inch) water in the bottom, which

will act as a *bain-marie* and prevent the custard from curdling. Heat gently, stirring frequently and allow to thicken until the mixture coats the back of the spoon. This can take as long as ¾ of an hour if one is being ultra cautious and keeping the heat very low.

Serve hot in a tall jug (a wide jug will allow a skin to form on top).

King George I Christmas pudding

TO SERVE FOUR

INGREDIENTS
225 g ($\frac{1}{2}$ lb) fresh
  breadcrumbs
225 g ($\frac{1}{2}$ lb) flour
350 g ($\frac{3}{4}$ lb) suet
225 g ($\frac{1}{2}$ lb) demerara sugar
225 g ($\frac{1}{2}$ lb) ordinary
  raisins
225 g ($\frac{1}{2}$ lb) large stoneless
  Malaga raisins
100 g ($\frac{1}{4}$ lb) sultanas
225 g ($\frac{1}{2}$ lb) mixed candied
  peel, lemon, orange and
  citron
$\frac{1}{2}$ teaspoon mixed spice
$\frac{1}{2}$ teaspoon ground nutmeg
1 teaspoon salt
4 eggs (size 2)
150 ml ($\frac{1}{4}$ pint) milk
1 wineglass brandy
Hard sauce
100 g (4 oz) softened butter
50 g (2 oz) castor sugar
2–3 tablespoons brandy
$\frac{1}{4}$ teaspoon grated lemon
  rind

This royal Christmas pudding is supposed to date from the days of George I and to have been in the possession of the Royal Family since then. Originally it was for three 1.4-kg (3-lb) puddings but it has been cut down to make two 900-g (2-lb) puddings.

In a large bowl mix together all the dry ingredients. Beat the eggs thoroughly until they are frothing, add the milk and brandy and stir the liquids into the fruit, flour, suet mixture. Cover the bowl and let it stand at room temperature for 12 hours – this is important as it gives the flavours a chance to mellow.

Now share the mixture out between two buttered 1-litre (2-pint) pudding basins. Leave at least 3 cm (1 in) headroom for the puddings to expand. Cover with a double sheet of greased greaseproof paper and then a layer of foil, tie it with string, crossing the string across the top to make an improvised handle to lift the puddings.

Place an upturned saucer in the bottom of a large pan of water and bring it to the boil. Lower in the puddings – the water should come to within 3 cm (1 in) of the top; bring it back to the boil, cover the pan and simmer steadily for 5 hours. Check the water level from time to time and fill up with boiling water when necessary.

When the puddings have had 5 hours cooking they should be covered with clean covers and put in a cool place to mature for at least a month.

On Christmas Day boil them for at least 2 hours before serving with hard sauce and a traditional sprig of holly.

Welsh amber pudding

A rich and very simply made tart with a subtle orange and lemon flavour

TO SERVE SIX

INGREDIENTS
2 whole eggs and 2 yolks
75 g (3 oz) sugar
peel of ½ a lemon
2 tablespoons of fine-cut
  marmalade
100 g (4 oz) butter, melted
175 g (6 oz) shortcrust
  pastry (*page* 212)

Beat together the eggs, egg yolks and sugar, the grated lemon rind and the marmalade. Whisk in the melted butter.

Line a greased 15-cm (7-in) tart tin with shortcrust pastry and bake it, pricked and filled with crumpled kitchen foil for 12 minutes at 220°C, 425°F, Gas Mark 7. Remove the foil, pour in the egg mixture and bake for 20 minutes at 190°C, 375°F, Gas Mark 5.

Welsh amber pudding, Ipswich almond pudding

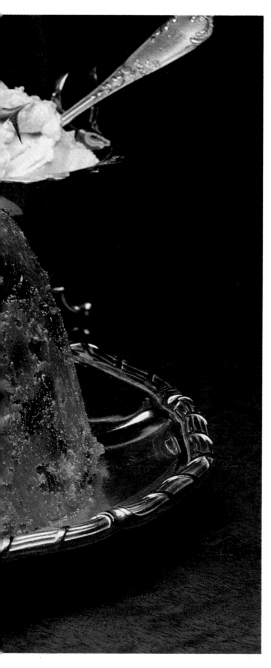

Hard sauce

Beat the butter and sugar together in the bowl, either with an electric mixer or by hand, until the mixture is light. Beat in the brandy and lemon rind.

Mound the mixture in a bowl or roll into little balls the size of walnuts and chill.

Senior Wrangler

This is a hard sauce, now usually known as brandy butter, to which has been added a few ground almonds, about a teaspoon of almonds for each tablespoon of butter.

Ipswich almond pudding

TO SERVE SIX

INGREDIENTS
150 g (5 oz) shortcrust
  pastry made with 75 g
  (3 oz) of plain flour, 25 g
  (1 oz) butter, 25 g (1 oz)
  lard, pinch salt (*page* 212)
50 g (2 oz) butter
50 g (2 oz) sugar
2 eggs
150 ml (¼ pint) milk
75 g (3 oz) ground almonds
2 tablespoons sherry
grated rind of ½ a lemon

This is rather similar to Bakewell tart, but without the jam, and the almond mixture is slightly richer.

Line a flan ring with the pastry, prick it well over the bottom with a fork.

Cream the butter and sugar together. Beat in the eggs, and milk, then add the almonds, sherry and lemon rind.

Spoon the mixture into the lined flan ring and bake in a hot oven, 220°C, 425°F, Gas Mark 7, for 10 minutes, then at 180°C, 350°F, Gas Mark 4, for a further 15–20 minutes. Serve hot with cream.

183

Plate pies

What could be simpler than lining a tin plate with pastry, filling it with fresh-picked fruits and covering the top with the leftover trimmings? Each top design was traditionally used for a different filling because all the pies for the week were cooked on one day – the baking day. The pies were made after the bread, when the oven was cooling. If you had seven identical pies in the larder you could easily get muddled, so you had wide strips for the apple pie, lattice – twisted or plain – for treacle tart, a star for a jam tart, often with jams of different flavours and colours in the different segments. A mince tart would often have a complete cover made with parallel cuts from side to side, and a rhubarb tart was completely covered but for a hole or two.

Back: Treacle tart, rhubarb plate pie, *front:* mince tart, apple plate pie

Treacle tart

TO SERVE SIX

INGREDIENTS
275 g (10 oz) shortcrust
  pastry made with 175 g
  (6 oz) flour, 75 g (3 oz)
  of butter, 25 g (1 oz) of
  lard (*page 212*)
40 g (1½ oz) fresh white
  breadcrumbs
1 egg beaten with a
  teaspoon of water
6 tablespoons golden syrup

The simplest of traditional tarts, treacle tart is sometimes made with lemon rind or lemon juice to take the edge off the sweetness of the syrup, but it is much nicer and more authentic without.

Line a 25-cm (10-in) pie plate with up to two-thirds of the shortcrust pastry. Spread the breadcrumbs over the bottom, and spoon on the golden syrup.
  Cut the remaining pastry into strips, and make a lattice top. Crimp the edge with a fork and a thumb so that you get a pattern round the edge of the plate and the lattice is firmly stuck down. Brush carefully with beaten egg. Bake at 220°C, 425°F, Gas Mark 7, for 12 minutes, then at 180°C, 350°F, Gas Mark 4, for a further 15–20 minutes. Allow to set for 5 minutes and then serve hot with cream.

Rhubarb plate pie

TO SERVE SIX

INGREDIENTS
250 g (9 oz) shortcrust pastry made with 175 g (6 oz) flour, 75 g (3 oz) butter, 25 g (1 oz) lard, pinch salt (page 212)
hazelnut-sized knob of softened butter
450 g (1 lb) young rhubarb washed, cut into pieces
50 g (2 oz) raisins
1 tablespoon flour
4 tablespoons sugar
pinch ginger
egg for glazing, beaten with $\frac{1}{2}$ a teaspoon of water
castor sugar

Divide the pastry into two. Roll out on a floured surface two discs to fit a deep tin plate about 25 cm (10 in) across. Butter the plate and lay one layer of pastry over, pressing it down lightly to exclude air. Brush the bottom with melted butter. Put in the wet rhubarb and the raisins, piling them up.

Mix the flour, sugar and ginger together in a cup and sprinkle over the top of the rhubarb. Wet the edges of the pastry. With a frilly-edged biscuit or pastry cutter, cut a hole in the centre of the second disc of pastry. Fold it over the rolling pin and place it on top of the pie with the hole in the centre. Trim the edges and press the two layers together with a fork using a criss-cross movement.

Brush the top of the pie with the beaten egg. Bake at 220°C, 425°F, Gas Mark 7, for 15 minutes to set the pastry, then at 180°C, 350°F, Gas Mark 4, for 20 minutes to cook the rhubarb. Sprinkle with castor sugar, and serve hot or cold with cream or custard sauce (see page 181).

Apple plate pie

TO SERVE SIX

INGREDIENTS
675 g (1½ lb) cooking apples such as Bramleys
75 g (3 oz) white sugar
25 g (1 oz) butter
good pinch ground cinnamon
good pinch ground cloves
1 strip lemon peel
1 tablespoon water
250 g (9 oz) shortcrust pastry made with 175 g (6 oz) flour, 75 g (3 oz) butter, 25 g (1 oz) lard, pinch salt (see page 212)
hazelnut-sized lump of softened butter
milk and granulated sugar for glazing

A piece of quince, if you can obtain this hard winter fruit, bright yellow and sweetly scented, gives a lovely old-fashioned flavour to apple pie; but if you can't don't worry. The aroma of the cinnamon and cloves alone will give the apples an extra fillip.

Peel the apples (and quince if you have one), quarter and core them. Place the quarters in a small casserole with the sugar, butter, spices, lemon peel, and a tablespoon of water (and the piece of quince if you have it). Cover the casserole, bring it to the boil and then let it simmer very gently either on top or in the oven for 30 minutes until the apples are like amber, and fairly dry. Let them cool.

Roll out the pastry on a floured board and use it to line a buttered pie plate or deep enamel plate about 25 cm (10 in) across. Brush the bottom with softened butter; this helps to prevent it from going too soggy, although it is bound to be softer than the uppercrust. Fill the plate with the apple purée which should be rather thick.

Roll all the trimmings and remaining pastry into a large piece and cut strips about 3 cm (1 in) wide. Lay them 3 cm (1 in) apart across the top of the tart. Now bring up the overhang all round the edge of the tart to cover the ends of the strips and crimp the edges, by pinching them with your left forefinger and thumb and pressing the middle of the pinch at the same time with your right forefinger.

Bake 220°C, 425°F, Gas Mark 7, for 15 minutes and then at 180°C, 350°F, Gas Mark 4, for a further 20 minutes. Brush with a mixture of milk and undissolved granulated sugar about 10 minutes before the end of the cooking to give a nice finish to the pastry. Serve hot or cold with cream.

Mince tart

TO SERVE SIX

INGREDIENTS
275 g (10 oz) shortcrust pastry made with 175 g (6 oz) flour, 75 g (3 oz) butter, 25 g (1 oz) lard, pinch salt (page 212)
hazelnut-sized knob of softened butter
400 g (14 oz) jar mincemeat (with a little brandy added) or 350 g (¾ lb) home-made mincemeat (page 224)
icing sugar

Divide the pastry into two and on a floured surface roll out two discs to fit a pie-plate or deep tin plate 22 cm (9 in) across. Butter the plate and lay one layer of pastry over, pressing it lightly to exclude air. Brush over the bottom with melted butter. Fill the plate with the mincemeat. Brush the edges with water and cut off overlap.

Fold the second disc in half and cut four parallel 8 cm (3 in) cuts across the fold. Open the disc out and place it, with the help of the rolling pin, centrally over the pie plate.

Press the edges together all the way round with a fork. Bake at 220°C, 425°F, Gas Mark 7, for 15 minutes, then at 180°C, 350°F, Gas Mark 4, for a further 20 minutes. Dust with icing sugar before serving – this is done by sprinkling it on through a wire sieve while the pie is still extremely hot.

Bread and butter pudding

TO SERVE FOUR

INGREDIENTS
5 slices bread and butter
   with crusts removed
50 g (2 oz) raisins
grated rind of $\frac{1}{2}$ a lemon
2 eggs
575 ml (1 pint) milk
25 g (1 oz) sugar
butter for the pie dish
a little granulated sugar

This recipe was devised to use up leftover bread and butter, which appeared daily on every tea table in the land, in Victorian times. This pudding is, however, so good that it is even worth cutting the bread and butter specially for it.

Butter a $\frac{1}{2}$-litre (1-pint) pie dish, and put in a layer of pieces of bread and butter cut in halves. Sprinkle with raisins and lemon peel. Fill the dish with more layers, ending with a layer of bread and butter.
   Beat the eggs in a bowl. Heat the milk with the sugar until it just reaches boiling point. Then let it cool a little. Pour it over the eggs, whisking to combine the two. Pour the mixture over the bread and butter and let it soak in for $\frac{1}{4}$ hour.
   Sprinkle a little granulated sugar over the top of the pudding and bake at 160°C, 325°F, Gas Mark 3, for $\frac{3}{4}$ hour, until the top is puffed and golden.

Brown Betty

TO SERVE FOUR–SIX

INGREDIENTS
175 g (6 oz) fresh
   breadcrumbs, mixed
   brown and white
75 g (3 oz) butter, melted
4 large cooking apples
   675 g (1$\frac{1}{2}$ lb)
100 g (4 oz) brown sugar
1 teaspoon ground
   cinnamon
grated rind and juice of
   $\frac{1}{2}$ a lemon
cream to serve with it

Put the breadcrumbs into a bowl and pour on the melted butter, mixing it in lightly with a knife.
   Peel and core the apples and slice them thinly. Mix them with the sugar and cinnamon, lemon peel and juice.
   Butter a 1-litre (2-pint) pudding basin and put in a thin layer of crumbs, then a layer of apples, then more crumbs, more apples and lastly a layer of crumbs. Cover with a sheet of foil.
   Bake at 180°C, 350°F, Gas Mark 4, for 20 minutes, remove the foil and bake a further 30 minutes, or until the top has browned nicely and the apples are tender. Serve hot with cream. The apples should have started to caramelize and become transparent and amber coloured.

Clockwise: Brown Betty,
bread and butter pudding,
blackberry cobbler

186

Apple crumble

TO SERVE SIX

INGREDIENTS
675 g (1½ lb) apples
1–2 tablespoons water
175 g (6 oz) soft light
  brown sugar or white
  sugar
100 g (4 oz) flour
1 teaspoon cinnamon
pinch salt
100 g (4 oz) butter
Whip sauce
425 ml (¾ pint) milk
2 level tablespoons castor
  sugar
1 strip lemon peel and
  grating of nutmeg or
1 teaspoon vanilla sugar
2 eggs, separated
1 level teaspoon cornflour
  mixed with 2 tablespoons
  cold milk

Peel, quarter and core the apples, slice them up and put them into a buttered 1-litre (2-pint) baking dish with 1–2 tablespoons of water and 25 g (1 oz) of the sugar.

Mix the remaining sugar with the flour, cinnamon, and salt and work in the butter, breaking it up with the fingers until it is like coarse crumbs. Sprinkle the mixture over the top of the apples and bake at 180°C, 350°F, Gas Mark 4, for 30 minutes, until the apples are soft and the top crisp and brown.

Whip sauce

Whip sauce, really a good home-made custard lightened to a foam with beaten egg white, is delicious with all tarts and pies, apple crumble and any fruit pudding.

Heat the milk and sugar in a saucepan together with the lemon rind and nutmeg or the vanilla sugar. Meanwhile, beat the egg yolks in a large bowl and whisk the whites to stiff peaks. As the milk comes to the boil, remove it from the heat and, vigorously stirring, add the cornflour. Return the pan to the heat and, still stirring, boil it for 2 minutes until the cornflour has done its work for thickening. Now allow your sauce to cool for 3 minutes and slowly pour it over the yolks, beating all the time. Return this mixture to the pan through a sieve, to catch the lemon if you have used it and any bits of egg. Stir over gentle heat for 2 minutes, then whip the egg whites into the custard. Whisk until it is light and frothy and serve straight away.

Blackberry cobbler

TO SERVE SIX

INGREDIENTS
900 g (2 lb) blackberries
  (plums or damsons will
  do)
100 g (4 oz) sugar
1 tablespoon flour
225 g (½ lb) self-raising
  flour
75 g (3 oz) granulated
  sugar
50 g (2 oz) lard
1 egg
milk to mix

A country dish with a short scone topping over blackberries cooked in their own juice.

First put the fruit, washed and sorted to remove all that are mouldy or unripe, in a large pie dish with the sugar mixed with a tablespoon of flour. Cover with foil and bake in a very slow oven until the juice runs and the fruit is tender. Then take it out of the oven and turn up the heat to 220°C, 425°F, Gas Mark 7.

Meanwhile make the scone topping. Sieve together the self-raising flour and the sugar and rub in the fat. Add the beaten egg and a little milk and mix to a light

dough. Roll out into an oval to fit the pie dish, then cut into squares about 4 cm (1½ in) across. Place these on top of the fruit, put the whole dish in the oven and bake for 10 minutes. Sprinkle the top with granulated sugar and bake for a further 5 minutes at 190°C, 375°F, Gas Mark 5. The scones mound up, looking very like cobblestones, which may be the origin of the name. It reheats well.

Dorset cream toast

A seventeenth-century regional recipe

INGREDIENTS

150 ml ($\frac{1}{4}$ pint) single
  cream
1 egg yolk
1 teaspoon sugar
grated rind of $\frac{1}{2}$ a lemon
6 slices French bread
  $\frac{1}{2}$ cm ($\frac{1}{4}$ in) thick
2 eggs
15 g ($\frac{1}{2}$ oz) butter and
  2 tablespoons sunflower
  oil for frying
castor sugar
1 orange cut in quarters, to
  squeeze on the 'toasts'

This is a very rich version of eggy-bread; it is similar to 'Poor Knights of Windsor' and was also known as Panperdy after the French *pain perdu* – lost bread.

Beat together the single cream and egg yolk with a teaspoon of sugar and grated lemon rind. Pour this mixture over the French bread and let it soak in.

Beat the eggs lightly on a plate or in a soup bowl. Dip the slices of bread into the beaten egg and fry them on each side, until golden brown, in foaming butter and oil.

Serve with castor sugar and quarters of orange, like pancakes.

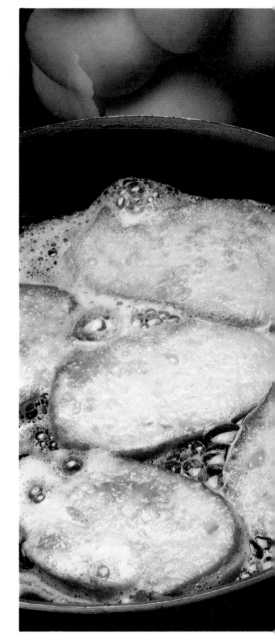

Apple fritters

INGREDIENTS

4 large apples
2 teaspoons icing sugar
100 g (4 oz) flour
2 eggs
275 ml ($\frac{1}{2}$ pint) light ale
25 g (1 oz) sugar
generous grating nutmeg
25 g (1 oz) butter
1 tablespoon oil
granulated sugar to serve
  with the fritters

The fritters should be eaten very hot indeed, so only start the frying when all the company is ready and waiting.

Core the apples with an apple corer, peel them and cut them into slices about $\frac{1}{2}$ cm ($\frac{1}{4}$ in) thick. Dust lightly with icing sugar.

Put the flour into a large bowl and make a well in the centre. Break in the eggs and stir them round, gradually adding the ale and drawing in the flour from the sides as you go.

Start beating with a wooden spoon and add enough ale to make a smooth batter the consistency of cream. Add the sugar and nutmeg and half the butter, melted, and beat well. Allow to stand for 3–4 minutes.

Heat the remaining butter and oil in a large frying-pan. Dip the apples into the batter and fry them on both sides until golden brown. Drain quickly and serve straight away, very hot, sprinkled with granulated sugar.

Pancakes

TO SERVE SIX

INGREDIENTS

150 g (5 oz) flour
pinch salt
1 egg (size 2)
250 ml ($\frac{1}{2}$ pint) milk and
  water mixed
25 g (1 oz) melted butter
1 teaspoon oil
hazelnut-sized knob of
  butter

Put the flour and salt in a large bowl and make a well in the centre. Break in the egg and start stirring it round with a wooden spoon, gradually incorporating the flour. As the mixture becomes thick add the milk and water gradually, beating all the time. When you have a smooth batter add the melted butter and beat thoroughly.

Allow the batter to stand for 30 minutes then beat again.

To make the pancakes heat a reliable small frying pan, one that you know will not stick. When it is hot put in a little oil and a hazelnut of butter, and swill it round to cover the bottom of the pan.

Now dip into the batter with a ladle and pour in just enough to cover the bottom of the pan. Tip the pan to spread the batter

evenly. Let it cook until all the batter is just set – it should be brown underneath, if it isn't the heat is too low. (If it is black the heat is too high.) Now slide a spatula under the middle and turn it. Cook the underside briefly and transfer it to a hot plate. Serve the pancakes as you cook them, with slices of lemon and castor sugar, or make a mound of them and keep them hot to serve all at once. If you want to keep them they can be allowed to cool, rolled up together and wrapped in foil. They will then keep for a day or two in the refrigerator, and can be filled with a stuffing and heated under the grill or in the oven.

Dorset cream toast, apple fritters, pancakes

Mrs Beeton's apple snow

A pretty supper dish

TO SERVE FOUR

INGREDIENTS
5 green cooking apples –
  Bramleys or Newton
  Wonder
4 tablespoons water
rind of 1 lemon
whites of 4–5 eggs
100 g (4 oz) castor sugar

This is a very good way of using up egg-whites after making mayonnaise or custard.

Peel, core and quarter the apples and place them in a saucepan with about 4 tablespoons of water and the lemon rind. Cover and cook them gently until they are tender and fluffy, then allow them to cool and remove the lemon rinds. Whisk them until they are light. Beat the egg whites until they are quite stiff.

Stir the apples into the meringue, then add the sugar gradually until it is a firm froth. Heap it in a glass dish and serve with cream or home-made custard sauce (*see page* 181).

This dish should be eaten at the very next meal and not kept standing about.

Moonshine

A light fresh lemon jelly

TO SERVE FOUR

INGREDIENTS
575 ml (1 pint) water
150 g (5 oz) sugar
rind and juice of 2 lemons
15 g ($\frac{1}{2}$ oz) or 1 packet
  gelatine

Put the sugar and the finely peeled rind of the lemons into a saucepan with the water. Bring it to a simmer, turn down the heat a little and let the lemon rinds infuse for 15 minutes without boiling. Let it cool, strain through a fine-meshed sieve, strain in the lemon juice.

Put the gelatine in a cup with 3 tablespoons of hot water and put it in a shallow pan of hot water over a low heat. Stir until the gelatine dissolves, then stir it into the cold lemon syrup.

Let it cool again and when just beginning to set, whisk the mixture until it looks like snow.

Turn it into a wet mould and chill thoroughly. It can be turned out and served with whipped cream.

Stone cream

TO SERVE SIX

INGREDIENTS
2 tablespoons apricot jam
rind and juice of 1 lemon
1 sherry glass of cream
  sherry
425 ($\frac{3}{4}$ pint) double cream
50 g (2 oz) castor sugar
15 g ($\frac{1}{2}$ oz) or 1 packet
  gelatine
425 ml ($\frac{3}{4}$ pint) creamy
  milk

Spread the bottom of a wide bowl with the apricot jam. Grate the lemon rind over the jam, and sprinkle it with the lemon juice and sherry.

Heat the cream in a small pan, when it reaches boiling point stir in the sugar and allow to cool.

Put the gelatine in a cup with 3 tablespoons of hot water, and stand it in a shallow pan of water over a moderate heat, stirring until completely dissolved.

Heat the milk, stir in the gelatine and when it is completely mixed in, add the cream and stir them well together. Allow to cool, then pour the whole mixture into a large jug. Whisk it lightly with a fork and then pour it from as high as possible above the dish, on to the jam, lemon and sherry mixture. Some cooks used to stand on a chair to perform this – the point of the exercise is to form as high a froth as possible on the top of the pudding. This is now left to stand overnight, when it will set to a foam. Serve it straight from the bowl.

Edinburgh fog

TO SERVE SIX

INGREDIENTS
275 ml ($\frac{1}{2}$ pint) cream
1 tablespoon castor sugar
1 teaspoon vanilla sugar
  (castor sugar in which
  your vanilla pod is
  stored)
50 g (2 oz) chopped
  blanched almonds
50 g (2 oz) tiny ratafias
  which are sold by the box
sherry for sprinkling

This extremely rich and delicious pudding should be served with fresh raspberries or some other fresh fruit.

Beat the cream to a soft light froth, flavour it with sugar and vanilla sugar and stir in the chopped blanched almonds. Spread out the ratafias, sprinkle them with the sherry and then stir them very briefly into the cream. Serve the 'fog' in a bowl, with a larger bowl of raspberries beside it.

Back: Edinburgh fog, *centre:* moonshine, stone cream, *front:* white bonnet, spring cream

White bonnets

TO SERVE FOUR

INGREDIENTS
450 g (1 lb) damsons or
  purple plums
150 ml ($\frac{1}{4}$ pint) red wine
50 g (2 oz) brown sugar
$\frac{1}{2}$ vanilla pod
150 ml ($\frac{1}{4}$ pint) whipping
  cream

This is fruit cooked in wine and served in glasses with whipped cream 'bonnets' on the top.

Stone the fruit. Crack half a dozen of the stones and put the kernels into a pan with the red wine, sugar and vanilla pod. Cook gently for 20 minutes, then put in the stoned fruit and poach it gently until it is just tender, about 15 minutes.

Let it cool, and meanwhile whip the cream to a soft snow. Spoon the fruit into glasses and pile a snowy bonnet of whipped cream on top.

Trinity cream

Also known as Burnt cream

TO SERVE SIX

INGREDIENTS
575 ml (1 pint) double
  cream
5 cm (2 in) piece split
  vanilla pod or 2 drops
  vanilla essence
4 egg yolks
castor sugar

This is a recipe supposedly of Scottish origin; it must have been brought over from France by Mary Queen of Scots and her entourage: it is similar to the delicious French *crème brulée* (hence burnt cream). This version, however, comes from Trinity College, Cambridge, and was a great favourite during May Week.

Bring the cream to the boil with the vanilla pod or vanilla flavouring.

Beat the egg yolks in a bowl. Take the cream off the heat and let it cool to just below boiling point before pouring it on to the yolks in a steady stream, whisking all the time.

Pour this custard into a nice flattish earthenware dish and bake in the oven for ½ hour at 160°C, 325°F, Gas Mark 3 for 25 minutes. Remove the dish, let it get cold. Chill it in refrigerator for an hour or two so that it becomes rather thick and solid.

Just before serving, preheat the grill. Sprinkle a fine layer of castor sugar over the top of the custard. Place the dish under the red hot grill and as close to it as possible, and let the sugar melt and caramelize to a deep brown and golden glaze, like tortoiseshell laid over the cream. As it cools the caramel will quickly set to a delicious sweet crust over the plain unsweetened custard. This dish is very rich.

Spring cream

A light mixture of rhubarb, spices and cream

TO SERVE SIX

INGREDIENTS
900 g (2 lb) rhubarb
rind of ½ a lemon
a little powdered ginger
1 stick of cinnamon
75 g (3 oz) soft brown
  sugar
275 ml (½ pint) double
  cream

Wash the rhubarb and cut into pieces. Put it in a saucepan with the lemon peel, finely grated, the ginger, cinnamon and sugar. Cook it over a gentle heat, stirring until it softens and then let it simmer on until enough liquid has evaporated to leave rhubarb like a soft pinky-green purée or jam. It can be sieved at this point, or it can be used without sieving.

Allow to cool, then stir in the very lightly whisked cream and serve, chilled, in a deep dish. This is a very welcome pudding in early spring as it brings a foretaste of the fruits of summer.

Fine almond flummery

TO SERVE SIX

INGREDIENTS
275 ml ($\frac{1}{2}$ pint) single
 cream
275 ml ($\frac{1}{2}$ pint) creamy
 milk
50 g (2 oz) ground almonds
50 g (2 oz) chopped
 almonds
50 g (2 oz) castor sugar
15 g ($\frac{1}{2}$ oz) or 1 packet
 gelatine
5 drops almond essence

Flummery, a lovely pale slippery pudding related to syllabub and custard, is a delicious pure white jelly, which used to be made with potato flour, rice flour or sago mixed and cooked long and slowly with the fruit juice, milk or cream. A more delicate version is made with ground almonds. Serve it with a very choice selection of small fruits, such as figs, greengages, raspberries, strawberries and blackberries.

Put all the ingredients except the gelatine into a saucepan and stir over a moderate heat until the cream just comes to the boil and all the sugar has dissolved. Let it cool.

Put the gelatine with 3 tablespoons of hot water into a cup and stand it in a pan of water over a moderate heat. Stir until the gelatine has dissolved. Pour the dissolved gelatine into the almond mixture and blend it in well.

Pour the mixture into a jelly mould; this is your chance to use an elaborate mould as the jelly sets well and is easy to turn out.

Put it in the refrigerator overnight to set, covered with a sheet of foil so that it does not absorb flavours from other foods. To turn it out dip it briefly into a basin of hot water. If kept for 2–3 days this pudding gets an interesting sharpness to the flavour.

Gooseberry fool

TO SERVE SIX

INGREDIENTS
450 g (1 lb) gooseberries
2 tablespoons water
175–225 g (6–8 oz) castor
 sugar according to how
 sour the goosberries are
275 ml ($\frac{1}{2}$ pint) double
 cream

The real old-fashioned gooseberry fool was not made with custard but with cream or milk and sugar, and was considered 'a very suitable preparation for children' partly because sufficient for five or six children cost 6d to make. Less cheap now, alas, but it is still a favourite pudding.

Top and tail the gooseberries and put them in a small thick saucepan with 2 tablespoons of water and two tablespoons sugar. Cover with a lid and stand it in a roasting tin of water. Place it over a low heat and let it stew very gently for $\frac{3}{4}$ hour until the gooseberries are soft. Beat them to pulp with a wooden spoon, sweeten them thoroughly and sieve the pulp through the coarse blade of a mouli-légumes and allow it to cool. It should be fairly stiff and a pretty, soft green.

Whisk the cream to a firm snow, fold in the fruit pulp and chill before serving.

Chranacan and raspberries

TO SERVE SIX

INGREDIENTS
50 g (2 oz) coarse oatmeal
425 ml ($\frac{3}{4}$ pint) cream
2 teaspoons Scotch whisky
1 tablespoon vanilla sugar
450 g (1 lb) raspberries

A delicious Scottish cream for eating with the prize local raspberries for which Ayrshire is so famous; it is also very good and delicate with blackberries or loganberries.

Spread the oatmeal in a baking tray and toast it in a moderate oven until the edges are just starting to get a brownish tinge. Let it cool.

Beat the cream to a soft light froth and stir in the whisky, cooled toasted oatmeal and sugar.

Serve chilled with a few spoonfuls of raspberries.

Chranacan and raspberries, marbled cream

Marbled cream

TO SERVE FOUR

INGREDIENTS
450 g (1 lb) raspberries
(or strawberries); these
can be slightly over-ripe
and mushy
175 g (6 oz) of castor sugar
275 ml ($\frac{1}{2}$ pint) double
cream

This delicate pink pudding can be made with raspberries or strawberries.

If you are using raspberries, put half of them into a saucepan, keeping several of the best and most beautiful ones on one side for decoration.

Add half the sugar to the pan and moisten with a tablespoon of water. Bring slowly to the boil and then simmer until the raspberries start to yield their juice.

Push the softened raspberries, pulp and juice through a sieve, with a wooden spoon, or use the finest blade of the mouli-légumes.

Whisk the cream until it is soft and thick, gradually adding the remaining sugar. Mash all but the reserved raspberries to a pulp and mix very roughly into the cream. Now add the cooked raspberry pulp, stirring just enough to give a marbled effect.

Decorate the top with the few remaining raspberries and chill in the refrigerator for about 3 hours before serving.

If you use strawberries, the process is identical, except that no cooking is involved. Instead, chop up the berries, and sprinkle with sugar. They will produce a quantity of lovely pink syrup: it will take them about an hour, and you could stir them about a bit to help the process along. After that, proceed as above, whipping the cream, sweetening it and adding the strawberries, crushed to a pulp, and their juices.

Carse of Gowrie fruit salad

TO SERVE FOUR

INGREDIENTS
The syrup
225 g ($\frac{1}{2}$ lb) sugar
275 ml ($\frac{1}{2}$ pint) water
1 wineglass red wine
juice of 1 lemon
dash of sherry
The fruit
2 fresh peaches
2 fresh apricots
1 orange
2 bananas
100 g ($\frac{1}{4}$ lb) raspberries
100 g ($\frac{1}{4}$ lb) redcurrants
100 g ($\frac{1}{4}$ lb) cherries

This is a very superior fruit salad from Scotland, to be made at the height of summer with all the most delicate of bush and tree fruits, together with a few old faithfuls, such as bananas.

Put the sugar, water and red wine in a small saucepan, bring to the boil and boil for 5 minutes. Allow to cool, then pour this syrup into a nice bowl, and stir in the lemon juice and sherry.

Dip peaches and apricots very briefly into boiling water and then skin them carefully. Slice them and put them immediately into the syrup.

Pare the skin and pith from the orange with a sharp knife and cut it into slices, catching the juice in a plate. Put orange slices and juice into the salad. Slice the bananas and add them too.

Lastly put in the raspberries, redcurrants stripped of their stalks, and cherries, halved and stoned. Spoon some of the liquid over the fruit and chill thoroughly before serving with or without whipped cream.

Carse of Gowrie fruit salad, summer pudding

194

Brown bread icecream

TO SERVE SIX

INGREDIENTS
2 egg yolks
75 g (3 oz) sugar
150 ml (¼ pint) single
  cream
275 ml (½ pint) double
  cream
2 teaspoons rum or brandy
100 g (4 oz) fresh brown
  breadcrumbs

This icecream, an Edwardian country weekend treat, has an elusive flavour which always seems to fascinate people. Make it in the freezer if you have one, otherwise in the ice-making compartment of the refrigerator. Eat within a day or two or the bread will become soggy.

Beat the egg yolks and sugar in a bowl until light and frothy. Bring the single cream to simmering point, remove it from the heat, let it cool for half a minute, then pour it on to the egg yolks, beating all the time. Put the bowl over a saucepan of simmering water and stir until the mixture starts to thicken. Allow to cool and thicken further.

Whip the double cream until it is soft and light and flavour it with the rum or brandy. Now fold in the cooled custard with a spatula and lastly the breadcrumbs.

Turn the mixture into a nice-looking container – a soufflé dish would be ideal – and freeze. No need to stir. Do not serve this rock hard, but just frozen, otherwise the breadcrumbs may seem too granular.

Summer pudding

TO SERVE FOUR

INGREDIENTS
450 g (1 lb) raspberries
225 g (½ lb) sugar
450 g (1 lb) blackcurrants
75 g (3 oz) sugar
175 g (6 oz) castor sugar
8 slices white bread,
  crusts removed

Make this a day ahead so that it has time to steep in its own juices.

Cook the raspberries briefly with the sugar until the juice runs out.

Cook the blackcurrants separately with 75 g (3 oz) of sugar and a tablespoon of water. Do not boil too fast, allow them to give up their juices slowly, or they will become a mush.

Take a 1-litre (2-pint) pudding basin and line it with slices of bread, cutting them to shape so that they all fit together

neatly. Fill the bread mould first with blackcurrants and then with raspberries. Cover the top completely with more trimmed slices of bread so that the fruit is completely enclosed.

Put a plate on top of the pudding and weight it down with a full bottle of something. Allow to stand overnight in a cool place.

Remove the weight and turn out the pudding carefully, the bread should be a uniform deep rosy red, and the fruit inside like delicious soft cheese.

Floating islands

TO SERVE FOUR

INGREDIENTS
Custard
575 ml (1 pint) milk
6 egg yolks
75 g (3 oz) castor sugar
1 tablespoon vanilla sugar
 or 3 drops vanilla essence
3 tablespoons single cream
Islands
6 egg whites
pinch salt
75 g (3 oz) castor sugar
Caramel
50 g (2 oz) sugar
2 tablespoons water

This sounds extravagant but in fact it contains very little more than the eggs, a little sugar and a few tablespoons of cream.

To make the custard
Bring the milk to the boil, then set the pan on one side.

Place the egg yolks in a bowl with the sugar and vanilla sugar or vanilla essence. Beat with an electric beater or wire whisk until thick and creamy. Stir the yolk mixture into the now considerably cooled

milk. Set the pan in a larger pan of water over a gentle heat and stir from time to time until the mixture coats the spoon – it can take 20–25 minutes. As soon as the custard has reached a velvety texture, stir in the cold cream to prevent it cooking any further – if it gets too hot it will curdle. Pour the custard into a wide deep dish.

To make the islands
Bring a large pan of water to a very slow simmer. Beat the egg whites to a firm snow with the pinch of salt.

Add three-quarters of the sugar and beat again until you have a firm fine smooth meringue – this should only take about 30 seconds with an electric beater. Fold in the remaining sugar lightly with a metal spoon (this is done by cutting the meringue and carefully turning it over – stirring the sugar in would knock out too much of the air).

Drop tablespoons of the mixture, smoothed to a round shape with your finger, into the hot water. Let the rounds poach for 2 minutes, then turn them and let them poach for a further 1½–2 minutes.

Lift them carefully from the pan, drain and cool them on absorbent kitchen paper, then place them on the custard.

They can be served as they are, or as a nice but rather French touch, laced with caramel made by boiling together, in a small saucepan, the sugar with the 2 tablespoons of water, until they become a deep golden brown. Let this caramel cool until it is thick and syrupy then drip it over the islands with a fork and trail backwards and forwards so that a web of golden threads covers the dish. This must be done almost at the last minute or it will dissolve.

Tipsy cake

TO SERVE SIX

INGREDIENTS
1 whole home-made sponge-
 cake with jam filling
2 wine-glasses sweet white
 wine, such as muscatel or
 sauterne
50 g (2 oz) blanched almonds
425 ml (¾ pint) rich custard
 (*see above*)
2 drops almond essence
½ small wine-glass brandy

This cake, called tipsy because it would make even the most adamant of teetotalers more than a little merry, without their even noticing it, is also known as Hedgehog.

Pierce the cake through in several places from top to bottom with a skewer, this helps the liquids to penetrate. Put the cake into a nice serving dish. Now pour on the wine, a tablespoon at a time, letting it soak in before adding the next spoonful.

Cut the blanched almonds into lengthwise slivers and stick them into the top of the cake so that it bristles like a hedgehog.

Make the custard, flavour it with 2 drops of almond essence and let it cool.

Just before serving pour the brandy over the cake, let it soak in completely, then spoon on the custard. You can decorate the top with whipped cream if you like.

Opposite : Sugarfrosted rose petals,
tipsy cake, chocolate mousse

196

Chocolate mousse

TO SERVE SIX

INGREDIENTS
3 egg yolks
75 g (3 oz) cooking
    chocolate
50 g (2 oz) sugar
425 ml (¾ pint) double
    cream

This is not strictly an English word but it exactly describes this rich and luscious Victorian pudding.

Beat the egg yolks thoroughly and put them into the top of a double boiler with the grated chocolate, sugar and 150 ml (¼ pint) of the cream. Stir them over a pan of gently simmering water until the mixture thickens, but take care not to overheat it or it will curdle – the addition of a tablespoon of cold milk will prevent this if it looks as if this is about to happen. Allow to cool and chill in the refrigerator until starting to thicken, then whisk with an electric beater until foamy and light.

Whip the remaining cream fairly stiffly and fold it into the chocolate mixture. Turn the mixture into a soufflé dish and chill.

Sugarfrosted rose petals

INGREDIENTS
1 egg white
castor sugar
pink rose petals

Frosted flowers were used a very great deal in Victorian times to decorate their elaborate desserts. Violets, lilac flowers, rose petals and mimosa balls were popular and mint leaves were also used. They do look a very great deal prettier than most bought decorations, their colours are so delicate and subtle.

Lightly beat the egg white. Use a pastry brush to paint the petals with a thin layer of egg white. While they are still wet dust them on both sides with castor sugar and leave them to dry in a warm place, or in a very low oven with the door ajar. Sugar-frosted petals can be stored in an airtight jar for a week or two.

198

Bread
and baking

Tea is a meal not to be missed. It comes during that dull part of the afternoon, half-way between lunch and supper, and brings zest to what can be a rather dispiriting time of day.

We all, in spite of the fact that it is often in reality no more than a cup of tea, have our own ideas about the perfect tea, whether it is hot buttered toast and fruit cake by the fire or cucumber sandwiches and Devonshire splits, with cream and jam, on the lawn.

And to prove that tea to the British is a serious institution, we have the most enormous and marvellous repertoire in the world of yeast-based tea breads and buns, of splits and scones, shortbreads from Scotland and fairings from Cornwall, with a specially good collection of recipes from bakers in Yorkshire, where buns and biscuits are made in quantity for the children's tea.

Home-made cakes, too, still figure largely in most households – many of the recipes we use now, such as our sponge cake, have developed from wonderful old 'receipts' calling for 18 eggs which had to be beaten for up to an hour by hand to lighten them, others like parkin are descended from sturdy concoctions designed to fill an empty stomach throughout the coldest winter's night, while tartlets such as Maids of honour were said to have been invented to tempt Queen Elizabeth I.

In our grandmother's day, special sets of china were kept for sociable, as opposed to family teas, and a good deal of attention was bestowed on these occasions, which were established so that a few friends, not too many, could talk comfortably and quietly: it was at these meetings, so useful before the invention of the telephone, that letters were shared and gossip exchanged.

Although the chilly coffee morning now prevails, and proper sit-down teas are more or less confined to Saturdays and Sundays, teatime is still a good moment for cosy conversations. And what is so cheering is that while ten years ago you might have been given chocolate biscuits for tea, today you are far more likely to find home-made shortbread or fruit cake instead.

The recent move towards home baking and simple traditional tastes has led, too, to a new enthusiasm for breadmaking. Taking pleasure in making bread must be very basic to human nature. Almost everybody enjoys it and if they can only turn out a good loaf, they seem to find it as good a way of relaxing as, for instance, reading a Sunday paper – or really rather better because at the end you can slice it up and eat it.

An early nineteenth-century bakery

200

Flour for breadmaking

To make white bread choose strong white flour. This can be bought either bleached or unbleached; unbleached contains some of the yellow pigment of the wheat germ, and has a warmer colour and slightly nuttier flavour than bleached flour. If you have only got ordinary plain white flour this can be used for breadmaking, but will make a rather crumbly, soft loaf.

To make brown bread or wheatmeal bread use 81% or wheatmeal flour. This contains most of the wholewheat but has had some bran sieved out. It makes a nutty loaf, with a good amount of rise to it.

To make wholemeal bread, choose 100% flour – wholemeal flour or wholewheat flour. This contains the whole grains and includes all the bran; it sounds dull but not only is it very good for you, it also gives the bread a lovely wholesome wheat flavour as well. 100% wholemeal flour can be finely ground or very coarse, according to the mill at which it was made. Wholemeal flour produces a somewhat heavier loaf with less rise to it than 81% flour, but it keeps very well, and is good even when stale if sliced very thinly.

You can of course blend your own flour, half 81%, half wholemeal gives a very splendid loaf with lots of character.

Yeast for breadmaking

Baker's yeast, not the same as wine-maker's or brewer's yeast, can be bought fresh or dried. Fresh yeast, which is the favourite with people who regularly make their own bread, can be stored for two to three weeks in a plastic container in the refrigerator or for several months in the freezer. Dried yeast granules can be kept several months. Where 25 g (1 oz) of fresh yeast is required, only about 15 g ($\frac{1}{2}$ oz) of dried yeast is necessary.

White bread

TO MAKE THREE LOAVES
AND SIX ROLLS

INGREDIENTS
1.4 kg (3 lb) strong white bread flour
40 g ($1\frac{1}{2}$ oz) fresh yeast or 25 g (1 oz) dried yeast
1 heaped tablespoon castor sugar
1 heaped tablespoon salt
25 g (1 oz) melted butter
850 ml ($1\frac{1}{2}$ pints) warm water
flour for dusting

Put the flour in a large bowl and warm it gently either on a warm grill or in a very low oven. Mix the yeast with about 150 ml ($\frac{1}{4}$ pint) of warm water, and stir in a teaspoon of sugar. Leave in a warm place to froth up. Mix remaining sugar, salt and melted butter into the rest of the water.

When the yeast is frothy pour it into the middle of the slightly warm flour. Add the remaining liquid, which should be just above hand-hot, and mix well to a soft dough. Let it rest for a few minutes to firm up a little, then knead the dough until it is fine and smooth, adding a little more flour if necessary, to prevent the dough from sticking to your hands or the board.

Put the dough back in the bowl in a well-rounded ball, and cover with a damp cloth and a piece of polythene. Leave to rise in a warm spot, until doubled in size, which will take about an hour although this rather depends on how warm the kitchen is.

Grease three 450-g (1-lb) tins. Now take out the dough, squash it down and knead again. Cut the dough into four pieces (3 large and one small), and use the three large pieces to make three sausage-shaped rolls. Do this by flattening each piece with the knuckles and then rolling it up. Tuck the ends under, and drop each into a tin, pushing it down round the edges so it forms a nice little dome. Cover loosely with the cloth and polythene and leave to prove (rise a second time), for about 30–40 minutes. With the remaining piece of dough make six rolls. Cut it into six equal pieces and knead each little piece, forming it into a nice round. Put on a greased and floured baking sheet. Leave to prove for 15 minutes, until puffy and risen.

Heat the oven to 220°C, 450°F, Gas Mark 7. First cook the rolls – give them 15–20 minutes, until they brown and sound hollow when tapped underneath.

Take them out and let them cool on a rack. Next put in the loaves, which should almost have filled the tins by now. Bake at 220°C, 425°F, Gas Mark 7 for 45 minutes, take them out of their tins and give them 5 minutes more baking until they sound hollow when tapped underneath.

A very nice finish can be given to white loaves by dusting the tops lavishly with flour before putting them in the oven.

Brown bread

TO MAKE THREE 450-G (I-LB)
LOAVES AND SIX ROLLS

INGREDIENTS
900 g (2 lb) 81%
  wheatmeal flour
450 g (1 lb) 100%
  wholemeal flour,
  preferably coarse ground
25 g (1 oz) fresh yeast or
  20 g ($\frac{3}{4}$ oz) dried yeast
2 level tablespoons brown
  sugar
2 level tablespoons salt
15 g ($\frac{1}{2}$ oz) butter, melted
850 ml (1$\frac{1}{2}$ pints) water, a
  few degrees hotter than
  hand hot

Mix the two kinds of flour in a large bowl and put in a warm place – a very low oven or on a gently heated grill until the bowl is becoming warm to the touch.

Dissolve the yeast in a cup with a few tablespoons of warm water, add a pinch of sugar and leave in a warm place (not hot or it will kill the yeast) until it becomes frothy.

Dissolve the salt and brown sugar in the remaining warm water and add the melted butter.

Make a well in the flour, pour in the yeast, add the warm water and mix with a wooden spoon at first and then with your hands, until you have a rough, warm lump of dough.

Turn the bowl upside down on the clean table or working-top and start working the dough with the heel of your hand, pulling it towards you and then pushing it back to roll and knead it on the hard surface. If it is too sticky add more flour by sprinkling it over the dough and working-surface.

When it is smooth, pliable and tense, put the dough back into the bowl and cover it with an oiled polythene sheet and a folded cloth. Leave in a warm atmosphere, kitchen or airing cupboard, until it has doubled in size.

When the dough has risen well and is quite puffy, which takes an hour or so depending on the warmth of the atmosphere, start the next stage.

Heat the oven, set at 230°C, 450°F, Gas Mark 8, so that the bread gets a blast of heat as it goes in.

Remove the dough from the bowl and push it down with your fists to expel the gas. Form it into a ball and cut it into four pieces (3 large and 1 small). Roll them up into balls. Grease three 450-g (1-lb) bread tins and a baking sheet with a piece of kitchen paper dipped into softened butter, lard or oil.

Spread one of the larger pieces of dough flat with your knuckles, and roll it into a tight roll. Fold the ends under on the side with the seam or crease, and place the roll in a greased tin with the seam underneath. Push it down round the sides to give a domed top. Repeat with the remaining tins. Leave them under a loose sheet of polythene and cloth to 'prove'. When they have doubled in size once more and are puffy and taut, they are ready for baking. This proving will take about 30–40 minutes.

Meanwhile cut the remaining dough into six pieces to make rolls and knead each one separately, forming it into a nicely rounded roll shape. Put on a greased baking sheet under a sheet of polythene and leave 15–20 minutes to prove.

Dust tops of rolls with flour and put them into the oven to cook. They will take 15–20 minutes. When they are done they will sound hollow when tapped underneath. Put them on a rack to cool.

Now dust the tops of the loaves with flour if you like, and push them into the oven. Let them bake for 20 minutes at the high temperature and then at 200°C, 400°F, Gas Mark 6 for a further 20 minutes or so. Take them out of their tins and tap them underneath to see if they are done; if they seem a bit soft put them back, on their sides, without their tins, for 5–10 minutes.

Cool them on a rack and eat, or freeze them straight away.

Quick brown bread

INGREDIENTS
225 g ($\frac{1}{2}$ lb) coarse
  wholemeal flour
225 g ($\frac{1}{2}$ lb) 81%
  wheatmeal flour
275 ml scant ($\frac{1}{2}$ pint)
  warm water, just above
  hand-hot
25 g (1 oz) fresh or 15 g
  ($\frac{1}{2}$ oz) dried yeast
$\frac{1}{2}$ teaspoon black treacle
25 g (1 oz) butter
15 g ($\frac{1}{2}$ oz) salt
squeeze of fresh lemon
  juice

This loaf should rise very fast. It tastes delicious but slightly lacks the elasticity of breads that take longer to make. It is the lemon juice which helps the yeast to grow so rapidly.

Mix the two kinds of flour together in a bowl and put it to warm, either on top of a very gentle grill or in a low oven. Measure out 275 ml ($\frac{1}{2}$ pint) of warm water, add the treacle and lemon and keep it warm.

Put the yeast in a cup and mix it with 3–4 tablespoons of treacly water. Leave in a warm place.

Add the butter, melted, and salt to the jug of warm water. When the yeast has frothed, stir it and the warm water into the flour, and mix it well with a wooden spoon.

Put the mixture into a greased 1-kg (2-lb) loaf tin and place inside a loose oiled polythene bag to rise. (Leave the bag slightly open to allow air to circulate.) Leave 30 minutes in a very warm place to rise to the top of the tin.

Preheat the oven to 220°C, 425°F, Gas Mark 7 and bake the loaf for 45–50 minutes. Cool it on a rack.

Barmbrack or Barmcake

This is a perfect tea bread and keeps extremely well, if uncut, for up to 10 days

MAKES TWO OR THREE TIN LOAVES

INGREDIENTS

900 g (2 lb) white strong flour
225 g (8 oz) butter or lard
40 g (1½ oz) fresh yeast
225 g (8 oz) raisins or sultanas
50 g (2 oz) shredded candied peel
175 g (6 oz) soft brown sugar
½ grated nutmeg
large pinch mixed spice
½ teaspoon salt
2 eggs
275 ml (½ pint) warm milk

Put the butter and flour in a slightly warmed bowl. Rub the butter into the flour as if you were starting to make pastry. Mix the yeast with a little of the measured amount of warm milk and pour it into a well in the centre of the flour. Flick flour over, stand the bowl in a warm place and wait until the yeast froths and cracks the flour. Add the fruit, sugar, salt and spices and the egg beaten with some of the milk and mix everything together, adding more milk as needed. Knead into a smooth and resilient dough and allow to rise for 2 hours or longer, even overnight, in a warm kitchen. Knock down the dough, divide it and push it into greased loaf tins, pressing it down well. Allow to prove for 30 minutes, or until doubled in size.

Bake in a preheated oven at 220°C, 425°F, Gas Mark 7 for 15 minutes, take the loaves out, brush them with top of the milk, turn them round and put them back to bake for a further 30–35 minutes at 190°C, 375°F, Gas Mark 5. Cool the loaves on a rack and keep in covered tins.

Background : brown bread, *foreground :* quick brown bread, barmbrack

Scottish baps

MAKES TWELVE–FOURTEEN

INGREDIENTS

450 g (1 lb) plain white flour

2 level teaspoons salt

150 ml (¼ pint) warm water

150 ml (¼ pint) milk

1 level teaspoon sugar

25 g (1 oz) fresh yeast or 15 g (½ oz) dried yeast

25 g (1 oz) melted lard

The bap is the Scottish version of the breakfast roll, and like all good Scottish food is puritanically simple in its ingredients, but when properly made it can 'justly be called noble' says Victor Mac-Clure, the knowledgeable Scottish epicure, author of *Good Appetite My Companion*.

Baps should be served warm, soft and dusted with a white powdering of flour.

Mix the flour and salt in a warmed bowl. Make a well in the centre. Cream the yeast with the water and sugar and leave in a warm place to froth up. Then pour into the well in the flour, together with the milk and melted lard. Mix everything together, form a mass, cover and allow to rest for a few minutes while you wash up the lard pan, etc. The dough will be more manageable after it has rested, and can be kneaded for a few minutes with floured hands on a floured worktop or board. When it is soft,

smooth and puffy, place it in the bowl, cover with a damp folded cloth and a sheet of polythene on top of the cloth. Allow to rise in a warm place until doubled in size, about 1 hour. Preheat the oven to 200°C, 400°F, Gas Mark 6. Now knead again on a floured board to knock it down. Cut into 12–14 pieces, roll them into balls and shape them into oval flattish rolls – 8 × 5 cm (3 × 2 in). Put them on two greased, floured baking sheets. Dust with flour and allow to rise, covered lightly with a cloth, for 15 minutes. Make a deep indentation in the middle of each with your finger and put them into the oven for 15–20 minutes.

The dough can be made the day before and left to rise overnight in the fridge. It is then ready for use and after 30 minutes in a warm kitchen can be shaped into baps ready for proving (second rise) and baking.

Scottish baps, muffins

Muffins

MAKES TWELVE–FOURTEEN

INGREDIENTS

450 g (1 lb) plain flour (not strong bread flour)

1 teaspoon castor sugar

25 g (1 oz) fresh or 15 g (½ oz) dried yeast

2 teaspoons salt

275 ml (½ pint) milk, warmed to just above blood heat

25 g (1 oz) butter, melted

The muffin man with his bell, once a familiar figure in our streets, has now disappeared but here is an authentic recipe to try yourself. If you are used to yeast cookery, then this should not be difficult. Keep the dough rather warm throughout so that the rising is rapid.

Cream the yeast and sugar with 150 ml (¼ pint) of the warm milk in a small bowl. Stir in 4 tablespoons of flour and stand the bowl in a warm place to froth up.

Put the remaining flour in a bowl and warm it slightly, either in a low oven or perhaps on top of the grill.

Now make a well in the flour and pour in the yeast, remaining warm milk, the salt and melted butter. Mix to a dough, adding more flour if the dough is too sticky. Knead it well, and when you have a smooth elastic dough put it back into the bowl, cover with a sheet of oiled polythene and a folded cloth and leave to rise in a warm place. When it has doubled in size knead the dough again and allow

to rise a second time. (The dough will have a better texture if you give it two risings but if you are in a hurry you can omit the second rise.)

Flour two baking sheets or boards. Now cut the dough into pieces the size of a small egg. Knead each into a flat, round shape, put it on to a board and keep it covered with a sheet of polythene and a light cloth. By the time the last are shaped the first ones will be ready to cook.

Heat a griddle or large frying pan and grease it very lightly with a piece of oily kitchen paper. Set the muffins, spaced apart, on the hot pan, and flatten them with the palm of your hand. Cook for 12 minutes over a moderate heat, turn them over, press lightly again and cook for 12 minutes more. When they are golden on both sides, cool a little, split, toast split sides, butter generously and eat at once.

Devonshire splits

MAKES TWELVE

INGREDIENTS
450 g (1 lb) plain white
    flour
15 g ($\frac{1}{2}$ oz) yeast
275 ml ($\frac{1}{2}$ pint) warm milk
50 g (2 oz) castor sugar
50 g (2 oz) butter
$\frac{1}{2}$ level teaspoon salt
275 ml ($\frac{1}{2}$ pint) clotted or
    whipped cream and
    350 g ($\frac{3}{4}$ lb) strawberry
    jam

These are the white fluffy buns piled high with clotted cream and strawberry jam, that holiday-makers in Devon hope to be offered when they see the sign 'Cream Teas'. They are much more easily made, in fact, than the difficulty of actually finding a teashop that will serve them would suggest.

Warm a large bowl. Melt the butter and let it cool. Stir the sugar into the warm milk until it has dissolved.

Mix the yeast in a small bowl with 3 tablespoons of sweetened milk. Put it in a warm place until it froths. Meanwhile put the flour in the warmed bowl and make a well in the centre; sprinkle the salt round the edge. Pour in the yeast, milk and melted butter and mix well to a soft dough. Allow to rest 4–5 minutes, then knead on a floured board with floured hands until smooth and elastic. Put back in the bowl, cover with a damp cloth and

a sheet of polythene and allow to rise until doubled in size, about 1 hour. Pre-heat the oven to 220°C, 425°F, Gas Mark 7.

Knock down, kneading well, and cut into 12 pieces, shape and knead them into round buns and place on a floured and greased baking sheet. Allow them to prove (rise for second time) in a warm place, covered lightly with a cloth, for 15 minutes until swollen and puffy. Place in the middle of the oven and bake 15–20 minutes.

Allow to cool on a rack. Split the buns from the top, diagonally across to the bottom, without cutting right through, and spread the split thickly on one side with clotted or whipped cream and on the other with strawberry jam. Arrange on a large, pretty plate and sieve a little icing sugar over the top.

Devonshire splits, hot cross buns

Hot cross buns

MAKES TWELVE–FOURTEEN

INGREDIENTS
450 g (1 lb) strong white
    flour
50 g (2 oz) castor sugar
25 g (1 oz) yeast or 15 g
    ($\frac{1}{2}$ oz) dried yeast
250 ml (just under $\frac{1}{2}$ pint)
    warm milk
1 egg
50 g (2 oz) butter
100 g (4 oz) currants
50 g (2 oz) mixed peel
1 teaspoon mixed spice
pinch of salt
For the glaze
1 tablespoon castor sugar,
1 tablespoon milk

'Hot cross buns, hot cross buns, one a penny, two a penny, hot cross buns.' Traditional folklore has it that hot cross buns, those familiar shiny round buns with their dark currants sticking out here and there, are descended from pagan days when the vernal equinox was celebrated. If properly made on the actual day – Good Friday – they are supposed to protect the whole family from fires, rats, accidents and shipwrecks. A cheap form of insurance.

Warm a large bowl. Melt the butter and let it cool. Cream the yeast in a small bowl with three tablespoons of warm milk and a teaspoon of sugar. Leave in a warm place to froth up. Sieve the flour and spice into the bowl and make a well in the centre. Pour in the yeast mixture.

Beat the egg, stir it and the remaining sugar into the warm milk. Pour it together with the warm, but not hot, melted butter into the well in the flour, add a pinch of salt and the currants and chopped candied peel, and mix until you have a sticky mass.

Allow to rest for 5 minutes, when it will become easier to handle, then place on a floured board and knead with lightly floured hands. When the dough is smooth and puffy put it back in the bowl, cover it with a damp cloth and then a sheet of polythene, stand the buns in a warm place and allow to double in size.

Preheat the oven to 200°C, 400°F, Gas Mark 6. Take out the dough and knead it again to knock it down. Cut it into 12 or 14 pieces, knead and shape them into small balls, place them on a greased baking tin and cover them lightly with a cloth. Leave them in a warm place to prove for fifteen to twenty minutes. When they are swollen and puffy mark a cross in the top of each with a knife. Put the buns in the middle of the preheated oven and bake for 15 minutes.

While they are baking make the glaze: dissolve the sugar in the milk in a small cup. Take the buns out, brush them with the glaze and put them back for 5 minutes to give them a lovely, shiny, sticky finish.

Guard's fruit cake

This is a mild, moist cake, and very good

INGREDIENTS
225 g (8 oz) self-raising
  flour
1 teaspoon mixed spice
¼ teaspoon grated nutmeg
1 small teaspoon
  bicarbonate of soda
100 g (4 oz) brown sugar
100 g (4 oz) butter
1 egg
100 g (4 oz) raisins
100 g (4 oz) currants
50 g (2 oz) mixed peel
150 ml (¼ pint) milk

Preheat the oven to 180°C, 350°F, Gas Mark 4.

Sieve the flour with the spices and bicarbonate of soda. Mix in the sugar by hand. Rub in the butter and add the fruit, shaken with a little flour from the measured amount.

Stir in the egg and milk, well beaten together. Beat the mixture well and turn out into a buttered and floured 18-cm (7-in) cake tin.

Bake for 1 hour 20–30 minutes in the middle of the oven, covering the top with a loose cover of baking foil or greaseproof paper if it becomes too dark. Allow to cool and set in the tin for 30 minutes before turning it out.

Cherry cake

INGREDIENTS
225 g (8 oz) glacé cherries
225 g (8 oz) butter
225 g (8 oz) castor sugar
3 eggs
225 g (8 oz) self-raising
  flour
½ teaspoon baking powder
100 g (4 oz) ground
  almonds

Icing
1 egg white
pinch salt
175 g (6 oz) sifted icing
  sugar
1 teaspoon double cream

This is a very good cake and looks appealing with a layer of matt white icing studded with whole cherries (you can halve them if you haven't got enough).

To prepare cherries for cakes and puddings put them in a wire sieve and let them stand over a pan of simmering water for 10 minutes, for the syrup to drip off. Now let them cool and dust them with some of the measured flour.

Sieve the remaining flour and baking powder together. Preheat the oven to 160°C, 325°F, Gas Mark 3.

Cream the butter and the sugar until they are white and fluffy. Beat in the eggs one at a time adding a tablespoon of flour with the last egg to prevent it curdling. When the mixture is smooth add the flour and almonds, mix them in as quickly as possible and lastly fold in the cherries.

Turn the mixture into a lined, buttered 20-cm (8-in) tin and put it in the middle of the oven.

Cook for 1¼–1½ hours, turning the cake round if your oven is uneven. Cover loosely with foil if the top starts to look too brown.

Icing
The cake must be cold before it is iced. Beat the egg white until stiff with an electric beater. Add the salt and then the sugar, still beating. When the mixture is soft and thick and stands up in peaks add the cream and beat again. Spread the icing over the cake and leave at least 4 hours to set.

Guard's fruit cake, cherry cake

Walnut cake

INGREDIENTS
100 g (4 oz) unsalted butter
100 g (4 oz) castor sugar
2 eggs
40 g (1½ oz) walnuts,
  coarsely ground
100 g (4 oz) self-raising
  flour

As any one over the age of thirty remembers, Fuller's tearooms used to be the place for an afternoon treat. The highspot of tea was the famous walnut cake, moist yet crumbly, with thick snow-white icing. The halved nuts sitting on top were spaced, blessedly, quite far apart: and each wedge, of course, had its own nut in the centre of its very broad end. This arrangement might have been designed expressly for schoolboys' appetites but it was also appreciated by their sisters and their cousins and their aunts. All will find this walnut cake nostalgic and delicious.

Preheat the oven to 180°C, 350°F, Gas Mark 4. Butter and flour a 15-cm (6-in) cake tin.

Cream the butter and sugar until light and fluffy. Add the eggs one at a time, beating the first one in very well before you add the second. Add the flour and the coarsely ground walnuts. Mix well together for a few seconds and turn into the prepared tin. Bake at 180°C, 350°F, Gas Mark 4 for 1 hour.

Allow to set for a few minutes before turning out to cool on a rack. Use the same icing as for cherry cake (*see facing page*) and decorate with walnut halves.

Madeira cake

This used to be enjoyed with the glass of Madeira that was the standard refreshment at formal visits.

INGREDIENTS
150 g (5 oz) plain flour
25 g (1 oz) cornflour
1 small teaspoon baking
  powder
100 g (4 oz) butter
150 g (5 oz) sugar
2 eggs
2 tablespoons milk
citron peel (or whole
  crystallized lemon or
  orange peel)
pinch salt

Preheat the oven to 180°C, 350°F, Gas Mark 4. Sieve together the flour, cornflour and baking powder. Cream the butter and sugar together until they are pale and light. Add one egg, beat it in, then add half the flour and beat it in; add the remaining egg and flour alternately. Finally beat in the milk. Turn the mixture into a buttered and floured 13-cm (5-in) cake tin. Bake in the middle of the oven for 1¼ hours; after 30 minutes decorate the top of the cake with a few pieces of citron peel. This is a very good, plain, moist cake, excellent in the middle of the morning with a glass of wine (or a nice cup of coffee or tea).

Tennis cake

INGREDIENTS
225 g (8 oz) butter
225 g (8 oz) sugar
grated zest and juice of
  ½ an orange
grated zest of ½ a lemon
4 eggs, at room
  temperature
50 g (2 oz) ground
  almonds
275 g (10 oz) self-raising
  flour
1 tablespoon of milk
175 g (6 oz) currants
175 g (6 oz) sultanas
50 g (2 oz) candied orange
  peel
50 g (2 oz) glacé cherries
25 g (1 oz) shredded
  blanched almonds
icing (*page* 206)

No country-house drawing-room used to be complete without the french windows admitting a white-flannelled figure crying 'Anyone for tennis?'; and no summer without its quota of tennis parties; and no tennis tea without its tennis cake.

Originally tennis cakes were round but later were always baked in an oblong (tennis court shape) tin. They should have marzipan and smooth glossy icing coloured in pale green, preferably flavoured with Kirsch (and they should have elaborate silver decorations – little tennis racquets and so on; but since tennis parties are few and this cake is terrifically good anyway, you could possibly get away without doing this bit).

Cream the butter and sugar with the orange juice and zest and the lemon zest until light and delicate. Add the eggs one at a time, beating in each one carefully to prevent the mixture from curdling. Next stir in the ground almonds, then the flour, and lastly the milk, the fruit, and the shredded almonds. Bake at 180°F, 350°F, Gas Mark 4 for 1¼–1½ hours.

Quick chocolate cake

One of the favourite cakes

INGREDIENTS
175 g (6 oz) sugar
4 tablespoons cocoa
75 g (3 oz) butter, melted
2 eggs
75 ml (3 fl oz) milk
250 g (9 oz) self-raising flour
pinch of salt
6 tablespoons boiling water

Chocolate butter cream
40 g (1½ oz) plain chocolate
1½ teaspoons water
175 g (6 oz) castor sugar
75 g (3 oz) fresh butter, softened to room temperature
2 drops vanilla essence

Chocolate icing
50 g (2 oz) plain or bitter chocolate
15 g (½ oz) butter
1 tablespoon water
100 g (4 oz) icing sugar

Preheat the oven to 190°C, 375°F, Gas Mark 5 and grease 2 18-cm (7-in) sandwich tins, then line them with a disc of greaseproof paper, greased and floured.

Put the ingredients into a bowl in the order given, sifting the sugar and cocoa together, adding the melted butter and eggs together, then the milk, sieving in the flour with a pinch of salt, and lastly adding the boiling water.

Beat until smooth and turn this mixture, which is very sloppy, into the tins and bake for about 25 minutes.

Turn out and when cold fill with chocolate butter cream and spread with chocolate icing.

Chocolate butter cream
Melt the chocolate in the water in a bowl placed over a saucepan of simmering water. Remove the bowl from the heat. Beat the sugar into the butter and when it is creamy, beat in the softened chocolate and vanilla essence.

Chocolate icing
Break up the chocolate and melt to a thick cream over a low heat together with the butter and water. Do not let it boil.

Remove from the heat, add the sifted icing sugar and stir until thick and shiny. To keep its gloss, warm it a little before pouring it over the cake.

Tennis cake,
quick chocolate cake

Real English sponge cake

INGREDIENTS
1 tablespoon flour
1 tablespoon granulated
  sugar
4 eggs
150 g (5 oz) castor sugar
150 g (5 oz) self-raising
  flour
grated rind of ½ a lemon

A real sponge contains no butter, and was originally made with eight or so eggs, which provided the necessary air and lightness. One early Victorian recipe for a rich sponge calls for 16 eggs. Nowadays we prefer to use fewer eggs and self-raising flour to obtain a light cake, so this recipe from an Edwardian cookery book is more to our taste.

Preheat the oven to 200°C, 400°F, Gas Mark 6. Mix the tablespoons of flour and sugar together. Butter two 18-cm (7-in) sponge or sandwich tins and sprinkle them thickly with the flour and sugar mixture to coat them inside.

Moisten the castor sugar with 2 tablespoons of boiling water. Let it cool. Put the eggs and sugar into a bowl and beat until creamy for about 5 minutes. Grate in the lemon rind.

Now stir the flour into the egg and sugar mixture, by hand. Turn the mixture into the sponge tins and bake for 20–25 minutes, at 190–200°C, 375–400°F, Gas Mark 5–6, until nicely crusted.

Allow to shrink away from the sides of the tin, then turn on to racks and leave in a warm place to cool slowly.

Spread the lower half with jam, preferably raspberry or strawberry, and the upper half with unsweetened whipped cream, and put the two halves together with the cream above the jam.

Opposite : real English sponge cake

Victoria sponge

INGREDIENTS
175 g (6 oz) butter
175 g (6 oz) castor sugar
3 eggs, well beaten
175 g (6 oz) self-raising
  flour

By Queen Victoria's day sponge cakes admitted butter into the ingredients to make a cake which was less likely to collapse and cause sadness in the drawing-room than the original butterless sponge.

Preheat the oven to 180°C, 350°F, Gas Mark 4. Butter and flour two 18-cm (7-in) sandwich tins.

Cream the butter and sugar together until light and pale, then add the egg, a little at a time, adding a tablespoon of flour when about two-thirds of the egg has been added. Lastly add the remaining flour, and stir it in briefly by hand.

Put the mixture into the two sandwich tins and smooth the tops.

Bake for 20–25 minutes until well-risen and brown. When they are cooked take them out and let them cool a little before turning them out on to wire cake-racks to become cold.

Spread with jam, sandwich the two halves together and dust the top with icing sugar.

Victoria sponge, Queen cakes

Queen cakes

MAKES TWENTY-FOUR

INGREDIENTS
100 g (4 oz) butter
100 g (4 oz) sugar
2 eggs
175 g (6 oz) self-raising
  flour
pinch sodium bicarbonate
pinch cream of tartar
a little milk

Preheat the oven to 190°C, 375°C, Gas Mark 5. Cream together the butter and sugar, beat in the eggs, one at a time, then stir in the flour sieved with the sodium bicarbonate and cream of tartar. Add enough milk to make a soft mixture, fill greased bun trays or paper cases and bake for 15–20 minutes until the cakes are an even golden brown colour.

Put a blob of white icing and half a walnut or half a cherry on each if you want to make them prettier.

Rough puff pastry

INGREDIENTS
100 g (4 oz) plain flour
pinch of salt
25 g (1 oz) lard, chilled
50 g (2 oz) butter, chilled
squeeze of lemon juice
3–4 tablespoons icy cold
  water

This is easier to make than the chef's favourite puff pastry, and amazingly useful for all sorts of pies and pastries, including the two following recipes – Eccles cakes and maids of honour.

Mix the flour and salt in a cold bowl. Cut the lard and butter into cubes the size of sugar lumps. Stir these lumps into the flour with the blade of a knife.

Add a squeeze of lemon juice and 2 tablespoons water, mix it in with the blade of a knife and keep mixing gingerly until you have a light mass. Now work it very lightly into a ball with your fingertips. Chill in the refrigerator for 15 minutes.

Roll into an oblong 1-cm ($\frac{1}{4}$-in) thick, fold it in three, pressing the edges with the side of your hand to seal in the air.

Turn the pastry by 90° so that you are now rolling in the other direction and repeat the same operation. If the pastry starts to get sticky and difficult to handle, put it back into the refrigerator for 10–15 minutes.

Repeat the same operation of rolling, folding, sealing the edges and turning the pastry twice more.

Chill the pastry once more and when rolling it out take care to keep it flat, to preserve the layers of air. Trimmings should be laid flat on top of each other and then folded over, rather than gathered into a ball as is usual.

Use this pastry for anything and everything. It is very delicious.

Eccles cakes

MAKES ABOUT TEN

INGREDIENTS
225 g (8 oz) rough puff
  pastry (see above)
The filling
25 g (1 oz) candied lemon
  peel
100 g (4 oz) currants
$\frac{1}{4}$ teaspoon ground allspice
$\frac{1}{4}$ teaspoon grated nutmeg
50 g (2 oz) castor sugar
25 g (1 oz) butter

These are crisp, crumbling, brown pies, reminiscent of mince pies, but fresher and simpler in their ingredients. Originally the Eccles cake was made with fresh blackcurrants and mint leaves.

Make the rough puff pastry and chill until you are ready to make the Eccles cakes.

Chop the peel finely and mix it with the other ingredients for the filling in a small pan, stirring it over a low heat until the butter has melted. Turn the mixture into a bowl and allow to cool.

Heat the oven to 200°C, 400°F, Gas Mark 6. Roll out the pastry fairly thinly and cut into 10-cm (4-in) rounds or squares.

Put a spoonful of the mixture on to each, brush the edges with top of the milk and fold them into the middle. Press together.

Turn the little pies over and flatten with the rolling pin until you can just see the currants under the pastry. Make small parallel slits in the top, brush with top of the milk and sprinkle with sugar. Lift carefully on to a greased baking tray and bake for 15–20 minutes until completely cooked and nicely browned. Sprinkle with a little more sugar and eat as soon as possible.

Maids of honour

MAKES TWELVE

INGREDIENTS
100 g (4 oz) rough puff
  pastry (see above)
850 ml (1$\frac{1}{2}$ pints) fresh
  milk
1$\frac{1}{2}$ tablespoons rennet
1 egg (size 4)
15 g ($\frac{1}{2}$ oz) butter, melted
25 g (1 oz) sugar
grated rind of $\frac{1}{2}$ a lemon

The recipe for these delicious little custardy tarts made with a sort of junket filling was a carefully guarded secret of the court kitchens from Anne Boleyn's day to George II's reign. Philip Harben gave the secret to the world at the Festival of Britain in 1951 and here is an adaptation of his recipe.

Roll out the pastry fairly thin and use it to line a deep tartlet tin, which you have first wetted slightly to prevent the pastry from sticking to it. Prick with a fork.

Heat the oven to 200°C, 400°F, Gas Mark 6. Warm the milk to blood heat, add the rennet. Allow to set, which should take 10–15 minutes, then turn into a sieve and allow to drip for 20 minutes. When you are left with a yoghurt-like curd push it through the sieve into a bowl and mix with the beaten egg, melted butter, sugar and lemon rind.

Half fill the pastry-cases and bake at 200°C, 400°F, Gas Mark 6, for 10 minutes and then at 180°C, 350°F, Gas Mark 4 for a further 15–20 minutes.

Shortcrust pastry

INGREDIENTS
175 g (6 oz) flour
75 g (3 oz) cold unsalted or
  slightly salted butter,
  taken straight from the
  refrigerator
25 g (1 oz) lard
about 3 tablespoons water

Put the flour into a cold bowl. Cut the butter and lard into pieces and put it in with the flour. Now keep slicing the butter and lard into the flour, with a small knife, until it is all cut up into small pieces. With cool fingertips rub the fat rapidly and lightly into the flour – do not rub it too much, it should still be in quite sizeable flakes. Stir in the water with a knife blade. When you have a crumbly mass work it quickly into a ball (this only takes a few seconds) and put it into a plastic bag in the refrigerator to rest for at least an hour. It is better still if you leave it overnight.

Everything should be kept very cool while you make the pastry and roll it out, and you should touch it as little as possible with your fingers. This is the secret of success.

Top : Eccles cakes, *left :* maids of honour, *right :* jam and marmalade tarts

Jam tarts

TO MAKE TEN–TWELVE

INGREDIENTS
4–5 oz shortcrust pastry
   (*see facing page*)
4 generous tablespoons
   strawberry jam
1 teaspoon brandy
butter for greasing tart tins

Heat the oven to 200°C, 400°F, Gas Mark 6. Roll pastry thinly and cut into rounds, 7–8 cm (2½–3 in) in diameter, to make 10–12 tarts. Prick lightly with a fork. Line a greased tart tin with the pastry and fill each one with one teaspoon of the strawberry jam which has been mixed with the brandy. Do not overfill. Bake for 10–12 minutes, then take them out of the tin and put them on a rack to cool.

Marmalade tarts
Using 4 generous tablespoons of marmalade mixed with an egg yolk, make just like jam tarts.

Welsh cakes

These are the famous bakestone (griddle) cakes of South Wales. If you do not have a griddle, a stout frying pan will do.

MAKES FIFTEEN–TWENTY

INGREDIENTS
225 g (8 oz) plain flour
½ teaspoon baking powder
pinch of salt
75 g (3 oz) fat (½ lard,
    ½ butter)
75 g (3 oz) sugar
50 g (2 oz) currants or
    sultanas
½ teaspoon mixed spice
    (optional)
1 egg
dash of milk

These are made very quickly. Sieve together or mix together with your hands the flour, baking powder and salt. Rub in the fat, add the remaining dry ingredients. Beat the egg and stir it in, then add a dash of milk to make a firm dough.

Roll out the dough to 1–2 cm (¼–½ in) thick, cut into 8-cm (3-in) rounds and cook on a hot, greased griddle or in a thick frying pan for about 10 minutes in all, turning when the underside is brown. Eat them hot or warm with butter and honey. They should be sandy-textured inside.

Ballater scones

From a Deeside town, not far from Balmoral, in Scotland

MAKES ABOUT TWELVE

INGREDIENTS
225 g (8 oz) self-raising
    flour
½ teaspoon bicarbonate of
    soda
¼ teaspoon salt
40 g (1½ oz) butter
either 150 ml (¼ pint) sour
    milk and 2 tablespoons
    cream, or 150 ml (¼ pint)
    buttermilk

The lightest scones were those made with buttermilk which reacted with the bicarbonate of soda and gave a soft, moist, well-risen result. If you can't obtain buttermilk you can use the above mixture of sour milk and cream.

Preheat the oven to 200°C, 400°F, Gas Mark 6. Sieve the flour, bicarbonate of soda and salt into a bowl and rub in the butter with your fingertips until the mixture is the texture of coarse breadcrumbs.

Add the milk and cream or buttermilk, mix to a dough, turn it out on to a floured board and roll out 2-cm (½-in) thick. All this must be done extremely rapidly and with a very light touch.

Cut the dough with a cutter into 5-cm (2-in) rounds, dust the tops with flour, put them on the baking sheets and bake for 10–15 minutes until puffed and golden brown. Cool on a rack and eat lukewarm, split in half rather than cut, and with plenty of butter.

Wheatmeal scones

These are even more delicious than white scones. They are made in exactly the same way, as the recipe above but self-raising 81% flour is used. This is brown flour with some of the bran extracted. They must be eaten soon after they are made, when they give a real farmhouse touch to a simple tea.

Top : Welsh cakes, Scotch pancakes,
centre : Ballater and cheese scones,
bottom : rock cakes, brown bread biscuits

Scotch pancakes

Also known as dropscones and pigs' ears, these thick little pancakes are great favourites with children.

MAKES ABOUT TWENTY-FOUR

INGREDIENTS
1 egg
425 ml ($\frac{3}{4}$ pint) milk
225 g ($\frac{1}{2}$ lb) self-raising flour
25 g (1 oz) sugar
$\frac{1}{2}$ teaspoon salt

Beat the egg and milk in a bowl. Put the flour in another bowl, make a well in the centre and beat in the milk and egg mixture gradually. Add the rest of the ingredients and beat well.

Heat a large frying pan, or griddle, oil it well with a wodge of kitchen paper soaked in oil and drop on the batter, well spaced, a dessertspoon at a time. Let the little pancakes cook on one side until they are set, then turn them and let them brown underneath. As they are cooked, put them inside a folded napkin on a heated dish to keep warm and soft, and eat at once with plenty of butter and honey.

Cheese scones

MAKES TWELVE

INGREDIENTS
225 g (8 oz) plain flour
1 level teaspoon sodium bicarbonate
1 level teaspoon cream of tartar
pinch of salt
50 g (2 oz) butter
50 g (2 oz) grated cheese
100 ml (4 fl oz) buttermilk or sour milk

Preheat the oven to 190°C, 375°F, Gas Mark 5. Sieve the flour, sodium bicarbonate, cream of tartar and salt into a bowl.

Rub in the butter, stir in the grated cheese, then make the mixture into a firm dough with buttermilk or sour milk.

Roll out 2 cm ($\frac{1}{2}$ in) thick on a floured board. Cut into rounds, dust the tops with flour and bake for 20 minutes.

Rock cakes

MAKES TWENTY-FOUR

INGREDIENTS
100 g (4 oz) butter
100 g (4 oz) demerara sugar
225 g ($\frac{1}{2}$ lb) self-raising flour
175 g (6 oz) sultanas and currants mixed
50 g (2 oz) chopped peel
1 egg
150 ml ($\frac{1}{4}$ pint) milk

Surely nobody but the British could give something as delicious as these quickly made little rounds of sugary, curranty crumble a title as prosaic as 'rock cakes'; but eat them the day they are made or they will begin to deserve the name.

Grease and flour two baking sheets and preheat the oven to 190°C, 375°F, Gas Mark 5.

Cream butter and sugar briefly, add the remaining ingredients, mix well and heap in little rough mounds on the baking sheets. Bake for 15–20 minutes.

Brown bread biscuits

From the Viscountess Falmouth, 1850

MAKES ABOUT THIRTY-TWO

INGREDIENTS
pinch of salt
15 g ($\frac{1}{2}$ oz) baking powder
450 g (1 lb) wholemeal flour
100 g (4 oz) butter
275 ml ($\frac{1}{2}$ pint) milk

Add the salt and baking powder to the flour, rub in the butter and mix to a soft dough with milk. Roll into small balls the size of a walnut, place on a buttered baking sheet and flatten with the palm of your hand. Bake at 190°C, 375°F, Gas Mark 5 for 15–20 minutes.

These crisp, tasty biscuits are excellent with cheese. They keep extremely well for at least a month in a really airtight biscuit tin.

Brandy snaps

MAKES TWELVE

INGREDIENTS
50 g (2 oz) butter
1 teaspoon brandy
100 g (4 oz) castor sugar
1 teaspoon lemon juice
50 g (2 oz) plain flour
½ teaspoon ginger
275 ml (½ pint) double cream

Brandy snaps, crisp delicate ginger-flavoured curls, were originally, as the name suggests, made with brandy, but are now often mixed with lemon juice; this recipe is made with both. They are very pleasing to make.

The biscuity flaps are curled up like cigars, usually round the handle of a wooden spoon, before they have time to set. They are then filled, when they are cool, with freshly whipped cream.

Melt the butter with the brandy. Put into the pan with the rest of the ingredients except the cream and cook for about 5 minutes. Meanwhile lightly grease three baking sheets.

Preheat the oven to 150°C, 300°F, Gas Mark 2. When the mixture is cooked, drop the batter in teaspoonfuls, widely spaced, on the baking sheets. Bake three or four at a time for 6–7 minutes until nicely lacy and golden brown. Take out and

Mulatto's stomach

This recipe is for the sticky moist variety of gingerbread that is so delicious eaten on Guy Fawkes' night to keep out the cold.

INGREDIENTS
225 g (½ lb) molasses
275 ml (½ pint) sour milk
100 g (4 oz) lard
1½ tablespoons ground ginger
350 g (12 oz) plain flour
1 teaspoon bicarbonate of soda

Spicy gingerbread has long been part of British popular culture. Dyed red with wine, made with honey and liquorice or studded with gilded cloves and *fleur-de-lis* made with leaves coated with harmless gold-leaf (hence the expression about putting the gilt on the gingerbread), or baked in moulds shaped like windmills or castles, farmers or queens, and decorated with red and white sugar, they were sold at fairs and festivities or given as presents on high days and holidays.

Preheat the oven to 180°C, 350°F, Gas Mark 4.

Put molasses, milk, lard and ginger in a saucepan and stir until melted. Beat the mixture for 10 minutes, dissolve the soda in a little boiling water and mix it in. Add the flour, gradually making a stiff batter and pour the mixture into well-greased tins, and bake for 1 hour until lightly browned, covering loosely with foil if the top gets too brown. This is a rich, soggy gingerbread.

Ginger nuts

MAKES TWENTY-FOUR

INGREDIENTS
1 tablespoon ground ginger
pinch powdered cloves
225 g (8 oz) plain flour
100 g (4 oz) butter
100 g (4 oz) sugar
4 tablespoons warmed golden syrup
½ wineglass sweet white wine

Sift the ginger, cloves and flour. Rub the butter into the flour, spices and sugar. Add the warmed syrup and then, very gradually, add the wine to make a dryish mixture.

Break off in lumps the size of a small walnut, flatten to make thinnish biscuits and bake in a slow oven, 180°C, 350°F, Gas Mark 4, for about 15 minutes. Be careful not to overcook them. They should not be too hard.

If you prefer to make these biscuits with fresh green ginger you will need a piece weighing about 25 g (1 oz). Pound it first and then add it to the mixture together with the syrup.

allow to rest for 1 minute while you put another lot in, then pick them up one at a time and roll them up, or place on the palm of the hand, place a wooden spoon-handle across the centre and press the snap gently to overlap in a tubular shape. Hold until set, then put on a rack and repeat with the others. When they are set, glossy and golden, fill with whipped double cream – unsweetened, as the brandy snaps will be very sweet indeed.

Cornish ginger fairings

TO MAKE TWENTY-FIVE

INGREDIENTS
100 g (4 oz) plain flour
1 level teaspoon of baking powder
1 teaspoon ground ginger
¼ teaspoon mixed spice
¼ teaspoon ground cinnamon
lemon rind or peel, if liked
50 g (2 oz) margarine
50 g (2 oz) sugar
2 tablespoons golden syrup

Shortbread

INGREDIENTS
150 g (5 oz) plain flour
50 g (2 oz) rice flour
175 g (6 oz) butter
50 g (2 oz) icing sugar

Top : brandy snaps, Cornish ginger fairings, *centre :* mulatto's stomach, *bottom :* ginger nuts, shortbread

These gingery cakes used to be sold at fairs and enjoyed by Old Uncle Tom Cobleigh and all, together with great draughts of spiced ale.

Mix all the dry ingredients together except the sugar. Rub in the fat and then add sugar. Preheat the oven to 190°C, 375°F, Gas Mark 5. Heat the syrup till it runs and add to the mixture. Shape and roll into balls the size of a walnut, place these on a greased tin on the top shelf of the oven. When the biscuits begin to colour, after about 10–15 minutes, remove the tin, bang it sharply on the table and put it on a lower shelf where the biscuits will flop and crack. Cook on for a further 5–10 minutes, then remove them and let them cool on the tin before transferring them to a rack.

Shortbread, in various forms, is liked all the year round, but Christmas is not complete without it. In Scotland, it is particularly eaten during the festive season between Christmas and Hogmanay, when it is always offered to 'first-footers': the first to cross the threshold of the house in the New Year.

Preheat the oven to 150°C, 300°F, Gas Mark 2. Put all the ingredients in a bowl and rub in the butter with your fingers until the mixture is like finest bread-crumbs. Then knead the mixture to form a smooth dough with no cracks. Turn it on to a board sprinkled with rice flour and form it into a flat round about 2-cm (½-in) thick.
Mark the edge all the way round with your fingers and mark into slices or prick with a fork.
Lay the round on a tin lined with buttered greaseproof paper and bake for 45 minutes. Cut it into pieces while it is warm, but allow it to cool on the tin.

Preserves
and pickles

The days when we needed to make great autumn preparations to provide ourselves with a hedge against winter starvation by filling the loft with apples, the cellar with root vegetables, and the larder with barrels of salt fish and pickled pork, are over (in spite of the occasional snowstorm to keep us on our toes). But it is still a satisfying pleasure to keep the memory of high summer in the winter by making jams, pickles and little preserves.

A few pots of jam, made in the fruit season – strawberry and raspberry in June, blackcurrant and redcurrant jelly in July, plum in August – can provide enough home-made jam for the tea table all through the winter. And with the flushes of eggs, apples, onions and tomatoes you can make a pot or two of old-fashioned pickles now and then, enough to fill the shelves and give an enormous boost to the degree of pride with which you can present cold meat or chicken, or dull sausages or hamburgers.

There is no need to make a great production out of pickling and jam-making. Although it is easier to make large batches of jam if you have a preserving pan, there is no reason why a large saucepan shouldn't be used, and jam made for pleasure, in small quantities, rather than in deadly earnest in vast amounts: 1 kg (2 lb) of fruit, with about 1 kg (2 lb) of sugar added, makes at least three well-filled pots of jam, a nice amount.

Making good jam takes only an hour or two of pleasant work; the atmosphere is invariably cheerful, everybody loves the smell and the old-fashioned ritual, the stirring and testing and tasting. And with the increase in 'pick your own fruit' farms, home-made jam has become a real possibility for everyone. Before you start, it is as well to know a few golden rules, to help produce well-set jam with good keeping qualities.

Opposite : strawberry, gooseberry and apricot jam

1. It is most important to have jars, saucepan or preserving pan and spoons ready and scrupulously clean before you start, so that you prevent any micro-organisms and bacteria from getting into the jam.
2. Choose sound firm fruit; a mixture of ripe and rather less ripe fruits is best, unripe fruits contain more pectin and fruit acid (both needed to obtain a good set) than ripe fruit.
3. Use fruit as soon as possible after picking. Wash only if necessary.
4. Cook the fruit with or without water for 20–30 minutes prior to adding the sugar. Simmer it gently to draw out the pectin.
5. Warm the sugar before adding it to the fruit, to help it dissolve quickly.

6. When you have added the sugar to the hot, softened fruit, stir it over a gentle heat until it has completely dissolved before returning the jam to the boil.
7. Boil rapidly until set, stirring from time to time to prevent sticking at the bottom; test frequently to avoid overcooking.
8. Testing for set: put a teaspoon of jam on a cold plate and let it cool. Push it with your finger; if it wrinkles and stays put it is ready to set. If it seems wet and runs about it is not ready to set.

Or let a teaspoon of jam get cool in your wooden spoon. Tip the spoon: if the jam drips off quickly it is not ready to set, but if it partly sets on the spoon and runs slowly into a large drop or 'flake' and then breaks off, it is ready.
9. Do not skim until the jam is ready, or you will waste jam.
10. Let the jam cool a little before pouring into jars, the slight thickening will prevent the fruit from rising to the top of the jars. Don't cool too much or you will get air bubbles in the jam.
11. Pour jam into clean hot jars standing on a wooden or laminated surface or on a layer of newspaper. Cover immediately with waxed paper discs.
12. As soon as the jam is cool put on the cellophane tops, slightly dampened. Label and store in a cool dry place.

Picking apples – a family affair in Victorian days

Strawberry jam

MAKES ABOUT 2.3 KG (5 LB)

INGREDIENTS
1.4 kg (3 lb) nice firm red
   strawberries, not too
   large
juice of 1 lemon
1.4 kg (3 lb) sugar

This is the jam that beats all others as a reminder of high summer; pretty, sweet and delicate, it is perfect eaten with scones and cream, or Devonshire splits, and makes a good filling for cakes and trifles.

Hull the strawberries and replace any bad ones with perfect ones. Put strawberries and lemon juice together into the preserv-ing pan, and heat gently. Simmer very slowly for 5 minutes, then add the warmed sugar, stir until it dissolves, then boil until setting point is reached. Do not overcook as the colour darkens during boiling and strawberry jam ought to be a nice clear red or at least a deep red. Skim, cool slightly until a skin starts to form on the jam and then pour into hot, dry, clean jampots.

Apricot jam

MAKES ABOUT 1.8 KG (4 LB)

INGREDIENTS
600 g (1¼ lb) sugar
1.4 kg (3 lb) fresh apricots,
   half ripe, half firm
150 ml (¼ pint) water

Warm the sugar. Cut the apricots in half and remove the stones. Crack the stones and blanch the kernels in boiling water for a minute or two to remove the skins.
   Put the apricots and water in a large pan and stew gently until the fruit is tender, about half an hour. Add the heated sugar and stir over a low heat until it dissolves.

Then boil rapidly until setting point is reached. (It is interesting that an apricot jam that sets straight away and is a clear orange doesn't taste half as delicious as one that has boiled for at least half an hour and has become a deeper chestnut colour.) Skim, then stir in the kernels, allow to cool a little before pouring into heated jars.

Green gooseberry jam

MAKES ABOUT 2.3 KG (5 LB)

INGREDIENTS
900 g (2 lb) green
   gooseberries
150 ml (¼ pint) water
1 kg (2¼ lb) sugar

Cut the larger ones in half and put the gooseberries to stew gently, covered, with the water. When the berries are soft and tender add the sugar and stir until it has quite dissolved, then boil rapidly until setting point is reached.
   If you want to give a strange musky flavour to the jam, it is quite traditional to put a head of elderflowers in with the gooseberries during their initial stewing. Remove it before adding the sugar and continuing the cooking.

Blackcurrant jam

MAKES ABOUT 2.5–3 KG
(6–7) LB)

INGREDIENTS
1.8 kg (4 lb) blackcurrants
575 ml (1 pint) cold water
1.8 kg (4 lb) lump sugar

This makes a soft and thick jam – so often blackcurrant jam is hard or has those little chewy currants that feel disagreeable between the teeth, but long, slow simmering before the sugar goes in softens the fruit completely.

With a fork, pick the stalks from the currants and remove all unripe fruit. Put the currants in a preserving pan with the water. Bring slowly to the boil and simmer for 30 minutes. Add the sugar and stir until it has dissolved before starting the simmering again.

Simmer for 15 minutes or until jam sets firmly. Skim well, stir and pour into heated pots.

Blackcurrant jam and redcurrant jelly

Redcurrant jelly

INGREDIENTS
To every 575 ml (1 pint) of
redcurrant juice obtained,
450 g (1 lb) preserving
sugar

This method is very extravagant but makes such superb jelly that if you have plenty of redcurrants it is well worth it. Choose slightly unripe berries as these have more acid and make better jelly. The amount of juice obtained will vary considerably according to the quality of fruit.

To extract the juice put the currants, which you have slightly mashed, into a bowl. Cover it. Stand the bowl in a large saucepan or deep roasting tin of water. Bring this to the boil and let it seethe away until the currants have sunk and their juice has run out. This will take perhaps 2–3 hours.

Hang the fruit in a jelly bag or a fine cloth, suspended over a bowl and let the juice run out overnight.

Measure the juice and put it in your preserving pan with the sugar, stir over a low heat until the sugar dissolves completely, then bring to the boil and boil rapidly until setting point is reached. Stir well and pour very quickly into clean, hot, dry jars. Cover when cool; do not tip or shake jars when jelly is cooling.

It should be a clear, bright, pale red. If this method seems too wasteful you can mash the berries to extract more juice before putting them into the jelly bag, but this will slightly darken the colour of the jelly and take the bloom from the beautiful flavour.

Clear breakfast marmalade

MAKES ABOUT 4.5 KG (10 LB)

INGREDIENTS
1.8 kg (4 lb) Seville
oranges
either 6 limes and 1 lemon
or 4 lemons
2.7 kg (6 lb) sugar
5 litres (9 pints) water

This is the transparent, finely cut marmalade, milder than darker kinds and better liked by children, but not by connoisseurs.

Pour boiling water over the fruit, which makes it easier to peel. Peel the fruit very thinly with a peeler. Coarsely chop the fruit, with its pith, and put it with its pips, into a large pan with 3 litres (5 pints) of water, bring to the boil and cook, covered, for 2 hours. Cut the peel into fine, even shreds and put it in another pan with 1.2 litres (2 pints) of water and cook, covered, for 1½ hours or until the peel is tender.

Strain the peel and add the liquid to the pulp. Strain the pulp through a cloth or jelly bag for 15 minutes, then return the pulp to the pan and cook it with the remaining 1.2 litres (2 pints) of water for a further 20 minutes. Strain again, for 1 hour, without pressing the pulp, and then throw the pulp away.

Put the juice in the preserving pan and bring it to the boil. Let it boil for 5 minutes, then add the sugar and dissolve thoroughly. Add the peel, bring to the boil and boil rapidly until setting point is reached. Skim, allow to cool a little, then pour into heated, sterilized jars.

Left: clear breakfast marmalade, *right:* all-year-round marmalade, *front:* Oxford marmalade

All-year-round marmalade

MAKES ABOUT 2.3 KG (5 LB)

INGREDIENTS
1 grapefruit
3 oranges
3 lemons
1.8 kg (4 lb) preserving
   sugar

This is an excellent marmalade for the end of the year, when you may run out of your home-made Seville orange marmalade before Seville oranges have come back on the market stalls.

Cut the fruit in half and scoop the pips into a small bowl with a teaspoon. Cover them with water and leave them to soak overnight, to give up their pectin. The fruit, peel, pith and pulp can be cut up by hand into fine slivers, or minced through the coarsest blade of the mincer. Put them in a bowl, pour on 1.2 litres (2 pints) of water and leave this too to stand overnight.

The next day when you are ready, put the peel, its water and the strained water from the pips into a large pan, and bring to the boil. Simmer until tender, about 15 minutes. Add the sugar, stir over a low heat until it has dissolved, then simmer for up to 2 hours, testing from time to time.

When it sets, pour into hot sterile jars and cover when cold.

Oxford marmalade

MAKES ABOUT 3–3.5 KG
(7–8 LB)

INGREDIENTS
1 dozen small Seville
   oranges
2.3 litres (4 pints) water
425 ml ($\frac{3}{4}$ pint) water for
   soaking pips
juice of 1 lemon
1.8 kg (4 lb) preserving
   sugar – 2.3 kg (5 lb) if the
   oranges are large

This famous chunky marmalade is a beautiful red-gold colour, but can be made considerably darker, in the true approved Oxford fashion, if 25 g (1 oz) of black treacle is added to the recipe.

Wash the oranges, which should be fresh and unwrinkled. Put them in a large pan with the water and let them boil, covered, for 1 hour. Take out the oranges and keep the water in which they were cooked.

Cut each orange in half and carefully scoop the pips into a jug containing 425 ml ($\frac{3}{4}$ pint) water. Now slice the oranges and pulp on a board, making the chips as thick and chunky as you like – about $1 \times \frac{1}{2}$ cm ($\frac{1}{2} \times \frac{1}{4}$ in) is the usual.

Put the orange cooking liquid and the sugar in a preserving pan and heat gently, stirring all the time with a wooden spoon until the sugar has completely dissolved.

Now turn up the heat and boil for 5 minutes. Skim round the sides of the pan with a plastic bowl scraper. Throw the orange chunks and lemon juice into the liquid. Add the treacle if you are after a really dark marmalade. Strain the pips into the liquid, pressing and rubbing them in the sieve with a wooden spoon to extract their pectin, essential to the setting of jam and marmalade.

Stir everything together, and bring to the boil. This marmalade should set in about 30–60 minutes. Test according to directions at the beginning of the chapter (*see page* 220) and when setting point is reached skim well, allow to cool a little, then pour into warm pots and cover.

Christmas mincemeat, rose-petal honey, gooseberry curd, lemon curd

Christmas mincemeat

MAKES ABOUT 2.7 KG (6 LB)

INGREDIENTS
225 g (8 oz) suet
450 g (1 lb) sultanas
450 g (1 lb) raisins
900 g (2 lb) cooking apples,
   peeled and chopped
225 g (8 oz) chopped
   blanched almonds
100 g (4 oz) mixed
   candied peel
450 g (1 lb) currants
grated rind 1 lemon
2 wineglasses brandy
$\frac{1}{4}$ teaspoon grated nutmeg
$\frac{1}{4}$ teaspoon ground
   cinnamon
$\frac{1}{2}$ teaspoon ground ginger

In the late sixteenth and early seventeenth centuries mincemeat appeared regularly on every table – as you might imagine from the name, not as a sweet dish, as it is now, but as a meat course; the mince was made up of mutton and veal seasoned with cinnamon and rosewater, and then mixed with eggs, sugar, orange and lemon peel, currants, dates, prunes and apples or pears.

The filling was baked into a 'savoury' pie and was traditionally part of an Elizabethan Christmas dinner.

Mince the suet, sultanas, raisins, apples, almonds and candied peel coarsely and mix them in a bowl with the other ingredients, but only half the brandy. Put them, covered, in a cool place and leave for 3 days, stirring daily, so that the flavours mellow. Add the remaining brandy. Put into sterilized jars, cover and keep until needed. This gives a very fresh mincemeat, rich without being the least bit cloying or oversweet.

Grapes preserved in brandy

INGREDIENTS
1 perfect bunch of black
   grapes weighing about
   450 g (1 lb)
450 g (1 lb) preserving
   sugar
150 ml ($\frac{1}{4}$ pint) cooking
   brandy

The prettiness of this recipe depends on using whole, perfect bunches of grapes. The brandy syrup in which they are preserved is excellent used in the making of puddings, or can be served in small glasses with the grapes as a dessert.

Wash the grapes very thoroughly and remove with scissors any that are at all bruised or imperfect. Prick each grape in 2–3 places with a needle, otherwise they will shrivel up.

Place the bunch in a wide-mouthed glass preserving jar, cover with the sugar, 225 g ($\frac{1}{2}$ lb) to each bunch of grapes, then pour on the brandy and seal the jars. Keep it in a cool dry place, turning it daily for a week or so to dissolve the sugar: the grapes are then delicious and ready to eat.

Lemon curd

MAKES ABOUT 1 KG (2 LB)

INGREDIENTS
3 lemons
100 g ($\frac{1}{4}$ lb) unsalted butter
225 g ($\frac{1}{2}$ lb) granulated
 sugar
2 eggs, beaten

This light fresh-tasting rich preserve is extremely easily made; originally it was thickened in a stone pot standing in a saucepan of water, and then put up on the still room or pantry shelf in the same jar. Nowadays it is made in a double boiler, put into glass jars and kept in the refrigerator.

Pare the rind very thinly from the lemons with a potato peeler. Squeeze the juice from the lemons and strain it.

Melt the butter in the top of a double boiler, add sugar, lemon juice, lemon peel and beaten eggs. Stir the mixture over hot water until it starts to thicken. Strain through a wire sieve to remove the rinds or simply scoop them out with a slotted spoon.

Continue cooking in the top of the double boiler until creamy, soft and thick.

Sterilize two glass jars by scalding with boiling water. Dry them upside down in a low oven.

Pour in the velvety yellow curd, cover the pots, cool quickly and store in the refrigerator. It keeps for at least two weeks.

Gooseberry curd

MAKES ABOUT 1 KG (2 LB)

INGREDIENTS
450 g (1 lb) green
 gooseberries
2 tablespoons water
100 g (4 oz) butter
225 g (8 oz) sugar
2 eggs, beaten

This is a delicate, beautifully pale green curd, very similar to lemon curd but more subtle in flavour. It is very special and keeps quite well for a few weeks in the refrigerator.

Slowly simmer the gooseberries with the water until they are soft, then rub them through a sieve. Now return the pulp to the pan, add the butter, sugar, and beaten eggs. Stir gently until it thickens but be careful not to allow it to boil or it will curdle. Pour into small pots and cover when the curd is cold.

Rose-petal honey

INGREDIENTS
rose-petals
450 g (1 lb) clear honey

On a warm sunny day, pack a 600-ml (1-pint) jug full of scented rose petals and a rose leaf or two. Wash them in cold water, shake in a cloth like a salad, then spread out the petals on the cloth to dry in the sun.

Bring the honey to the boil, then throw in all the petals and leaves and let them simmer for a few minutes. Remove the pan from the heat, and leave it to stand for a few hours. Bring to the boil again and strain back into the pot, pressing the rose petals with a wooden spoon. Keep this honey in the refrigerator as it becomes a bit liquid after the heating.

Pickled peaches

INGREDIENTS
7–8 ripe peaches – about
 900 g (2 lb)
juice of $\frac{1}{2}$ lemon
4 cloves to each peach
275 ml ($\frac{1}{2}$ pint) white wine
 or cider vinegar
275 ml ($\frac{1}{2}$ pint) water
450 g (1 lb) white sugar
2 sticks cinnamon

Pickled peaches traditionally used to be served with cold ham, cold duck and cold roast pork, but they are equally delicious with a freshly cooked ham or a hot roast. They also made a very good addition to fruit salads.

Put the peaches in a bowl and pour boiling water over them. Remove them after 1 minute and take off the skins. Squeeze lemon juice over them. Stick each peach with 4 cloves.

Bring the vinegar, water, sugar and cinnamon sticks to the boil and simmer for 5 minutes.

Cook half the peaches, gently poaching them in the syrup until they are tender. Take them out with a slotted spoon and repeat with the remaining peaches.

If there seems to be too much syrup at this point, remove the peaches and reduce it a little by boiling.

Spoon the peaches into heated sterile glass jars, pour the syrup over to fill the jars and keep for a month before eating.

Pickled eggs

INGREDIENTS
16 eggs
1.2 litres (2 pints) malt
  vinegar, preferably spiced
  (*see below*)
12 peppercorns
1 small whole red chilli
Spiced vinegar
1.2 litres (2 pints) malt or
  cider vinegar
3 5-cm (2-in) cinnamon
  sticks
2 heaped teaspoons whole
  cloves
10 blades mace
2 heaped teaspoons whole
  allspice
2 heaped teaspoons black
  peppercorns

This is excellent with salad, or served as an appetizer with celery salt.

The eggs should be about one week old. Hardboil them for 12–15 minutes, cool in cold water, peel them and put them into sterile jars.
Pour on the spiced vinegar, add peppercorns and chilli and cover. Keep for 10 days, when the eggs will be ready to eat.

Spiced vinegar
Heat the vinegar with the spices in a covered basin standing over a pan of hot water. When the water boils remove from the heat, allow to cool, and infuse for 2 hours. Store with the spices in it, in covered bottles; and strain before use. The pickle can be used at once but if you keep it for some months, it will improve and intensify the flavour.

Curried apple and pepper chutney

MAKES 2.7 KG (6 LB)

INGREDIENTS
225 g ($\frac{1}{2}$ lb) raisins
225 g ($\frac{1}{2}$ lb) currants
6 firm red tomatoes
6 small onions
3 red peppers
12 eating apples
450 g (1 lb) light brown
  sugar
1.2 litres (2 pints) white
  distilled vinegar,
  preferably spiced (*above*)
2 tablespoons each whole
  mustard seed and salt
2 teaspoons whole
  coriander
1 tablespoon curry powder
$\frac{1}{2}$ teaspoon cayenne pepper

Soak the raisins and currants in warm water for $\frac{1}{2}$ an hour to plump them up. Peel and chop the tomatoes and onions. Remove the seeds from the peppers and shred them into strips. Peel, quarter, and core the apples. Combine the sugar, vinegar, spices, salt, curry powder and cayenne in a large heavy saucepan, and bring slowly to the boil, stirring to dissolve the sugar.
Add the tomatoes, onions, peppers, raisins and currants, and simmer gently for 45 minutes. Now add the apples and 2–3 tablespoons of water. Bring the mixture slowly back to the boil and simmer, stirring occasionally, until the apples are soft, and the mixture is thick and an appetizing russet colour.
Spoon into sterile glass jars and cover when cool.

Rhubarb and raisin relish

MAKES ABOUT 900 G (2 LB)

INGREDIENTS
225 g (8 oz) brown sugar
275 ml ($\frac{1}{2}$ pint) cider
  vinegar, preferably spiced
  (*above*)
150 ml ($\frac{1}{4}$ pint) water
$\frac{1}{2}$ teaspoon each whole
  allspice, salt, and
  whole cloves
1 teaspoon mustard seed
$\frac{1}{4}$ teaspoon celery seeds
2 onions
450 g (1 lb) rhubarb
225 g (8 oz) raisins

This is very useful in springtime when last season's chutneys are beginning to run out.

Combine the sugar, vinegar, water and spices in a heavy-based pan. Bring to the boil and boil for 5 minutes. Chop the onions and cut the rhubarb into small pieces. Add the onions and the rhubarb and cover the pan. Simmer gently for 45 minutes. Now add the raisins to the pan and cook on, uncovered, stirring from time to time, for about 1 hour until the mixture is thick and ploppy. Pour it into clean hot jars, cool and cover.

Tomato ketchup

MAKES ABOUT 1.5 LITRES
(2½ PINTS)

INGREDIENTS
2.7 kg (6 lb) ripe tomatoes
10 shallots
1 5-cm (2-in) piece root
  ginger, bruised with a
  hammer
3 cloves
225 g (½ lb) white sugar
1 level teaspoon cayenne
  pepper
2 level tablespoons salt
575 ml (1 pint) spiced
  vinegar (*see facing page*)
juice of 2 lemons

This is only one of many ketchups or 'catsups' that were once the stock-in-trade of Victorian cooks, who used them liberally – all too liberally – to improve their sauces and gravies. But while mushroom ketchup and walnut ketchup have gone the way of the comfortable railway waiting-room, where they used to be dispensed from the buffet, tomato ketchup has become the one essential sauce with all children and quite a number of adults too.

Quarter the tomatoes and peel and chop the shallots. Put them in a large saucepan and add the bruised root ginger and the cloves. Cook until the shallots are tender, then rub through a sieve or purée in the mouli-légumes, to remove spices and tomato skins and seeds.
  Put the pulp back into the cleaned pan and add the sugar, cayenne pepper and salt. Cook until the sauce thickens – it takes up to 2 hours – then add the spiced vinegar and lemon juice. Cook again until the sauce reduces to a moist purée.
  Pour into sterilized jars or bottles and seal firmly; allow to mature for a least 1 month before use.

Green tomato chutney

MAKES 3.2 KG (7 LB)

INGREDIENTS
1.8 kg (4 lb) small green
  tomatoes
1 teaspoon celery salt
450 g (1 lb) cooking apples
  (Bramleys)
550 g (1¼ lb) shallots
2 red or green peppers
6 red chillies
450 g (1 lb) brown sugar
(1 pint) cider vinegar,
  preferably spiced (*see
  facing page*)
450 g (1 lb) red tomatoes

This is an extremely good way of using up the small unripe tomatoes left on the plants as autumn arrives.

Cut the green tomatoes into very thin slices and sprinkle them with salt. Let them drain for an hour or two. Peel and mince the apples and shallots. Grill the peppers, skin them and cut them into short strips.
  Tie the chillies in a piece of fabric. Put all the ingredients except the red peppers and ripe tomatoes in a pan, having just rinsed the tomatoes, and bring to the boil. Simmer for a while until the liquid has somewhat evaporated, then add the peppers and the ripe tomatoes, skinned and chopped. Simmer until thick, remove the chillies and pour the mixture into clean pots and cover with lids or waxed paper. Jam-pot tops will not do as they allow the chutney to shrink.
  This is more of a relish than a chutney.

Top: pickled eggs, tomato ketchup, *centre:* curried apple and pepper chutney, *bottom:* rhubarb and raisin relish, green tomato chutney

Cheese

The renewed interest in our British regional cheeses means that more and more people are learning to distinguish between them. These cheeses are easily identifiable, and so outstanding (as great as any in the world), that it is well worth getting to know the different types, their flavours, colours and textures. It makes a great deal of difference, whether you are shopping for cooking cheese or eating cheese, if you know what you are looking for. Roughly speaking, our cheeses can be divided into three types, hard cheeses such as Cheddar, blue cheeses such as Stilton and fresh cheeses – these include cottage cheese. The hard cheeses include Cheddar, Leicester, Lancashire, Wensleydale, Derby and Sage Derby, Gloucester and Caerphilly; they range in colour from red-gold to white and in texture from firm to crumbly. The flavours vary widely too; not only because of the different traditional methods of making cheese but also because of the varying soils; sandy soil produces very different grass to heavy clay and this naturally affects the texture and flavour and quality of the milk. In the past, the milk of different breeds of cow was used to make different cheeses, and fortunately, although up-to-date farming has almost done away with many of the low-producing specialized breeds such as the Gloucester, which was considered in the old days to be the only cow for making Double Gloucester cheese, there are still enthusiasts who keep the old breeds going.

Blue cheese is made by the same methods as the hard cheese, but certain desirable micro-organisms or moulds are encouraged to get to work on the cheese as it matures. The result is the well-known sharp-flavoured marbling of greeny or blue veins that thread their way through the cheese and give it its 'bite' and its appetizing quality and character.

Lastly, there are the fresh soft cheeses: full-fat cream cheese, low-fat cottage cheese, and curd cheese which is generally made with skimmed milk. They vary greatly in the amount of fat (or cream) they contain, but all are white or creamy-white and fresh-tasting. It is curious that although we live close to Normandy, the home of so many of the world's favourite soft 'ripe' supple cheeses, such as Camembert and Pont l'Evèque, we have not developed any of these soft cheeses ourselves, partly because they do not keep well. I therefore intend to concentrate on the long-maturing, hard or semi-hard varieties.

It is marvellous to see the traditional farmhouse Cheddars, huge boulders of cheese, waiting in rows in their dark store rooms, labelled, dated and marked with their name. Each batch is individually known to the farmer who made it, and he really knows his cheese, taking a pride in producing a fine-flavoured, mature product.

But to the layman, knowing and choosing a good piece of cheese is more difficult. Obviously, if you want a cheese of great character you will choose a farmhouse cheese, with a visible rind, and you will buy it at a shop which takes the trouble to keep good cheeses in stock, and to keep it in good condition. There are still some expert grocers who cut cheese off the whole round with a cheesewire. The cheese can then be cut into suitable pieces and fitted back together like a jigsaw puzzle so that it keeps its moist condition. But, wrapped or unwrapped, cheese should never be oily or cracked nor show a wet glistening surface or traces of surface mould.

When people said that the moon is made of green cheese they were thinking of pearly white, round little curd cheeses, made in cottages all over England from milk that had been skimmed of its cream for butter making.

Caerphilly (1)

This is one of the mildest, crumbliest and softest of our 'hard' cheeses and was once known as 'miner's cheese' since it was a favourite lunch at the coalface. It is a distant relation of Cheddar and Cheshire, but ripens more quickly. Although now mostly made in the West Country, Wales and on the borders, it originated in the Welsh village of Caerphilly, and is one of the cheeses for which the Welsh are famous today. In the past too they were renowned for having a way with cheeses. One of Shakespeare's characters said he would rather trust a Welshman with his cheese than any other nationality. Even earlier, a Welsh cheese joke had made the rounds. Andrew Boorde tells us that heaven was one day overwhelmed by the ringing chatter of Welshmen, so St Peter stepped outside the pearly gates and cried 'Toasted cheese', whereupon all the Welsh rushed out. St Peter closed the gates on them and celestial peace was restored. However, Caerphilly, which is no more than 160 years old, is not the best toasting cheese, but a sandwich or after-dinner cheese.

It is mild, slightly acid and fresh, excellent with bread and butter and celery, or with salads.

Cheddar (2)

Cheddar, prince, if not king, of British cheeses, is so popular that copies are made all over the world. It is a cheese of character. Ripened to full maturity it can take over a year to make, and ten times its own weight of milk is compressed into it, to give it its full, sweet, sharp flavour, mild when young, and nutty when mature.

The largest Cheddar ever made, weighing a grand 11 hundredweight, was given to Queen Victoria in 1840 as a wedding present by the farmers of Pennard, one of the Cheshire villages, where it was traditionally made.

Although classed as a hard cheese, Cheddar was originally only found on the tables of the rich, since it contained large quantities of cream. Peasants and labourers had to make do with harder, poorer, cheeses, notably those from Suffolk, of bad reputation, which contained no cream and really were like rock. 'Hard cheese' was a true sad fact long before it became schoolboy slang, and nobody liked it much. There was a song about it: 'They made me harder than the devil . . . knives won't cut me . . . dogs bark at me but can't eat me', and 'hunger will break through stone walls and anything but Suffolk cheese'.

It was a happy day when Cheddar began to be more easily and cheaply made and more readily available, and took its place as the mainstay of the ploughman's lunch.

It is now our very best all-purpose cheese, excellent for eating, grating, cooking, in sandwiches, salads and with the port. One of its great advantages is that even the hardest old ends will still grate well and can be used for cooking.

The colour of Cheddar varies from golden yellow to quite pale primrose, and the texture when freshly cut is like fine suede. The outside or rind, unless the Cheddar has been made in blocks (as is now mainly done), is hard, having been compressed and tightly bandaged in its early stages. Australia, New Zealand, and Canada all make their own quite good versions of Cheddar, but for the best Cheddar of all, look for mature English farmhouse Cheddar and eat one of the world's greatest cheeses.

Cheshire cheese (3, 4, 5)

The oldest of our golden cheeses, having been mentioned in the Domesday Book, Cheshire is also the most highly praised by cookery writers from Sir Kenelme Digby to Ambrose Heath, a great connoisseur and lover of British cheeses.

There are three Cheshires to choose from, the red (3) or coloured, which varies from a deep marigold orange to a golden yellow, the white (4) which is a pale creamy colour and the blue (5) which is golden, veined with green. (There is also to be found a blue farmhouse Cheshire called Blue Fade.) The red is crumbly, nutty and salty; it makes excellent eating as well as first-class rarebits and soufflés. It has the reputation, in fact, of being one of the very best cooking cheeses in Europe, was already renowned in Charles I's day, and was described by Sir Kenelme Digby as 'a quick, fat, rich well-tasted cheese to serve melted on toast'. A good blue has a buttery texture, and an added piquancy, richness and saltiness which are definitely not liked by everybody but are prized by connoisseurs; while the white is still sharp, it has a somewhat salty tang and an excellent after-dinner flavour for a winter's evening. Unfortunately the white, with age, can develop a bitter taste which may discourage people from trying it again, which would be a great pity.

Cotherstone and Cottenham

Cotherstone from Yorkshire, a blue-veined cheese sometimes called Yorkshire Stilton, and Cottenham, said to be from Cambridgeshire, another Stilton type, are mourned in passing, since neither has been available since the 1930s.

Cream cheese (6)

The true sort is very little made today either domestically or commercially. It is both rich and delicious. There are, however, many 'creamy' cheeses, correctly described as medium and full-fat soft cheese.

Crowdie

This is a home-made Scottish cheese now becoming rare, made with skimmed milk, curdled with rennet and enriched occasionally with sour cream. It is drained and then allowed to mellow a little, when it becomes smooth and creamy. Try this excellent fresh cream cheese with brown bread and butter and a glass of white wine.

Curd cheese (7)

This is the simple cheese that was at one time made in cottages all over England for family eating. At its most basic it is made from the curd of soured skimmed milk; the whey is dripped off through a fine muslin cloth. It is then eaten very fresh.

Other recipes, more complicated, stem

'The honest Ancient English Farmer's Wife in the Dairy at her proper Employ.'

from this one; in some parts of the country rennet is added to produce a curd in fresh milk; in others the cheese is salted and wrapped in leaves. 'After it has done wetting,' runs one old recipe, 'set it on sharp-pointed dock leaves or nettle leaves to ripen'; the leaves, with their network of veins, provide a perfect draining platform for any remaining moisture; these little white cheeses were called nettle cheeses. In other areas the salted cheeses wrapped in leaves and cloth were buried deep in the ground for 3–4 days, while in Scotland they would be embedded in a box of oats.

There were many variations of this simple cheese – the country people made it more interesting with the addition of herbs and spices, while Elizabeth I had egg yolks mixed into her favourite cheese.

The tradition of making cheese at home lasted well into this century. Alison Uttley, author of *Recipes from an Old Farmhouse*, remembers being sent to pick the prettiest hazel leaves she could find to make a green mat for the cheese. But the custom dwindled with the arrival of refrigerators; perhaps because it meant there was less sour milk available.

Derby and Sage Derby (8, 9)
A good, plain cheese resembling Cheddar, Derby (8) is often sold young, but is much better if left to mature.

At one time a variation of it, Sage Derby (9), was made by placing chopped fresh sage leaves between the layers of curd as they went into the press. Sometimes the green colour was enhanced by the addition of spinach juice, particularly if 'figure Derby' was in the making.

These figured cheeses were masterpieces in which green arabesques were inserted into plain cheeses, like marquetry into a cabinet. Another good Christmas present was the 'chequerboard Derby' made of sage-green squares alternated with golden squares tinted with marigolds as so many of the older golden cheeses were.

Today, unfortunately, although some originals are still to be found, most Sage Derby has become a very dull product indeed, layered with green streaks bearing little resemblance in colour or flavour to the original sage. So look for the marbled Derby, mottled with fine streaks of a natural sage green.

Plain matured white Derby has an interesting and strange flavour – rather strong, ripe, and pungent.

Dorset Blue Vinney, Dorset Blue, Blue Vinney
A certain amount of mystery surrounds the Dorset Blue, a white cheese with a bright blue mould. At one time the farms where it was made would not divulge their names; it was whispered that since the characteristic mould came from the proximity of the cheeses to old leather harness and working boots, the cheesemen were afraid they might be closed down if their whereabouts was known.

Nowadays Blue Vinney can be bought, hygienically made, in a few select places, mainly in the West Country, and is reliably good. It has thick rind, which can become hard as iron with age – legend has it that a train once ran on Blue Vinneys instead of wheels – and an open texture, crumbly when young, firm when mature.

Unlike its grander relative, Stilton, it is made from skimmed milk, and therefore lacks the richness and creaminess associated with this type of cheese, but when mature it has a very pleasing astringency and a moist firm texture and is delicious with cider in a ploughman's lunch, together with pickled shallots and the little hard rolls called Dorset Knobs.

Gloucester, Single and Double (10)
On May Day in the city of Gloucester a huge golden wheel of cheese, festively garlanded, used to be carried in procession round the town. It was the great Double Gloucester of which the county was justly proud. It is a splendid golden cheese, tending to dryness but with a full rich flavour, sometimes sharp and pungent. Single Gloucester, now obsolete, was a smaller cheese, which matured more quickly and had a milder flavour.

Double Gloucester is a good eating cheese and equally good cooking cheese. Use it for the making of Welsh Rarebit and cheese straws.

Lancashire (11)
There are two types of Lancashire cheese, an excellent sharp-flavoured softish white cheese, crumbly when young, becoming more creamy and mellow as it gets older, and a yellow, fatty type.

Since they do not travel particularly well, they are mostly eaten by the residents of Lancashire, who enjoy them tremendously with their lunchtime glass of beer; they are also excellent cooking cheeses, making a superb Welsh Rarebit.

These cheese vary in size but are sometimes made in 'truckles' (these are small cheeses about 25 cm (10 in) deep and 18 cm (7 in) across) which real cheese enthusiasts call 'monstrous midgets' as they sometimes do not reach the peak of flavour usually achieved by a full-sized cheese.

Leicester (12)

'Many's the long night I've dreamed of cheese, toasted mostly', said Benn Gunn, in R. L. Stevenson's *Treasure Island*. The chances are that he was a Leicestershire man: Leicester is a fine, mild deep reddish-gold cheese, marvellously rich and mellow-looking on a cheese board, and really excellent for toasting and cheese sauces.

It is the sort of cheese that the Elizabethans liked prodigiously, eating it toasted or 'roasted' although their physicians decried it as 'more meet to bait a trap than to be received into the human body'.

However, cheese-toasting didn't noticeably abate because of their warnings and Georgian wives still regretted their husbands' enthusiasm for 'this strong-smelling, coarse kind of thing'.

In fact, today's Leicester is 'mild-smelling' and excellent with a sweet nutty flavour and a moist, flaky texture.

Stilton (13)

This is the most aristocratic of our cheeses and, along with Cheddar, the most famous. When perfectly made and ripened it was 'the delicatest, rainbow-hued, meltingest cheese' ever tasted by Charles Lamb. While delicate might seem a strange word to use, subtle being perhaps more apt, his description does conjure up the creamy, veiny surface of a cut, mature Stilton.

True blue Stilton is made in the Vale of Belvoir and Dove Valley, according to traditional methods, and is protected by a Certification trade mark. In fact Stilton was never made in Stilton at all, but it was there, at the historic Bell Inn on the Old North Road, that it was first offered in quantity to stagecoach travellers, by a Mrs Paulet. Its fame spread, although Daniel Defoe described it as 'brought to the table with mites and maggots round it so thick, they bring a spoon with them to eat the mites with'. (It is never like that today.)

It is still the custom to scoop Stilton from the middle with a silver spoon without disturbing the crusty rind. However, this can only be advised if the cheese is to be eaten quickly, or it will dry out.

To preserve a Stilton (or half a Stilton), traditional centrepiece of the Christmas table, in as good condition as possible, cut it horizontally halfway across, then cut your slices from one side, cutting it with the rind still left on. Gradually work your way down the cheese.

Store it wrapped in a cloth. If it should come too dry, revive it by wrapping it in a damp cloth, and leave it until it regains its proper consistency.

If you have a bottle of port, do not pour it into the cheese but drink it with it, and

serve perhaps a few fresh walnuts or inner sticks of celery to go with both.

Stilton can be used in cooking too: it is excellent crumbled into a green salad, or whipped into a mousse; it has even been frozen into ice-cream but this is perhaps going too far with such a noble cheese.

White Stilton (14)

This is a plain unripe Stilton, usually not more than two weeks old; it is chalky and sour-tasting, but pleasant and mild. It doesn't, however, have the outstanding character of ripe blue Stilton.

1, 2. Caerphilly and Cheddar
3, 4, 5. Red, White and Blue Cheshire
6, 7. Cream and Curd cheese
8, 9. Derby and Sage Derby
10. Double Gloucester
11. Lancashire
12. Leicester
13, 14. Stilton and White Stilton
15, 16. White and Blue Wensleydale
17. Caboc
18, 19. Orkney and Caithness
20. Cotswold chive
21. Ilchester
22. Red Windsor

Wensleydale (15, 16)

> But I, when I undress me,
> Each night upon my knees
> Will ask the Lord to bless me
> With apple pie and cheese
>
> Eugene Field (1850–1895)

The White Wensleydale is the one and only cheese, according to Yorkshiremen, to eat with apple pie; it is also delicious with Cox's orange pippins if you like the North Country association of apples and cheese. It is mild, moist, and delicate with a flaky texture and a subtle fruity flavour.

The Blue Wensleydale is claimed by locals to be better than Stilton, and they even suggest that Stilton is no more than an upstart version of their original blue cheese.

This blue-veined, creamy version is hard to find, but worth seeking out; it has a sweet delicate, nutty flavour and a nice moist creamy texture.

New cheeses

Amongst the most interesting new cheeses being made in Britain are the following three Scottish cheeses:

Caboc (17), a mild double cream cheese rolled in pinhead oatmeal, has a very pleasant buttery taste and texture. Some say it is a descendant of the old crofters' home-made cheeses which were matured in barrels of oatmeal.

Orkney (18) is a small round disc of Dunlop cheese, slightly rubbery in texture but with a delicious tangy Cheddar-like flavour.

Caithness (19) and **Islay** are similar well-flavoured small cheeses, Islay being rather flaky and crumbly and Caithness semi-soft and rich in texture.

Cotswold chive (20) is a golden cheese, similar to a Gloucester, but moister, and speckled with mild-flavoured fresh chives. Delicious in small quantities.

Ilchester (21) is a soft Cheddar mixed with beer and herbs.

Red Windsor (22) is a moist Cheddar impregnated with elderberry wine. It has a gaudy red veining and is really not to be compared with our great traditional cheeses.

Applewood is the name for small bars of smoked Cheddar cheese.

Keeping cheese at home

Broadly speaking, any cheese can be kept in good condition for a reasonable time, if you wrap each piece individually in foil, cling film or greaseproof paper, and put it into an airtight plastic box in the bottom or least cold part of the refrigerator. Remember to remove the cheese an hour or so before eating to give it time to recover from the cold and release its flavour. But try not to keep cheese for too long – and most particularly do not leave it exposed to the warm air of kitchen or dining room for long periods: the warmth will cause it to sweat and release the fat from the curd. The cheese will never recover, although the cracked outside layer can be cut away and used for cooking, a purpose for which English cheeses are particularly well suited.

Index

Acknowledgments

The producers of this book would like to thank the
following for their help:
Christine Lloyd, Martin Newton, Derek Witty
(design and photography); Caroline Ellwood, Diana
Marchant, Joanna Percival (home economists);
Veronica Willans (index).

Also the following for kindly allowing us to take
photographs on their premises:
R. Allen and Co. Ltd., 117 Mount Street W1
J. F. Blagden, 64 Paddington Street W1
Butcher and Edmonds Ltd., 1 Grand Avenue,
  Leadenhall Market EC3
Paxton and Whitfield Ltd., 93 Jermyn Street SW1

Also the following companies for the kind loan of
accessories for the photography:
John Baily and Son Ltd., 116 Mount St W1
W. Bainborough, 75 Elizabeth Street SW1
British Crafts Centre, 43 Earlham Street WC2
Burgess and Leigh, Middleport Pottery, Burslem,
  Stoke-on-Trent
Butlers of Sheffield, 101 Matilda Street, Sheffield
  S1 3PY
Conran Shop, 77 Fulham Road SW3
Craftsmen Potters Association of Great Britain,
  William Blake House, Marshall Street W1
Dartington Glass Ltd., 4 Portland Road W11
David Mellor, 4 Sloane Square W1
Denby, 58–59 Great Marlborough Street W1
Designers' Guild, 277 King's Road SW3
D. H. Evans, 318 Oxford Street W1
Dickens and Jones, 224 Regent Street W1
Divertimenti, 68 Marylebone Lane W1
Elizabeth David, 46 Bourne Street SW1
General Trading Company Ltd., 144 Sloane Street
  SW1
Gered Wedgwood, 158 Regent Street W1
John Gow Ltd., 55 Connaught Street W2
T. and G. Green, Church Cresley, Burton-on-Trent,
  Staffordshire
Habitat Ltd., 156 Tottenham Court Road W1 and
  206 King's Road SW3
Harvest (Covent Garden), British Crafts,
  40 Tavistock Street WC2
The Irish Shop, 11 Duke Street W1
Laura Ashley, 40 Sloane Street SW1
John Lewis, Oxford Street W1
Liberty & Co. Ltd., Regent Street W1

Minton, 46 Pall Mall W1
Peter Jones, Sloane Square SW1
Portmerion (Potteries Ltd.), 4 Portland Road W11
The Reject Shop, 209 Tottenham Court Road W1
Royal Doulton, 46 Pall Mall W1
Royal Worcester Spode (Showroom), 31a St George
  Street W1
Sally Lawford's Country Kitchen, 241 Royal College
  Street NW1
Temple & Crook, 3 Kinnerton Street SW1
Thorn Domestic Appliances (Electrical) Ltd.,
  New Lane, Havant, Hampshire
Tile Mart Ltd., 151 Great Portland Street W1
The Wedgwood Group, 34 Wigmore Street W1
Wedgwood, Oxford Circus, 270 Regent Street W1
The White House, 51 New Bond Street W1

Black and white illustration acknowledgments
The producers of the book would like to thank the
following who kindly supplied us with photographs:
14 Mary Evans Picture Library
15 Radio Times Hulton Picture Library
24 Mansell Collection
40 Ford Jenkins, The Studio, 11 The Bridge,
  Lowestoft, Suffolk
41 (top) Mansell Collection
  (below) Ford Jenkins
62 Victoria and Albert Museum
63 Mansell Collection
87 Museum of English Rural Life, University of
  Reading. Original in possession of the
  Agriculture Economic Research Institute,
  Oxford
88 Victoria and Albert Museum
122 Mansell Collection
132 Radio Times Hulton Picture Library
133 Radio Times Hulton Picture Library
150 John Freeman
160 The Rainbird Publishing Group Ltd.
176 Weidenfeld and Nicolson (reproduced by
  permission of Viscount de L'Isle, VC, KG, from
  his collection at Penshurst Place)
177 Exeter Public Library
200 Museum of English Rural Life, University of
  Reading
220 Mary Evans Picture Library
231 Mansell Collection
232 John Freeman